GRASSROOTS LITERACY

'*Grassroots Literacy* helps us see the realities of inscription – writing in longhand – at the non-elite peripheries of our globally stratified system of communication. Two Congolese texts, one autobiographical, one historiographic, float upward and inward like messages in a bottle: in telling their story, Jan Blommaert illustrates and passionately advocates for an ethics of interpretation that confronts and overcomes the tiers of exclusion that otherwise mute such writers' voices.'

Michael Silverstein, University of Chicago, USA

What effect has globalisation had on our understanding of literacy? *Grassroots Literacy* seeks to address the relationship between globalisation and the widening gap between 'grassroots' literacies, or writings from ordinary people and local communities, and 'elite' literacies.

Displaced from their original context to elite literacy environments in the form of letters, police declarations and pieces of creative writing, 'grassroots' literacies are unsurprisingly easily disqualified, either as 'bad' forms of literacy, or as messages that fail to be understood. Through close analysis of two unique, handwritten documents from the Democratic Republic of the Congo, Jan Blommaert considers how 'grassroots' literacy in the Third World develops outside the literacy-saturated environments of the developed world. In examining these documents produced by socially and economically marginalised writers Blommaert demonstrates how literacy environments should be understood as relatively autonomous systems.

Grassroots Literacy will be key reading for students of language and literacy studies as well as an invaluable resource for anyone with an interest in understanding the implications of globalisation on local literacy practices.

Jan Blommaert is Finland Distinguished Professor of Linguistic Anthropology at the University of Jyväskylä, Finland, as well as Professor of Linguistic Anthropology at Tilburg University. His publications include *Debating Diversity* (co-author, Routledge, 1998), *Language Ideological Debates* (editor, 1999) and *Discourse: A Critical Introduction* (author, 2005).

LITERACIES
Series Editor: David Barton
Lancaster University

Literacy practices are changing rapidly in contemporary society in response to broad social, economic and technological changes: in education, the workplace, the media and in everyday life. This series reflects the burgeoning research and scholarship in the field of literacy studies and its increasingly interdisciplinary nature. The series aims to provide a home for books on reading and writing which consider literacy as a social practice and which situate it within broader institutional contexts. The books develop and draw together work in the field; they aim to be accessible, interdisciplinary and international in scope, and to cover a wide range of social and institutional contexts.

LITERACY, LIVES AND LEARNING
David Barton, Roz Ivanic, Yvon Appleby, Rachel Hodge and Karin Tusting

LITERACY AND GENDER
Gemma Moss

HIPHOP LITERACIES
Elaine Richardson

LITERACY IN THE NEW MEDIA AGE
Gunther Kress

CITY LITERACIES
Learning to Read Across Generations and Cultures
Eve Gregory and Ann Williams

LITERACY AND DEVELOPMENT
Ethnographic Perspectives
Edited by Brian V. Street

SITUATED LITERACIES
Theorising Reading and Writing in Context
Edited by David Barton, Mary Hamilton and Roz Ivanic

MULTILITERACIES
Literacy Learning and the Design of Social Futures
Edited by Bill Cope and Mary Kalantzis

GLOBAL LITERACIES AND THE WORLD-WIDE WEB
Edited by Gail E. Hawisher and Cynthia L. Selfe

STUDENT WRITING
Access, Regulation, Desire
Theresa M. Lillis

SILICON LITERACIES
Communication, Innovation and Education in the Electronic Age
Edited by Ilana Snyder

AFRICAN AMERICAN LITERACIES
Elaine Richardson

Editorial Board:

Elsa Auerbach *Boston University*
Mike Baynham *University of Leeds*
David Bloome *Vanderbilt University*
Norman Fairclough *Lancaster University*
James Gee *University of Wisconsin*
Nigel Hall *Manchester Metropolitan University*
Mary Hamilton *Lancaster University*
Peter Hannon *Sheffield University*
Shirley Brice Heath *Stanford University*

Roz Ivanic *Lancaster University*
Gunther Kress *University of London*
Jane Mace *Southbank University*
Janet Maybin *Open University*
Greg Myers *Lancaster University*
Mastin Prinsloo *University of Cape Town*
Brian Street *University of London*
Michael Stubbs *University of Trier*
Denny Taylor *Hofstra University*
Daniel Wagner *University of Pennsylvania*

GRASSROOTS LITERACY

Writing, identity and voice in Central Africa

Jan Blommaert

LONDON AND NEW YORK

First published 2008
by Routledge
2 Park Square, Milton Park, Abingdon, Oxon OX14 4RN

Simultaneously published in the USA and Canada
by Routledge
711 Third Avenue, New York, NY 10017, USA

Routledge is an imprint of the Taylor & Francis Group, an informa business

© 2008 Jan Blommaert

Typeset in Baskerville
by The Running Head Limited, Cambridge

All rights reserved. No part of this book may be reprinted or reproduced or utilised
in any form or by any electronic, mechanical, or other means, now known or
hereafter invented, including photocopying and recording, or in any information
storage or retrieval system, without permission in writing from the publishers.

British Library Cataloguing in Publication Data
A catalogue record for this book is available
from the British Library

Library of Congress Cataloging in Publication Data
Blommaert, Jan.
Grassroots literacy : writing, identity, and voice in central Africa / Jan Blommaert.
p. cm. — (Literacies)
Includes bibliographical references.
1. Anthropological linguistics—Congo (Democratic Republic) 2. Literacy—Congo (Democratic
Republic) I. Title.
P35.5.C75B56 2008
306.44096751—dc22
2007048548

ISBN10: 0–415–42631–6 (hbk)
ISBN10: 0–415–42630–8 (pbk)
ISBN10: 0–203–89548–7 (ebk)

ISBN13: 978–0–415–42631–2 (hbk)
ISBN13: 978–0–415–42630–5 (pbk)
ISBN13: 978–0–203–89548–1 (ebk)

FOR GUNTHER KRESS

CONTENTS

List of figures	xi
Preface	xiii

PART I
Grassroots literacy   1

1   Introduction: grassroots literacy and literacy regimes   3
Yes I can write 3
Writing 4
Grassroots literacy 7
Ethnographies of text 12
Globalisation 23

PART II
The lives of Julien   27

2   Three lives for Mrs Arens   29
Three versions of a life 29
Writing with an accent 30
Julien's life: a storyline 35
Writing (as) a (way of) life 37
Context and pretext 40

3   Genres and repertoires   42
Resources 42
On genre 43
Emerging genres in an emerging tradition 47
Histories and letters 49
The repertoire 68
The misfit 72

CONTENTS

4   Writing, remembering and being   74
Emerging genres, emerging lives 74
Writing and remembering 75
Who is Julien? 85
Textuality and subjectivity 95

PART III
Tshibumba the historian   **97**

5   Tshibumba: artist, painter, historian   99
Paintings, conversations and texts 99
Tshibumba Kanda Matulu 103
The storyline 108

6   The aesthetics of grassroots literacy   113
Writing as drawing 113
Tshibumba's writing and drawing 118
Tshibumba's voice 129
A disciplined voice 135

7   Sources as resources   137
The archive again 137
A national history with local resources 140
Tshibumba's voices 162

8   The grassroots historian's craft   165
Tshibumba's historiographic methodology 165
Grassroots historiography and popular consciousness 171
Artist, painter, grassroots historian 180

PART IV
Julien, Tshibumba, and beyond   **183**

9   Reflections   185
Lives, literacy, subjectivity 187
The skeleton of literacy practices 191
Grassroots literacy in globalisation 194
History from below 197
Conclusion 199

Notes   203
References   209
Index   215

FIGURES

1.1	Democratic Republic of the Congo	25
1.2	The Katanga and Kasai region of the Democratic Republic of the Congo	26
2.1	Copy of 1/5	32
3.1	Copy of 2/14	57
3.2	Copy of 3/20	63
5.1	Copy of pages 31–2 of Tshibumba's *Histoire*	106
6.1	Tourism assignment, Wesbank	115
6.2	The six drawings in the *Histoire*	124–5
7.1	The empty chapters, pages 10–11 of the *Histoire*	159
9.1	Questionnaire response, Wesbank	195

PREFACE

In an ideal world, this book would be three times its current size, two-thirds of which would be consumed by an appendix in which I present facsimiles, transcripts, translations and annotations of the texts on which most of the discussion is based. This would have had the advantage that the materials would be open for inspection by others, and that, perhaps, others might be infected by the endless fascination I have for them. All the same, this would make the production of the book complex and expensive, and would so risk making the retail copies unaffordable for most of the readership I hope to reach. I will have to find another channel and format for presenting the documents. Given this constraint, this book is necessarily a compromise which I tried to turn into a benefit. Rather than focusing on a critical edition and detailed exegesis of the documents I chose to focus on the general issues they raise.

These issues are, I think, fundamental. Globalisation is a process that forces us to take the world as a context. This world is complex and highly diverse, and developments in the 'centre' of this world – the development of new telecommunication systems and media, for instance – have effects on the 'margins' of the world. Literacy is a case in point, and what the documents I examine here show us is that there is a growing gap between different literacy regimes in the world. Texts such as the ones I will discuss here do not quickly or easily communicate the messages they contain. Their meanings increasingly disappear in the widening gap between literacy regimes in diverse parts of the world. The problem is obviously not academic but very real, of immediate life-or-death importance to many people. Voice is a pressing concern in a globalising context in which less and less can be taken for granted with respect to the communicative repertoires of people interacting with one another. I have addressed these concerns in an earlier book called *Discourse: A Critical Introduction* (Cambridge University Press 2005), and in many ways the present study is a sequel to *Discourse*. It picks up, and develops, points embryonically made there, focusing on literacy because of the reasons specified above, and bringing literacy analysis into the same theoretical field of force as the one described in *Discourse*.

This purpose offers me the opportunity to write about a corpus of texts that has puzzled, intrigued and mesmerised me for more than a decade. I came

xiii

PREFACE

across Julien's life histories in the mid-1990s, by what I would call 'structured accident'. The documents are rare instances of grassroots life-writing, and they offered me more theoretical and descriptive challenges than I could imagine at the time. My encounter with these documents coincided with a period in my life when I was deeply engaged with Johannes Fabian's work. I had read and reviewed his *History from Below* (Fabian 1990a), and few books ever had such a profound impact on me. Fabian has definitely been one of my *maîtres à penser* and the present book is, consequently, very much the upshot of a protracted dialogue with Fabian's work. This dialogue intensified when, again by accident, I started working on a handwritten history of the Congo written by the Congolese painter Tshibumba, about whose historical paintings Fabian had published the magnificent *Remembering the Present* (Fabian 1996). I received a copy of this massively intriguing document from Bogumil Jewsiwiecki, and quickly spotted the similarities between this history and Julien's life-writing. Both displayed the constraints of sub-elite writing, and both produced a grassroots voice on history. In both, the very act of writing appeared to produce all sorts of things: texts, but also particular positions, subjectivities. The question guiding my work then became: *what does this kind of grassroots literacy make possible* for people such as Julien and Tshibumba?

I had, in the meantime, started realising that the notion of *constraint* is central in considering this issue. Since the mid-1990s, I had frequently been requested by my national authorities to translate written statements by African refugees and Africans arrested by the police. Gradually, a corpus of texts had emerged in which I clearly saw that literacy achievements that had some value in sub-elite African contexts rather systematically failed to be seen as valuable in Belgium. The question about the possibilities of grassroots writing thus acquired a dimension of globalisation: 'grassroots' equals local, and the local effectiveness and adequacy of communicative resources raises questions of *mobility*. Texts travel, and they do not necessarily travel well. In the transfer from one place to another, they cross from one regime into another, and the changed orders of indexicality mean that they are understood differently. Having clearly understood that both Julien's and Tshibumba's texts were *mobile texts* – both were written for addressees in the West – I started realising that these documents might offer exceptional possibilities for exploring and identifying the main issues of literacy in the age of globalisation: issues that have to do with the locality of literacy regimes, with mobility and inequality.

This is the story of this book. There is irony in the story, because, naturally, it was hard not to reflect on my own writing practices while I was investigating those of Julien, Tshibumba and others. I saw my own literacy regime in action – writing in a globalised language that is not my own, in a particular register and genre, on a sophisticated laptop, in a solitary comfortable space surrounded by an archive and a working library, and with Google on the toolbar. All these material conditions: I don't take them for granted anymore. There is so much inequality inscribed in the production of this book. The main inequality is in

xiv

PREFACE

the result: voice. I can produce a globalised voice, they can't; I can produce a prestige genre, they can't; I can speak from within a recognisable position and identity, they can't.

There are ethical issues here. I can write about Julien and Tshibumba in ways they themselves could not, for reasons that will become all too clear in the chapters of this book. And I could not consult them while writing. I never had contact with Julien, only with his patron, Mrs Arens. She informed Julien about my academic work on his texts, and she gave me, on his behalf, permission for pursuing it. As for Tshibumba, he disappeared from the radar screen and no one has been able to inform me of his whereabouts. Julien and Tshibumba, we should recall, live in the southern part of the Congo, in an area marked by deep poverty and marginalisation, and torn by unrest and war since the second half of the 1990s. As for the refugees and police suspects whose documents I have analysed, I hardly ever had any contact with them either, often because I did not even know their names and because my role as state-appointed translator proscribed contacts with these subjects.

I am aware of these issues, have reflected on them over and over again, and come across the bitter irony of contemporary realities. Customary ethical codes for research presuppose a particular socio-political environment in which every-one has a name, an administrative existence, a recognisable and recognised subjectivity that demands respect and distance. We can only use a pseudonym when people's real names are known and when knowledge and possession of that name is connected to inalienable rights, to subjectivity and, consequently, to norms that separate the public from the private sphere. Underlying is the image of a fully integrated Modern society in which such elementary features are attached to everyone and recorded – officially – somewhere. Real societies, alas, are different. There are people in our own Modern societies that do not possess such elementary features and rights. Illegal immigrants have no name and no identifiable 'official' existence. Their 'lives' and stories are, for all prac-tical purposes, non-existent. Their anonymity is not the result of a desire for 'privacy', it is the effect of erasure and silencing; not of choice but of oppres-sion. And there are even more people elsewhere in the world to whom these conditions apply. African works of art kept in museums are only rarely attrib-uted to an individual artist, they are attributed to an ethnic group or to a region somewhere in Africa. Millions of people there live 'unofficial' lives, and no one cares about their names, birth dates, addresses, or, in a wider sense, subjectivity. I write about their subjectivity, about their existence and lives – or seen from a different perspective, I invade their privacy – because I have voice and they don't. I can invade their privacy because I have shaped a private sphere for them, and this act is an effect of global inequalities. I am not comfortable with that situation. But I believe there is great virtue in caring about their lives and in getting to know them, and if that exposes me to ethical criticisms, I will live with that. It is a lesson I have already learned about research in contemporary societies. I have also learned that it is good to stop and reflect on such questions,

PREFACE

and to realise (in Gunnar Myrdal's footsteps) that existing ethical codes do not solve the moral dilemmas of social research. They merely highlight them.

Given the many years that I have worked, talked and lectured on these texts, I cannot possibly mention everyone who ever had an influence on what this book has now become. I must however, acknowledge my debt of gratitude to several people. First I need to thank the people I have dubbed Mrs and Mr Arens, as well as (a real name) Bogumil Jewsiwiecki. They were the ones who gave me the documents that became the core of this book, and they talked or corresponded with me about their features and significance. Those were acts of generosity that triggered a long process of reflection and writing, and led to this product. Johannes Fabian has already been mentioned as an obvious source of inspiration for work along the lines developed in the following chapters, and Michael Silverstein, Dell Hymes, John Gumperz, Aaron Cicourel, Sue Gal, Kit Woolard and Misty Jaffe, among others, have been influential beyond measure on my work and have always been wonderful interlocutors on all sorts of issues.

I wrote this book at a time when I was leaving the Institute of Education of the University of London. The years spent in close proximity with Gunther Kress – to whom I dedicate this book – were invaluable humanly and intellectually, and much of what I was able to put in the pages of this book was learned in conversations with him, Diane Mavers, Mary Scott, Brian Street, Ben Rampton, Jeff Bezemer, Cathie Wallace, Adam Lefstein, Norbert Pachler and other members of the London Gang. Many of them read draft chapters of this book and commented perceptively on them. David Barton gave me excellent feedback on the draft, and Thomas Bearth, Michael Meeuwis, Katrijn Maryns and Vincent de Rooij offered important suggestions on parts of it. If this book is judged to be good, it is largely because of their impact on it; if it is judged to be bad, I take full responsibility for it.

Part of the research that went into this book was facilitated by a personal research grant from the Belgian National Science Foundation-Flanders (FWO-V) in 1998 and 1999. The greatest facilitators, however, were Pika, Frederik and Alexander, who sacrificed part of their summer holiday to enable me to write this book.

Antwerp, November 2007

Part I

GRASSROOTS LITERACY

1

INTRODUCTION
Grassroots literacy and literacy regimes

Yes I can write

> baKANGi NGAi NAYibi , eZALi YALoKuTA
> baKANGi NGAi na biLamba minei
> 4 Pantalon na yebi batu te mosusu
> oyo bazxLati na MAGAĐiN te

This text was written by a woman from the Congo, who was arrested by the Belgian police on grounds of shoplifting. The text was written on official police stationery. In the Belgian legal system, everyone has the right to go on record with his/her own account. That means: one would be asked whether one 'can write', and if so, one would be invited to write one's own account of the events. This document, then, becomes a legally consequential element in the criminal prosecution case: it is 'the story of the accused' and both the defence lawyer and the prosecution will refer to it as such. Observe that under Belgian law, suspects have the right to write in a language of their choice. In this case, the woman obviously confirmed that she 'could write', and she chose to write in Lingala, the lingua franca of Kinshasa and of the Congolese diaspora.

The phrase 'can write', however, is deceptively simple. In a country such as the Congo, literacy skills are generally rare and access to advanced and sophisticated forms of literacy is severely restricted. That means: while Congolese say they 'can write' when they are able to perform basic writing skills, that description would not cover the production of a long, nuanced and detailed written narrative in a standard, normative language variety and a standard orthography. Let us have a closer look at what and how the woman wrote. Here is a transcript of the text, followed by a translation. In the transcript I will try to preserve the graphic features of the original:

BaKANGI NGAI NAYIBI, eZALI YALOKUTA
baKANGI NGAI na bilamba minei
4 Pantalon na yebi [ɳɓ]atu te moSuSu
oyo baZALAKI na MAGASIN te

> They caught me (because) I had stolen, that is a lie
> They caught me with four pieces of clothing
> 4 *pantalons* I don't know the other people
> who were with me in the *magasin*

This text, I should emphasise, enters an institutional space of literacy, a rather strict and punitive one. And if we take this strict and punitive viewpoint, the woman – even if her writing was procedurally prefaced by a clear affirmation that she 'could write' – obviously struggles with several very basic literacy requirements. There is orthographic instability articulated through the alteration of upper case and lower case; punctuation is erratic, and several corrections betray a struggle with the grammatical and narrative norms she knows are at play here. She also switches to French – 'pantalons', 'magasin' – and so offers us a glimpse of the vernacular everyday (but 'non-standard') Lingala she speaks. And finally, she manifestly fails to produce a narrative that can stand as her 'account of the events'. There is no sequential development of actions, no plot nor storyline, no argued conclusion. The woman has written *something*, but in the legal procedure this something will not be of much use to her. Her writing has failed to produce voice in the specific communicative environment in which it was produced, and writing here silences her voice. The simple question 'can you write?' seems to be one that does not withstand the test of globalisation. Answers to it refer to practices and skills that belong to local, and very divergent, economies of literacy. Institutional regimes that emphasise uniformity in communication practices will exclude, marginalise and silence people whose repertoires do not match the normative expectations. Globalisation is likely to intensify this form of exclusion, because the super-diversity it spawns precludes any presupposability of linguistic or literacy resources among growing numbers of people. Processes and phenomena such as those are the topic of this book.

Writing

What we, in everyday parlance, call 'writing' is a very complex set of semiotic practices that involve the visualisation and materialisation of ideas and concepts, their archivability and transferability across time and space. Any consideration of writing, consequently, is forced to address material aspects as well as ideational ones, and both categories of aspects are of course in turn lodged in social, cultural, historical, economic and political contexts. The complexity that is hidden by the simple word 'writing' is tremendous, and many studies of writing have been plagued by the legacies of this suggestive simplicity, assuming a degree of homogeneity in the practices of writing, and their products and functions, which can no longer be sustained. As Hymes (1996: 35) observed, '[w]riting is usually seen as a record of something already existing'. Writing is an ethnographic object *par excellence*, something which, because of its sheer complexity and context-dependence, can only be fully understood when an

INTRODUCTION

analytical tactic is used that focuses on the object in relation to its contexts and relinquishes a priori claims about what this object would or should mean to the people who use it. For underneath every examination of writing – or literacy more generally – there is the question: *what counts as writing* for people who write and read? What is the meaning of writing practices for those who deploy them as well as for those among whom the products of writing – 'texts' or 'documents' – circulate?

The question can be reformulated sociolinguistically as: *what is the particular place of writing in the sociolinguistic repertoire of people* (Hymes 1996: 36)? And right from the start we can state that the answer to this is by no means easy or predictable. A repertoire comprises communicative resources as well as knowledge about their function and their conditions of use, and all of this is a very concrete matter. It is not enough to say that 'literacy' is part of someone's repertoire: it matters *which particular literacy resources* are there. It is evident that there is a difference between someone who is able to write with pen and paper and someone who in addition to that skill also writes on a keyboard; between someone who is able to read short and simple texts in one language variety and someone who is a competent reader of multiple genres in multiple languages and language varieties. Thinking about repertoires forces us to abandon totalising notions in the field of language and communication, and to replace them with terms that identify actual, specific practices. The range of factors we need to consider in analysing literacy, consequently, is expanded and now includes social, cultural, historical and political factors.

The distinctions made above do not usually occur by accident: they can be *systemic*, be part of the general structure of societies and characterise societies in distinction from others. Thus, keyboard writing on a computer and access to the kind of reading environment created by broadband internet are more or less widely distributed in a small number of societies while being extraordinarily rare in most other societies. Where such 'computer literacy' occurs, it quickly occupies a status position in the repertoires of its users as a 'higher' and more sophisticated form of literacy; it starts dominating certain genres of writing and transforms them – think of email as the new form of 'correspondence'. Becoming educated and getting access to middle-class jobs then depends on being competent in these particular forms of literacy, and while keyboard writing was until recently a highly specialised professional skill (I wrote my very first article with pen and paper and had it typed by an obstinate departmental typist), it is now a skill that defines a large middle-class educated cohort in societies such as mine. To be computer illiterate these days equals being illiterate *tout court*. As soon as I leave my society, however, or even as soon as I leave my middle-class environment, I find myself in a world where keyboard writing is all but absent, and where people pride themselves on being able to produce handwritten texts in a more or less stable orthography and language variety. We see differently organised repertoires there, and the repertoires reflect wider societal divisions and inequalities. Thinking about repertoires thus not only compels us to focus on actual practices, but it also compels us to set these practices in a field of power and inequality. Repertoires are internally and externally stratified, with all kinds of internal distinctions marking differences between 'better' and 'worse' resources, and external distinctions defining the resources from one repertoire as 'superior' or 'inferior' to those of others (Hymes 1996; Blommaert 2005a). Literacy is organised in *literacy regimes*, in structures of distribution, access, value and use that are closely tied to the general make-up of societies.

Most of what I have said so far is fairly common and hardly controversial sociolinguistic knowledge. The fact that literacy practices need to be seen and understood as contextualised, socially and culturally (ultra-)sensitive is the cornerstone of the New Literacy Studies and I do not feel I can add much to the arguments developed in some outstanding work within that paradigm (e.g. Gee 1990; Barton 1994; Graddol, Maybin & Stierer, eds. 1994; Baynham 1995; Besnier 1995; Collins 1995; Street 1995; Prinsloo & Breier, eds. 1996; Barton & Hamilton 1998; Collins & Blot 2003). The matter gains complexity as soon as we move these issues into the field of globalisation, when literacy products – texts and documents – move from one society into another in an ever-intensifying flow. What is correct in one society becomes an error in another society; what is perfectly appropriate writing in one place becomes a meaningless sign system in another. Texts may travel easily, but the system of use, value and function in which they were produced usually does not travel with them. Globalisation imposes a new grid on our analysis: we are now facing the task of designing an ethnography, not of locality but of transfer, of mobility – not of product but of process, and not in one 'ecologically' described community but across communities. These are poorly charted waters, and that is where I let my story begin.

This book is an attempt towards an ethnographic understanding of grassroots literacy in an age of globalisation. It will examine documents from the 'periphery': two sets of handwritten texts written by people from the southern province of Katanga in the Democratic Republic of the Congo. Both documents are exceptional with respect to their formal features – their length, for instance, and their genre characteristics – as well as with respect to the communicative framework in which they came into being: both are written for a specific purpose and for a 'Western' readership. Both, thus, are instances of grassroots literacy written *for* globalisation, with the explicit purpose of being read by people from outside the community of their composers. The two sets of documents are exceptionally large and complex bodies of grassroots literacy, and it is precisely their exceptional nature and scope that offers us opportunities for generalisation and extrapolation, as I hope to demonstrate in the chapters of this book.

The particular histories of these texts as well as of how they became my data will be told later on in the book. Now, I must introduce some of the basic theoretical considerations that will underlie this study: I must unpick and unpack what I mean by 'an ethnographic understanding of grassroots literacy in an age of globalisation'.

INTRODUCTION

Grassroots literacy

Grassroots literacy is a label I use for a wide variety of 'non-elite' forms of writing (and the elite forms will be flagged by means of the hyphenated 'ortho-graphy' – 'writing right' – in this book). It is writing performed by people who are not fully inserted into elite economies of information, language and literacy. The term can only be defined in a loosely descriptive way here; the analysis further in the book should add detail and clarity. In the materials I examine, grassroots literacy can be identified by:

1   *Hetero-graphy*. The deployment of graphic symbols in ways that defy *ortho-graphic* norms. This is manifest in (i) spelling difficulties – words are spelled in different ways, and very often reflect 'accent', the way in which they are pronounced in spoken vernacular varieties. (ii) It is also manifest in erratic punctuation and the use of upper and lower case without clear rules apparently guiding their usage. (iii) The texts very often look like 'drafts': there are corrections and additions, often revealing uncertainty about linguistic and stylistic rules. (iv) At the same time, and apparently paradoxically, we also often see a clear dimension of *visual aestheticisation* of documents: texts would be 'drawn', so to speak, and they would often contain sketches, drawings and other visual means of structuring and representing information. Grassroots writing often looks like calligraphic writing.

2   *Vernacular language varieties being used in writing*. The 'code' in which documents are written often betrays absence of access to 'Standard' normative (and thus prestige) language varieties. People write in local, so-called 'sub-standard' varieties of language, they use code-switching, colloquialisms and other 'impurities' in their written texts.

3   *Distant genres*. People write in genres to which they have only been marginally exposed and for whose full realisation they often lack the required resources. The genres often evoke (and suggest) distant *sources* for the texts: texts are 'assembled' out of the available and accessible materials in attempts to construct such perceived genres.

4   *Partial insertion in knowledge economies*. People often construct texts on the basis of locally available knowledge resources: the things they can find out by asking or listening rather than by searching in literate corpuses.

These four characteristics combined lead to a fifth one:

5   *Constrained mobility*. Texts are often only *locally* meaningful and valuable. As soon as they move to other geographical and/or social spaces, they lose 'voice'. This is a derived feature of grassroots literacy, and it bears on the ways in which in times of globalisation, grassroots literacy products and resources move around.

A description of texts these days must therefore necessarily have two sides: one, a description of the *local* economies in which they are produced, and two, analyses of what happens to them when they become *translocal* documents. The two corpuses of text I shall examine in the main body of this book have been moved around, they have travelled, and part of the analysis will address their problematic uptake elsewhere. They have been produced in a local literacy regime and then projected into translocal trajectories, but their reception was, in both cases, problematic.

I came across the term 'grassroots literacy' in Fabian's *History from Below* (Fabian 1990a). This remarkable book discusses a printed booklet from Lubumbashi, called the *Vocabulaire de Ville de Elisabethville*. The text is a local (or regional) history of the city, written by a former houseboy called André Yav. It is 33 pages long, typewritten and reprographed, with illustrations and other embellishments that make the document visually appealing. Fabian presents a facsimile edition, a 're-oralised' transcript, a translation, and linguistic (by Walter Schicho, Schicho 1990) and anthropological notes. In the preface to this book, Fabian writes:

> The *Vocabulaire* is a document of grass-roots literacy; it remains rooted in orality. Texts of this sort, as we shall see, cannot be read (understood, translated) by outsiders except 'ethnographically', by way of 'performing' the written script according to the rules that govern oral communication in this culture.
>
> (Fabian 1990a: 2)

It is this connection of a written document with an oral substrate culture that motivates Fabian's 're-oralisation' procedure. In a later paper reflecting on the work on the *Vocabulaire*, Fabian returns to the issue of grassroots literacy, and I quote him at length (Fabian 1993: 90):

> Apart from its extraordinary content, it was its literacy, or more specifically, its graphic form that made the *Vocabulaire* such a challenge. I referred to it as an instance of 'grass-roots literacy', that is, of the appropriation of a technique of writing by speakers of Shaba Swahili which was relatively free from the ideological and technical constraints that characterized literacy taught to the same speakers in other languages (French, some regional languages, and a variety of Swahili spoken by no one but considered fit for literacy). From the results [. . .] we can infer that it is a literacy which works despite an amazingly high degree of indeterminacy and freedom (visible in an erratic orthography, a great disdain for 'correct' word and sentence boundaries and many other instances of seemingly unmotivated variation).

This concern for 'graphic form' was central to Fabian's analysis of the *Vocabulaire*, and he formulates it as a thesis: 'much of *what* the document tells us about

INTRODUCTION

colonial history and experience is inscribed in *how* it was conceived, composed, presented and diffused' (Fabian 1990a: 164) because 'we want to read the features of a text, a static record, as evidence for process. Patterns we detect can then be made to tell the story of events in the work of producing this document' (204).

Later in this book, I will discuss the epistemological and methodological issues involved in this view. In a nutshell and roughly put, documents such as the *Vocabulaire* and the texts I will examine here are so packed with features that defy our expectations of 'full' literacy that we stop *reading* them and treat them as things that require *reconstruction*. Fabian's re-oralisation procedure is one tactic for reconstructing the document; seeing the document as primarily *visual* and *material* is another. In both cases, however, we will have to be careful not to invite abstract distinctions between 'form' and 'content'; we must be aware that, in the end, we are *always* looking at something material and visual (let us not forget that our own texts are material and visual objects), and that we *always* face an object that intentionally conveys meaning.

Fabian's description of the literacy variety in the *Vocabulaire* was, as I said, my first encounter with the term 'grassroots literacy', as well as an introduction to a particular way of analysing documents. We shall see that I will have to take my analysis in different directions than Fabian's. One reason is that I am not comfortable with the connection between a literate document and an 'oral culture' sketched here. Naturally this connection is based upon a distinction between a dominant orality and a peripheral literacy, in which only a hierarchical and unidirectional influence can occur: from orality into literacy. This, to my taste, smacks a bit too much of Great Divide images of orality and literacy, and it presupposes the primarily 'oral' character of the local culture (see Street 1995 for an elaborate discussion). In the data I shall discuss, I'm afraid things are rather more complex and nuanced. I have not felt any need to use the notion of an 'oral culture' as an element of explanation and I will not be forced to make statements about African cultures as 'primarily oral'. The fact that I am examining written documents demonstrates that such cultures are *literate* as well. The literacy we observe there may very well be described as grassroots, peripheral, but it is literacy nevertheless – a cultural product that shapes cultural subjects. That is not to say that there is no connection whatsoever between forms of language in oral versus in written use. There is *always* a trace of 'spoken language' in 'written language': everyone 'writes with an accent', but when we encounter such accents in writing we usually call it 'style'. I will address the matter of accent in writing at great length, hoping that it will demonstrate more precise and useful ways of treating orality and literacy.

A second element in Fabian's description from which I gradually learned to keep my distance is the image that grassroots writing is relatively 'free from the ideological and technical constraints' that characterise schooled, normative literacy. I find the distinction between grassroots literacy and schooled literacy less than useful, because (as we shall see) schooled literacy can be very 'grassroots'.

9

Fabian also talks about 'a literacy which works despite an amazingly high degree of indeterminacy and freedom' and in both statements there is an image of grassroots writing as a liberating (and/or liberated) practice of expression. 'Freedom', I started realising, is not an appropriate term for grassroots literacy. Grassroots literacy has its own constraints. Even more: I am convinced (and will attempt to demonstrate) that we can only understand grassroots literacy when we see it *in terms of constraints*, not just of opportunities (cf. Blommaert 2004). Grassroots literacy is only *locally* liberating and free; *translocally*, however, it can be oppressive and disempowering. The example with which I opened this chapter illustrates this.

There is, in general, methodological uneasiness among scholars facing grassroots literacy texts. One of the reasons is that such texts violate our conceptions of textuality and do not match our textual expectations. Scholars, to be sure, have *used* such texts. But often they have insufficiently attended to the features that make such texts into what they are: products of grassroots literacy that demand close inspection of their formal features, the linguistic, stylistic and material resources that were used in them, and the various constraints that operated on this process. Thus, whereas scholars seemed rather at ease methodologically in ethnographies of oral performance data, their treatment of text was often less than ethnographic: texts were not presented as they were but *normatively reorganised* (or re-entextualised) and the status of the texts remained methodologically unclear. Three examples can illustrate this.

Pat Caplan's *African Voices, African Lives* (1997) is an admirable study of the life of Mohammed, a small farmer from the Tanzanian coast. It is one of the very few in-depth ethnographies of an African life, and a source of inspiration for the present book. An important part of the material used by Caplan is a diary written by the man on her request. The status of this material, however, is unclear. Caplan has obviously worked from a *transcript* of the diary (the diary is described as a typescript: 1997: 61), and during the transcription process, the man asked her to include several *spoken* additions. The material, here, is a further stage of the text trajectory, and the original document is not the basis for the analysis – that is, the 'diary' used as 'data' is a seriously edited and reorganised textual format. Caplan also gives reasons for that. She mentions the option to publish 'as much of the diary in as unedited a form as possible' but discarded that 'because of the style in which the diary is written, as well as because of the complexity of its content which would have required a large amount of commentary and footnotes in order to render it intelligible' (63). As to style, Caplan saw an immediate obstacle for documenting a life history: 'Mohammed does not write in totally chronological order' (63). A life history is here conceived as a chronological sequence; I shall have to show in later chapters that chronology is *necessarily* a problematic genre feature. She also mentions, as a stylistic problem, the fact that 'Mohammed frequently utilises direct speech' (64) where reported speech (a more 'objective' entextualisation of cultural encounters) would be expected and preferable. Here, too, we see how a genre feature which is culturally sensitive – the preference for a 'factual' report – is projected onto the diary.

INTRODUCTION

Caplan's use of the text written by Mohammed illustrates some general problems. The grassroots written document does not fit the expected genre in writing, and the analyst consequently 're-orders' the text. In doing so, a whole range of features that uniquely represent the position from which the document has been written are erased, and much of what the document effectively *is* and *represents* as an act of subjectivity is lost. The document, manifestly, cannot speak with its own voice. We see similar unfortunate interventions in another remarkable and very stimulating book, Bogumil Jewsiwiecki's *Naître et Mourir au Zaïre: Un Demi-Siècle d'Histoire au Quotidien* (1993). Jewsiwiecki presents a unique collection of grassroots writings from the Congo, documenting the way in which people experience life in their society and the often conflictual changes therein. His presentation of these texts aims at authenticity: he has 'opted for maximum respect for the specific character of each text'. And indeed, no attempt has been undertaken to 're-write' the texts into polished autobiographical prose. But he adds: 'thus only manifest errors in orthography, syntax, and, occasionally, in vocabulary have been corrected' (1993: 15, French original). This textual intervention naturally destroys a good deal of the evidence of the grassroots character of the text. In an attempt to make texts 'readable' to a highly educated international audience, the genre features of the texts have been reorganised.

Liisa Malkki's *Purity and Exile* (1995) is a classic ethnography of displacement in post-conflict situations. Malkki investigated the narratives and experiences of Hutu refugees from Burundi living in a Tanzanian refugee camp and in the Tanzanian town of Kigoma, where they had fled after the 1972 political troubles in their country. The book contains a powerful postscript called 'Return to Genocide'. The postscript treats the predicament of her informants during the Rwandan genocide of 1994, which caused another exodus and put many of the people Malkki had worked with in very precarious situations. In this part of the book, Malkki works on the basis of letters sent to her from the refugee camps. And here a remarkable epistemological and methodological break occurs: whereas the narratives of the refugees were analysed as 'mythico-history' in the main body of the book, and whereas this aspect of mythical-historical patterning in narratives was crucial in her understanding of the condition of displacement, the letters in the postscript are treated as neutral, factual accounts of events. They are accepted on face value, as 'evidence' of historical events and situations. The critical distance that Malkki maintained throughout the book suddenly disappears when the letters are discussed. The letters, of course, are not presented in their original form; they, too, are generically reorganised in 'factual' narratives that can then be treated as such. The epistemological and methodological confidence the book exudes disappears as soon as the letters appear. They are written and synchronic, as opposed to the oral narratives on a more remote past that formed the core of the book. And Malkki, in discussing them, is no longer an observer but a participant who intervenes – not just in the situation of the people but also in their textual accounts.

11

These few examples show how uncomfortably grassroots literacy texts are treated in much scholarship, even in some of the most distinguished examples of it. The particular material shapes of such literacy products, and the way in which these shapes distort dominant images of what a text is and should be, and the functions of such shapes in conveying meaning: all of this is a methodologically underdeveloped domain. What is needed, I believe, is an ethnography of text.

Ethnographies of text

In a seminal paper published in 1974, Keith Basso observed:

> [. . .] the most conspicuous shortcomings of traditional studies of writing is that they reveal very little about the social patterning of this activity or the contributions it makes to the maintenance of social systems.
>
> (Basso 1974: 431)

Basso's proposals for an ethnography of writing were those of early (Hymesian) ethnography of speaking: an ethnography of writing should be an approach to writing directed towards understanding its role and function in social life, the way in which writing involved and drew in (or excluded) participants, the way in which it could be divided into genres within a repertoire and a community. The approach was mainly descriptive – though this description was a theorised description, a *descriptive theory* (Hymes 1972: 52). That is: the conceptual apparatus deployed in this description was designed so as to allow comparison and generalisation across cases. And the fundamental theoretical assumptions were general too: writing was seen as a *practice*, a *situated*, contextualised practice that needed to be understood as such. Texts no longer had an isolated existence: they were now firmly locked into a wider complex of human contextualised activities. A text is always connected to the practice of its production, circulation, uptake, re-use and so forth. This central theoretical point (rather than the actual descriptive grid of such an ethnography) became the keystone for later developments in the ethnography of literacy practices (e.g. Fabian 1990a; Besnier 1995; Street 1995; Barton & Hamilton 1998), including historical analyses of early literacy (e.g. Rafael 1993). This central ethnographic perspective also informed studies on the transmission of texts across contexts in which such transmissions were seen as complex re-orderings of textualised meaning (Silverstein & Urban, eds. 1996).

Such work is still relatively rare. As noted earlier, anthropologists still seem to prefer oral data and display uneasiness when written data have to be addressed. On the side of applied linguistics, educational linguistics and sociolinguistics, the ethnographic terrain is often only superficially explored. Studies on narrative have yet to begin to attend to the wealth of written narrative material; for

INTRODUCTION

the moment, the focus is firmly on oral narrative (see e.g. De Fina, Schiffrin & Bamberg, eds. 2006; Bamberg, ed. 2007). We shall not be discouraged by this absence of a huge and diversified literature. Much of what is there is of excellent quality, and we have a relatively sound theoretical basis to start from. Let me now try to summarise my own views.

Texts and practices

I will work on texts. The core data for this book are two sets of documents: one consisting of three versions of a life history from the Congo, the other a handwritten 'history of the Congo' by a popular painter from the Congo, Tshibumba. I have not met the authors of these documents; I have not been able to conduct interviews with them, to observe them while they were writing, talk to members of their community, and so on. In short, this is not a fieldwork-based book. To some, this suffices to disqualify it as ethnographic.

This is a very misguided view, and I will give two major reasons. The first one is simple: reducing ethnography to fieldwork yielding a particular kind of data, reduces ethnography to a collection of *methods and techniques*. It so discards most of what is valuable about ethnography: the fact, for instance, that it is (and always has been) a *theoretical perspective* on human behaviour. That means: ethnography includes a particular epistemological and methodological position which is different from other approaches. This position is characterised by features such as (i) an assumption about the situated (contextualised) nature of human actions; (ii) an interpretive stance and a reflexive awareness of 'bias' in all stages of research; (iii) a commitment to comprehensiveness and complexity – ethnography does not attempt to reduce the complexity of human conduct and does not try to reduce it to 'core' features – and (iv) an assumption that small things (analytic detail) can shed light on bigger things, or, in another jargon, we can explore macro-structures through micro-details (see Blommaert 2005b, 2007 for a more elaborate discussion). When it comes to methods, ethnography has always been characterised by eclecticism and *bricolage*: the ethnographer thinks and develops methods in response to features of the object of inquiry. I don't believe I need to expand on this issue; it is a matter of record and there is very good reflective literature on this topic (Hymes 1996; Fabian 2001; Wacquant 2004). The bottom line is: ethnography is a theoretical position, not one of method.

The second argument cuts deeper and is more particular to the ethnography of literacy. It seems to me that the notion of 'practices' is artificially separated from that of 'products'. Texts – as products of literacy practices – appear often to be seen as just the accidental outcome of a far more interesting 'practice'. Therefore, when the practice is not observable, analysis is thrown back to formal description and cannot be ethnographic. This line of argument rests on a *prima facie* distinction between processes and products which denies a rather elementary set of observations: that 'practices' always yield 'products', that such

13

'products' therefore contain traces of practices and can disclose the nature of such practices, and that the 'products' themselves yield practices. The whole idea of text is so deeply connected to ideas we have about cultural transmission and social reproduction that extracting them from that complex of practices amounts to the de-materialisation of such processes. It also leads to a view which is even less sustainable: that of the 'context-less' text. There are no 'context-less' texts: every text displays features of its unique context-of-production as well as of the potential it has to move across contexts. Thus, even a text of which we have no 'contextual' information will be analytically contextualised. The fact that we don't know its authors, the language in which it was cast, its original function and audience, its uptake by that audience – all of that does not mean that the text has no context. It means that we have to contextualise it, fill in these contextual blanks by means of rigorous ethnographic interpretation.

Let me comment further on the ways in which texts display traces of contexts. The point should be easy to understand. When we see a nail in a piece of wood, we know that someone put it there; we know that, normally, someone has used a particular tool for doing that – a hammer – and we can imagine the specific activities involved in that process. We can even do more and develop hypotheses about the particular function of that activity from looking at how the nail has been fixed. If it connects two beams in a wooden building, we can guess that the nail has been put there by someone who was building a house, and that it needed to be there in order to give stability to a fragile structure. In all likelihood, the one who performed that practice was an adult with fairly developed building skills. If we don't find such clues, we can suggest that, perhaps, this was a kid trying his/her hand at hammering a nail into a piece of wood, just for fun.

I hope my readers appreciate that I have not been making wild guesses here. I have made *inferences* that are based on plausibility: a somewhat tortuous construction for which we have a simpler word, *hypotheses*. On the basis of a single detail, I have constructed a range of hypotheses about what this detail means in relation to wider frames of human knowledge and behaviour. I have, in yet another reformulation, provided contextualising inferences for the detail. The detail is now connected with a *category* of such details, it has become a token of a type, and I can start the verification process of my hypotheses. These now have a clear direction: I do not need to speculate but I can perform checks on my conjectures.

This very simple everyday procedure is, in fact, a scientific methodological paradigm of considerable respectability: it is the cornerstone of the 'inductive' paradigm. Ethnography belongs to a range of other scientific disciplines in which induction rather than deduction is the rule – history, law and archaeology are close neighbours. Inductive sciences usually apply what is called the *case method* (see e.g. Shulman 1986). This case method builds upon a much older tradition, which Carlo Ginzburg (1989) calls the '*evidential or conjectural paradigm*': evidential because it uses (inductive) empirical facts as its point of departure,

INTRODUCTION

'conjectural' because these facts are seen as *probably* meaning this-or-that. The facts generate hypotheses that can then be verified. This paradigm is epitomised by Sherlock Holmes, who was able to deduce more insights from a cigarette butt left in an ashtray than his rival police inspector could by deploying his elaborate (deductive) forensic investigation tactics.

Ginzburg finds ancient roots for this paradigm in divination – where the divinator would examine small things in order to predict big things – and he nicely summarises the case:

> the group of disciplines which we have called evidential and conjectural [. . .] are totally unrelated to the scientific criteria that can be claimed for the Galilean paradigm [in which individual cases do not count – JB]. In fact, they are highly qualitative disciplines, in which the object is the study of individual cases, situations, and documents, precisely *because they are individual,* and for this reason get results that have an unsupressible speculative margin; just think of the importance of conjecture (the term itself originates in divination) in medicine or in philology, and in divining.
>
> (Ginzburg 1989: 106)

History, philology, psychoanalysis, archaeology, medicine, law, art history: these are the companions of ethnography in a long and venerable tradition of scientific work. In fact, every truly *social* science falls in this category. Chomsky's linguistics was an attempt to bring the study of language – a social science, evidently – into the orbit of Galilean science. To Chomsky and his followers, linguistics would be a deductive science in which individual *performance* had no place, because individual cases could never invalidate the generalisations made from theory. In other social sciences as well, we have seen how strong the appeal of a deductive Galilean model of science was. The effect has been that the existence, and the validity, of this evidential and conjectural paradigm have been largely forgotten. Yet, it is the methodological basis for generalisation in ethnography, and it is a very firm basis.

Ethnography and philology

As I said above, ethnography is eclectic when it comes to methods. There is no reason why, for instance, conversation analysis would be intrinsically more 'ethnographic' than, say, phonetics. One can imagine perfectly sound ethnographic work based on phonetics and very un-ethnographic conversation analysis. Work is ethnographic when it subscribes to the fundamental assumptions sketched above. And in this book, I will present what can pass as an ethnographic philology. I will analyse texts in ways clearly reminiscent of a long philological tradition; the questions guiding this analysis, as well as the finality of this analysis, will be ethnographic. There are precedents for that approach, and I drew my inspiration from Hymes' views of 'ethnopoetics'. Ethnopoetics is an analytic strategy aimed at disclosing implicit poetic and aesthetic form in oral narratives. Hymes himself elaborated the strategy in trying to 'restore' Native American oral narratives to their original function. His views deserve some comments.

Hymes sees ethnopoetics as a form of structural linguistics, more precisely of 'practical structuralism' – 'the elementary task of discovering the relevant features and relationships of a language and its texts' (Hymes 2003: 123).[1] It is about describing *what exists* in language and texts, and when applied to texts it is a form of *philology*. But even if '[t]his kind of linguistics is old, known as philology [. . .], [t]he kind of discoveries it makes are new' (Hymes 1998: ix). It is an eclectic and composite philology, one that has been composed out of classical philological principles (the collection and meticulous analysis of texts), anthropological heuristics (the Boasian and Whorfian emphasis on cultural categories, on culture as an organising principle for linguistic form), and ethnographic epistemology (the principle that things can only be found out by structured attention to situated contextualised behaviour). This philology is oriented towards discovering verbal *art*, organised in a (structurally described) 'grammar' of discourse which yields implicit patterns and principles of organisation, allowing us to see 'artistry and subtlety of meaning otherwise invisible' (Hymes 2003: 96).[2] It comes down to 'considering spoken narrative as a level of linguistic structure, as having consistent patterns – patterns far less complex than those of syntax, but patterns nonetheless' (97).

Such patterns, I will argue, can also be detected in written texts. In order to detect them, however, one must adopt the analytic strategy proposed by Hymes: abandon received wisdom about the 'normal' (overt) structure of text, and delve into its deeper fabric in a search for principles of organisation that are 'emic', so to speak. They reflect the 'methods' employed by the author in constructing the text. These 'methods' are particular models that have been followed, as well as judgments about the usefulness and validity of particular textual resources: the language or code, the particular script, the graphic organisation of a text, and so on. Such methods have been described as language ideologies (Silverstein 1979; Schieffelin, Woolard & Kroskrity, eds. 1998): local beliefs and perception of what linguistic resources are, what they are there for, and what their use tells us about the act of communication and those who perform it. The latter is indexicality (Silverstein 2006; Agha 2007). We can *indexically* infer all kinds of contextual features from observing the patterns in the text, because they reflect the ways in which people organise communicative resources such that they produce *specific* meanings. People don't normally just shoot meanings in the air: they target them and are quite specific about how they want others to construe their acts of communication.

This kind of analysis is an analysis of *voice*. Let us turn back to Hymes and follow his argument in some detail:

INTRODUCTION

> The work that discloses such form can be a kind of repatriation. It can restore to native communities and descendants a literary art that was implicit, like so much of language, but that now, when continuity of verbal tradition has been broken, requires analysis to be recognized.
>
> (Hymes 1998: vii)

In order to understand this argument, the decor of our discussion needs to be slightly changed, from the texts themselves to the tradition of recording and analysing them. Hymes is critical of the linguistic and folkloristic traditions of scholarship on 'oral tradition', claiming that they produced a record which has dismembered the very traditions *as traditions*, i.e. as something deeply connected to culture and cultural activity – as performable, poetically organised narrative, operating as a cognitive, cultural, affective way of handling experience. Losing that dimension of language means losing the capacity to produce voice – to express things on one's own terms, to communicate in ways that satisfy personal, social and cultural needs – to be communicatively *competent*, so to speak.

Voice – this is what functional reconstruction is about. Ultimately, what this analysis does is to show voice, to represent the particular ways – often deviant from hegemonic norms – in which subjects produce meanings. In Hymes' view (most eloquently articulated in Hymes 1996), voice is the capacity to make oneself understood in one's own terms, to produce meanings under conditions of empowerment. And in the present world, such conditions are wanting for more and more people. The Native Americans in Hymes' work are obvious victims of minorisation, but Hymes (1996) extends the scope of ethnopoetic reconstructions to include other disenfranchised groups – African Americans, working-class college students, other minorities. Such groups frequently appear to be the victim of the negative stereotyping of part of their repertoire, the dismissal of their ways of speaking as illegitimate, irrational, not-to-the-point, *narrative* rather than factual; and 'one form of inequality of opportunity in our society has to do with rights to use narrative, with whose narratives are admitted to have a cognitive function' (1996: 109).

This argument, of course, can easily be extended to cover texts in general. Some people's texts are not taken into account; they are struck from the record or dismissed as nonsense, curious or funny. Hymes observes (alongside many others, e.g. Gumperz, Labov, Bourdieu) that 'making sense' in actual fact is about 'making sense *in particular ways*', using very specific linguistic, stylistic and generic resources, thus disqualifying different resources even when they are perfectly valid in view of the particular functions to be realised. It is in this world in which difference is quickly converted into inequality that attention to 'emic' forms of textual organisation takes on more than just an academic import and becomes a political move, aimed at the recognition of variation and variability as 'natural' features of societies, and at recognising that variation in cultural behaviour can result in many potentially equivalent solutions to similar problems.

This, consequently, radicalises the issue of diversity, because it shifts the question from one of latent potential equivalence to one of effective disqualification and inequality. If all languages are equal, how is it that some (many!) are not recognised even as languages? How is it that the latent and potential equivalence of languages, in actual practice, converts into rigid language hierarchies? That potential equality is matched by actual inequality? That 'unfamiliar pattern may be taken to be absence of pattern' (Hymes 1996: 174)? Part of Hymes' answer is that diversity still requires deeper understanding as to its actual forms, structures and functions. Misunderstanding of such aspects of diversity, often resulting from errors in past work or sloppiness in current work, precludes appreciation of diversity *as a solution*. Finding the unexpected patterns in 'strange' texts could recast visions of diversity:

> In sum, there lies ahead a vast work, work in which members of narrative communities can share, the work of discovering forms of implicit patterning in oral narratives, patterning largely out of awareness, *relations* grounded in a universal *potential*, whose *actual* realization varies. To demonstrate its presence can enhance respect for an appreciation of the voices of others.
>
> (Hymes 1996: 219)

This is no longer just about developing a better, more accurate philology of native texts; ethnopoetics here becomes a program for understanding voice *and the reasons why voice is an instrument of power* with potential to include as well as to exclude. It becomes a critical *ethnographic and sociolinguistic* programme that offers us a way into the concrete linguistic shape of sociocultural inequality in and across societies.

Visuality, materiality, textuality

The platform from which I will address the texts in this book has now been sketched. I have specified my epistemological and methodological stances and the main lines of my analytical tactics. I will try to perform 'the elementary task of discovering the relevant features and relationships of a language and its texts' (Hymes 2003: 123) by looking at forms of text organisation that appear to be governed by locally valid norms, rules, and economies of semiotic resources – in short, by a particular literacy regime from which such things are derived and given function and value. This approach is aimed at uncovering voice – at *reconstructing* voice that was denied because of the effect of such regimes. And I will do so on the basis of two bodies of texts from the Congo. These two sets of documents will be introduced in detail later: they are both exceptional documents, 'historiographic' in the broad sense of the term, and produced under the kinds of 'grassroots' constraints specified earlier. The question will be: how does the *specific* textuality of these documents – their textual architecture and

INTRODUCTION

make-up – explain issues of voice that emerged in their reception? Both sets of documents were written for people who were, to use a silly but momentarily useful descriptor, 'Westerners', and both sets of documents were rather coolly received by them. They failed to get their voices across to their readers. The question is: why?

I will begin by looking at documents produced by a man I call Julien. Julien was a former houseboy who worked for a Belgian family in Lubumbashi, the Arens family. He wrote three versions of an autobiography for Mrs Arens, and each of these versions is an instance of deep grassroots writing. When we analyse his versions, however, we will see a gradual increase of structural tightness. Julien has a genre in mind – let us call it 'historiography' – and his writings are increasingly oriented towards an ideal type of that genre. I will first address some general issues, focusing on the history of these texts as 'data' and on the tremendous writing effort that went into them (Chapter 2). Next, I shall examine the issues of genres and repertoires. Genres require particular resources, and such resources are grouped and organised in a repertoire. From the way in which Julien writes – he writes in Shaba Swahili and French – we see how he selects and *develops* resources to fit the genre he intends to realise (Chapter 3). This genre, however, remains 'incomplete', because some formal resources are out of reach, and some other material and informational resources are absent as well. Julien works without an 'archive' and he has to remember his life from scratch in each writing exercise. We can see this from the way in which his versions show an increasing chronological tightness: remembering, for Julien, is remembering a particular precise chronology to events. This, then, shows something about the connections between writing and subjectivity. An elementary act of subjectivity – the story of one's 'life' – appears to be controlled by the possibility of performing particular genres. Julien had no life prior to writing it down in specific ways (Chapter 4). Consequently, the way in which we can understand this subjectivity – his voice – requires elaborate analytical reconstruction.

Tshibumba was a popular painter from Lubumbashi whose work became internationally acclaimed due to the influence of scholars who worked with him in the 1970s, the most prominent of whom were Johannes Fabian and Bogumil Jewsiwiecki. Tshibumba painted a magnificent series of 101 works on the history of the Congo; he also wrote such a history and sent it to Jewsiwiecki. In contrast to Tshibumba's painting, this handwritten document remained underexposed. Yet it is a document of tremendous value. I will introduce the text and its relation to the paintings and conversations on history he left on record (Chapter 5). I will then address the aesthetics of Tshibumba's historiography. As a painter, Tshibumba's historical work was characterised by his use of sometimes lengthy inscriptions. His visual work was textual. His written work, however, is disciplined, orthodox writing, and Tshibumba appears to have surrendered some of his best resources when he decided to write. This reveals particular genre notions and ideologies of text to us, and there appears the problem of the resources available for this demanding genre (Chapter 6). Some

19

of these resources, when writing history, have to do with 'sources': Tshibumba's text shows a diffuse range of sources that he used for constructing his history, ranging from political propaganda and colonial schoolbooks to locally circulating rumours. The notion of 'local' is relevant here. Another striking feature of his text is that Tshibumba literally writes 'from Katanga', from the place where he lives. He looks at his country from within its south-eastern corner, and this informs us about the economy of knowledge and information in which he is locked. He constructs a national history with local resources (Chapter 7). Yet, Tshibumba repeatedly and emphatically claimed a particular identity: that of a *historian*. And he wrote as a historian, too: he spent pages on methodological and meta-historical reflections, which articulate a deep awareness of crucial intellectual issues in an exercise such as that of historiography. The issue of subjectivity emerges here, as in Julien's case, as one of genres and resources: the identity he claimed needed to be produced through a particular genre in writing. For this genre, he needed particular resources, and many of them were out of reach. Thus, he remained 'memorable' as a painter, not as a historian (Chapter 8).

The detailed analysis I shall provide of these documents illustrates widespread patterns of 'hetero-graphic' textual organisation. 'Hetero-graphy' stands in contrast to 'ortho-graphy'. The latter is the normative deployment of graphic signs in writing; the former is the deployment of such graphic signs for unexpected functions and purposes. A lot of grassroots writing displays such hetero-graphic features, and seeing them not as deviations from a (presumed universal) norm, but as effects of the local organisation of resources, casts light on a range of theoretical, methodological and ethical issues which I shall try to review in Chapter 9.

As can be seen from this brief survey of the chapters, my ethnographic philology is informed by relatively 'un-philological' concerns: a concern for sources and resources that can often only be detected from a thorough review of the visual and material characteristics of documents. Recall Fabian's words, '[m]uch of *what* the document tells us [. . .] is inscribed in *how* it was conceived, composed, presented, and diffused' (1990a: 164). This attention to visual and material features is crucial for understanding the constraints under which such grassroots documents emerge – indeed, it is crucial for understanding what 'grassroots' means. In that sense, my analysis aligns with contemporary approaches to multimodality (e.g. Kress & van Leeuwen 1996) – including a healthy scepticism about the nature and functions of texts, which, for instance, questions the old assumptions that 'texts' are primarily 'for reading'. Often, we can only read when we have *looked* at the documents.

Congo and Zaire

Many readers may find it hard to situate what goes on in the chapters unless they familiarise themselves with some basics about the country where the action takes place: the Democratic Republic of the Congo (not to be confounded

INTRODUCTION

with the République du Congo, also known as Congo-Brazzaville, adjacent to the D.R. Congo). One can refer to the maps provided here, and several good sources of information can be consulted. But I must provide a number of basic elements before I embark on my analysis. I do this with an important caveat in mind. We shall see in the subsequent chapters that the very concept of 'historical facts' is strongly tied to regimes of literacy, in which 'facts' derive from generically regimented work for which particular positions are required. I cannot claim to be a master of such work, and it would please me if readers see what follows here not as a conclusive statement on the history of the Congo but as an *aide-mémoire*, a glossary if you wish, to clarify some of the things Julien and Tshibumba write. I will restrict myself to things that are directly relevant for the discussion in the subsequent chapters.[3]

Summarising the colonial and post-colonial history of the Congo, we can roughly distinguish between five periods, four of which will be relevant for our discussion of the documents.

1 The first period is that of the Congo Free State, and it was preceded by a phase of exploration in the 1870s, in which Henry Morton Stanley was the most visible and energetic character. During the 'scramble for Africa' in the third and fourth quarter of the 19th century, King Leopold II acquired a huge territory as an effect of the Berlin Conference of 1885. That conference was called by him under the pretext of the scientific exploration of Central Africa. Leopold uniquely acquired *private* control over this vast territory, and between 1885 and 1908, the country was effectively turned into a robbery economy in which mercenaries, private enterprises, missionaries and a small administrative cadre operated. The rubber campaigns of this period were genocidal; the military campaigns broke the back of the local political structures; but Leopold was seen by many as a philanthropist. Major industries – mainly mining – were set up in the Katanga region (where both Julien and Tshibumba lived), and the *Union Minière du Haut Katanga* (UMHK) became one of the most formidable industrial powers in Africa.

2 Due to massive financial problems, Leopold donated the Congo to the Belgian State in 1908. From 1908 on, Belgium officially *colonised* the Congo, and our second period is the colonial period, 1908–60. Belgium was a reluctant coloniser, and opted for *direct* rule (as opposed to 'indirect rule' in the British Empire). The colony was governed from Brussels and, locally, by a vast administrative apparatus and an army, in close collaboration with Catholic Missions who took charge of most of the education system. The Congo effectively became a province of Belgium, and significant numbers of Belgian settlers moved to the Congo. After the First World War, Belgium acquired the former German colonies of Rwanda and Burundi as a mandate. During the Second World War, the Congo remained unoccupied and became crucial in the Allied war effort. Katanga had been developed into one of the richest mineral-extraction fields in

21

the world, producing copper, cobalt and uranium (uranium for the first atomic bombs came from Katanga). In Kasai, rich diamond fields were discovered and exploited. From the 1950s on, modest independence movements emerged among the new class of local 'clerks'. In the late 1950s, a series of disruptions of public order precipitated the process of independence – clearly inspired by the fear of violence. A Round Table conference was organised in Brussels in 1960, elections were called, and on June 30, 1960 the Congo became an independent republic. The first President, Joseph Kasavubu, shared power with Prime Minister Patrice Lumumba, who had won the elections with his non-ethnic and non-regional nationalism party.

3 The third period begins with independence in 1960 and ends with the military coup of Joseph-Désiré Mobutu in 1965. The period was one protracted 'Congo Crisis' in which distinct Cold War notes could be discerned: The Congo was a major industrial force in Africa and Western powers were anxious to avoid alignment between the Congo and the USSR. In July 1960, Katanga proclaimed its independence under the local leader Moïse Tshombe, strongly supported by the industrial powers in that region. This secession initiated a period of military campaigns and further regional secessions (of Southern Kasai, under Albert Kalonji), with the intervention of UN troops in late 1960, the assassination of Lumumba in January 1961 and a Belgian military intervention in 1964 as landmark moments. The country staggered through a period of chronic instability and destruction, which ended when the Chief of Staff of the Army, Mobutu (with the agreement of the US government), deposed the government, disbanded parliament and the political parties, and proclaimed a period of law and order in 1965.

4 The fourth period, then, is Mobutu's reign, from 1965 until 1997. Mobutu developed quickly from a Congolese nationalist into a classic dictator. Having disbanded and prohibited political parties he started the *Mouvement Populaire de la Révolution*, MPR. MPR was the single party, and the country was defined as a 'parti-état', a state that completely coincided with the single party. In 1971, he proclaimed the 'Zairianisation' of his country. The Congo was renamed 'Zaire', the Congo River became the Zaire River, and cities and regions were renamed as well: Katanga became Shaba, Elisabethville became Lubumbashi, Jadotville became Likasi, and so on. Personal names were changed as well, because Mobutu now insisted on African authenticity. *Authenticité* became the cornerstone of '*Mobutism*', the official ideology of the parti-état Zaire. The country slipped quickly down the slope of economic decay with the nationalisation of key industries. The UMHK was nationalised as well, and became the '*GECAMINES*'. Massive corruption and the brutal repression of dissidents led to the complete collapse of the state system, including the education system. While Mobutu retained a measure of popularity in the 1970s, this popular support dwindled in the 1980s. In 1977–8, former Katangese secessionist militiamen

INTRODUCTION

invaded Katanga and Mobutu needed the help of French, Belgian and Moroccan troops to curb the invasion. As a result of political unrest and international pressure, Mobutu abolished the MPR parti-état and allowed political parties during a brief moment of 'democratisation' in 1990. This process was, however, undercut by MPR-affiliated bogus parties and deliberately fuelled regionalisms, and led to more civil unrest. In the wake of the Rwanda crisis of 1994, a rebellion emerged in Eastern Congo, led by Laurent-Désiré Kabila and supported by Uganda and Rwanda. The rebel movement marched through the country at an amazing pace; the Mobutu regime ended with the occupation of Kinshasa in May 1997. Mobutu fled the country and died shortly afterwards.

5 The final period, less relevant to our concerns here, is the period since Kabila assumed power in 1997. Most of the Zairianisation measures were abolished at once, and the country was renamed the Democratic Republic of the Congo. The Shaba province became Katanga again, but most of the names of towns retained their Mobutu-era names. Thus, Kinshasa is still Kinshasa and Lubumbashi is still Lubumbashi. The end of the Mobutu era did not, unfortunately, mean the end of terror and poverty. The country found itself locked in an international war (with involvement from Zimbabwe, Rwanda and Uganda, notably), while its industrial riches were quickly sold off to less than scrupulous foreign high-risk entrepreneurs. Since 1997, an estimated 4 million people have died in the Congo as an effect of the chronic conflicts and violence.

In the chapters that follow, I have chosen to use the current names for places, including for the Congo. Different names – the colonial ones as well as those of the Zairianisation period – will be given when they reflect the voices of Julien and Tshibumba. It is important to know that Julien and Tshibumba were born in the late 1940s and grew up in the late days of the Belgian colony. Their documents were written between 1980 and 1997, which was a period in which the Mobutist state system completely decayed and in which violence, corruption and abject poverty had very much become the state of things in the Congo. There was very little cause for optimism among non-elite Congolese in those days.

Globalisation

I see this analysis as having immediate relevance for analyses on globalisation, and I will go into considerable ethnographic detail in order to demonstrate this. This may seem counter-intuitive, for the documents I examine are deeply 'local', were it not for the fact that they crossed half of the world to find their addressee (and in the event, also their analyst). The phenomenon that stares us in the face is, of course, that even very 'local' documents such as these are mobile, travel and find uptake (even if lukewarm) elsewhere. The document with which I opened this chapter illustrates the nature of such mobility: the

23

documents reflect a literacy regime that operates in one part of the world and is then moved into a very different regime, where it loses voice and creates 'misunderstandings'. Such 'misunderstandings' (ironically) are barely understood. They are very often the effect not just of *difference* but of *inequality*: of the hierarchical organisation of our ways of thinking about communication, in which certain forms of communication (certain *genres*) rank higher than others.

I consider such processes of communicative inequality to be at the heart of contemporary globalisation processes. The more frequent and intense we see processes of mobility become, the more we will see patterns of 'structured' misunderstanding – forms of misunderstanding that are predicated by the structural inequalities in the world, part of which is reflected in the communicative repertoires of people. It is not that I believe that we can understand contemporary globalisation processes *only* by looking at language and communication; it is that I firmly believe that we cannot understand them *without* attention to language and communication. For one thing, we need to understand what exactly – in actual ethnographic detail – happens in the 'flows' that are supposed to characterise contemporary globalisation (Appadurai 1996), or in the 'networks' that co-exist now with more enduring social structures (Castells 1996). We need to understand what happens when people perform that most elementary form of human social behaviour, communication, in the patterns of human and semiotic mobility that now define our societies. And in all of this, we ought to be aware of the bias that characterises our own stance in such acts of communication. In other words, we need to come to terms with why others fail to get their meanings across to us *as well as* with why we fail to understand them.

My own views of globalisation have been strongly influenced by the works of Immanuel Wallerstein (e.g. 1983) and Eric Hobsbawm (e.g. 1987, 2007). Both would emphasise, and compellingly demonstrate, that the current wave of globalisation is a stage in a much older process of capitalist expansion, the key to which is not uniformisation but inequality. Globalisation in its current form is one stage in that process, a stage of acceleration and intensification, and it is driven by technological innovations in mass media and communication technology. The foundations of the globalised world system – its economic and political structures – have remained essentially stable for about a century, and are not likely to change dramatically soon. We can expect that, given the structural 'underdevelopment' of the Third World, patterns of worldwide inequality will become even more outspoken in this phase of acceleration and intensification. Texts will travel in greater numbers and at greater speed, and as an analysis of email fraud from Nigeria demonstrated (Blommaert & Omoniyi 2006), decoding such processes demands a great amount of attention to textual, stylistic and genre detail. The *prima facie* assumption of comprehensibility based on the superficial observation that we now all use the same communication tools – the internet and English, for example – is dramatically wrong. Issues of literacy will acquire a tremendously important place in the social-scientific interpretation of globalisation.

INTRODUCTION

In this respect, one final disclaimer is needed. I am aware that I treat here just one aspect of what is called 'literacy': writing. Contemporary approaches to literacy would refuse to separate writing from other aspects of literacy – reading, design, processing – and relatively little attention has gone to writing itself as a complex literacy practice. I do believe, however, and I hope the reader will also understand, that the particular forms of writing I examine here do shed light on wider literacy issues. I will highlight how writing practices proceed under conditions that severely constrain what can be written. These conditions are material, socio-economic and cultural, and they are structural. Highlighting the problem of structural constraints on writing should, I trust, teach us a thing or two about literacy in the world today. With these restrictions and limitations in mind, we are now ready to have a look at some fascinating documents. Let's go.

Figure 1.1 Democratic Republic of the Congo

GRASSROOTS LITERACY

Figure 1.2 The Katanga and Kasai region of the Democratic Republic of the Congo

Part II

THE LIVES OF JULIEN

2

THREE LIVES FOR MRS ARENS

Three versions of a life

The things we call data often come to us, rather than us going out to find them. And they come to us because of what we can call 'structured accidents': coincidences that are influenced by one's particular position. In the winter of 1994, a Belgian lady whom I shall call Mrs Helena Arens sent a handwritten text to my friend Marcel Van Spaandonck, with a request to translate it into Dutch. Van Spaandonck, who had just retired as Professor of Swahili at Ghent University, passed it on to me. The text was written partly in Shaba Swahili, partly in French. It was an autobiographical account written by a Congolese man whom I shall call Julien and sent to the Belgian lady as a form of symbolic repayment. The Belgian lady was Julien's former employer: Julien had been her houseboy while she and her husband lived in the Congo in the late 1960s and early 1970s. After her departure, and systematically since 1973, she had sent him money and goods to support him and his family. When he raised the issue of repayment, Mrs Arens suggested that instead of the rather hopeless prospect of raising cash, Julien should write the story of his life in what the lady believed to be his mother tongue, Swahili. I translated the text for the lady, and afterwards published (with Mrs Arens' permission) an edited and annotated version (Blommaert 1996).[1] Between 1994 and 1997 I had frequent contacts with Mr and Mrs Arens. I visited the couple, interviewed them, and saw part of the voluminous correspondence Julien had maintained with them.

The text I had translated turned out to be the second version of Julien's life history. A first version had been sent in 1992. The second version came through in 1994, accompanied by a letter in which Julien expressed his dissatisfaction over the first version. And in 1997, Julien sent a third version of his autobiography, entitled *Ukarasa wa pili (2° partie)* ('Page two (second part)'). So in the end, we were confronted with a corpus of three versions of the same life history, marked by considerable differences. Let me try to summarise the characteristics of the three versions in schematic form.

29

THE LIVES OF JULIEN

	First version *1991–2*	*Second version* *1994*	*Third version* *1997*
page length	9 pages	17 pages	20 pages
number of lines	282	503	504
language	Shaba Swahili	Shaba Swahili 1–14 French 14–17	Shaba Swahili 1–18 French 19–20
text title	none	Récits Maisha yangu	Ukarasa wa pili (2° partie) [Récits]
chapter titles	page 5 onwards	systematic	systematic

The first version is by far the shortest of the three. It is written completely in Shaba Swahili, it carries no title, and chapter titles only occur halfway through the text. The second and third versions bear considerable resemblances. Both are long handwritten texts, largely in Swahili but ending with a French part which is generically different. These two versions are signed by Julien. Both carry a title: the second version carries the generic qualifier 'Récits' ('stories') on the first page followed by a chapter title that probably covers the whole of the text, 'maisha yangu' ('my life'); the third version, as noted above, is entitled 'ukarasa wa pili (2°partie)' on the first page, and has 'Récits' written upside down on the last page of the text (probably added after the completion of the writing process, as we shall see). Both versions also use chapter titles throughout and in a relatively systematic way. In version two, the transition from Swahili to French in the text happens through a new chapter; in version three, there is no chapter break but the French text starts on a new page.

Writing with an accent

Julien writes with an accent: an accent that reflects his location as a man with a particular regional and sociolinguistic background, gender, age, social status and experience with literacy. His writing is definitely sub-elite. In the Shaba Swahili parts we notice considerable difficulties with orthography proper as well as with other literacy conventions such as hyphenation. Consider the following fragment, part of page 5 of the first version. I will mark some features with numbered arrows and will comment on them below (see also figure 2.1).

> Niliuzinika sana juu ya safari yao kwasa
> babu, nilikuwa na mawazo yakutayarisha
> maisha yangu kwa kazi yangi, ata kwa
> Verstappen nilituka paka mwaka monja
> wao pia wakarudi kwao lote, niliw*e*za
> kuwatumia wao pia mabarua, ila ha   ←[1]
> wakuweza ku*n*ijibu. KAZi zote nililo

THREE LIVES FOR MRS ARENS

bakia kutumika Lubumbashi, hazikwe- ←[2]
ndelea nikanjaa kazi ya kuchoma Makala
haikwendelea, NiKAkamata mali ya de- ←[3]
ni kwa Kalonda, ZAïRE mia tano, na kila
mwezi kumurudishia FAida *y*ʸa ZAïRE mia
(250). *M*ia mbili na makumi tana ama (←[4]
cinquante pour Cent). yapata muda wa
miezi saba nika*wa*ᴺᵃZAïRE ELFu-Moja- ←[5]
na mia mbili ikawa Nguvu kwa mie
kumurudishia Feza yake, nikapata aki
li yakumwandia MKOMBOZI wangu bibi ←[6]
Hèlena ARÈNs, yeye akaniambia asema ←[7]
Kwa apa sasa hakuna namna yakukutu
mia FRaNKA Elfu innen (quatre Mille FRancs - ←[8]
Belges). hatuna nayo, sikuwa na ngishi hata Mtu
wakunisaidia ao kunikopesha feza nilipe
*d*eni ya KOLONDA. ←[9]

Translation:

I was very sad because of their journey because
I was thinking how to prepare my life
for my work, even with
the Verstappen [family] whom I had left a year ago
they too had all returned, I managed
to send them letters too, to which
they could not reply. All the work I
continued to do in Lubumbashi, it did not
progress and I started burning charcoal
that too did not progress, I borrowed money
from Kalonda, five hundred Zaire, for me
to return him every month an interest of more than hundred Zaire
(250) two hundred and fifty, that is (
cinquante pour cent). I got seven
months for twelve hundred Zaire
it became very tough for me to
repay him his money, I got the wisdom
to write to my saviour madam
Hèlena Arèns, she told me that
It was impossible for the moment to send you
Four thousand Francs (*quatre Mille Francs-*
Belges). We don't have it, I had no way out not even anyone
To help me or to give me money so that
I could repay the debt to Kolonda

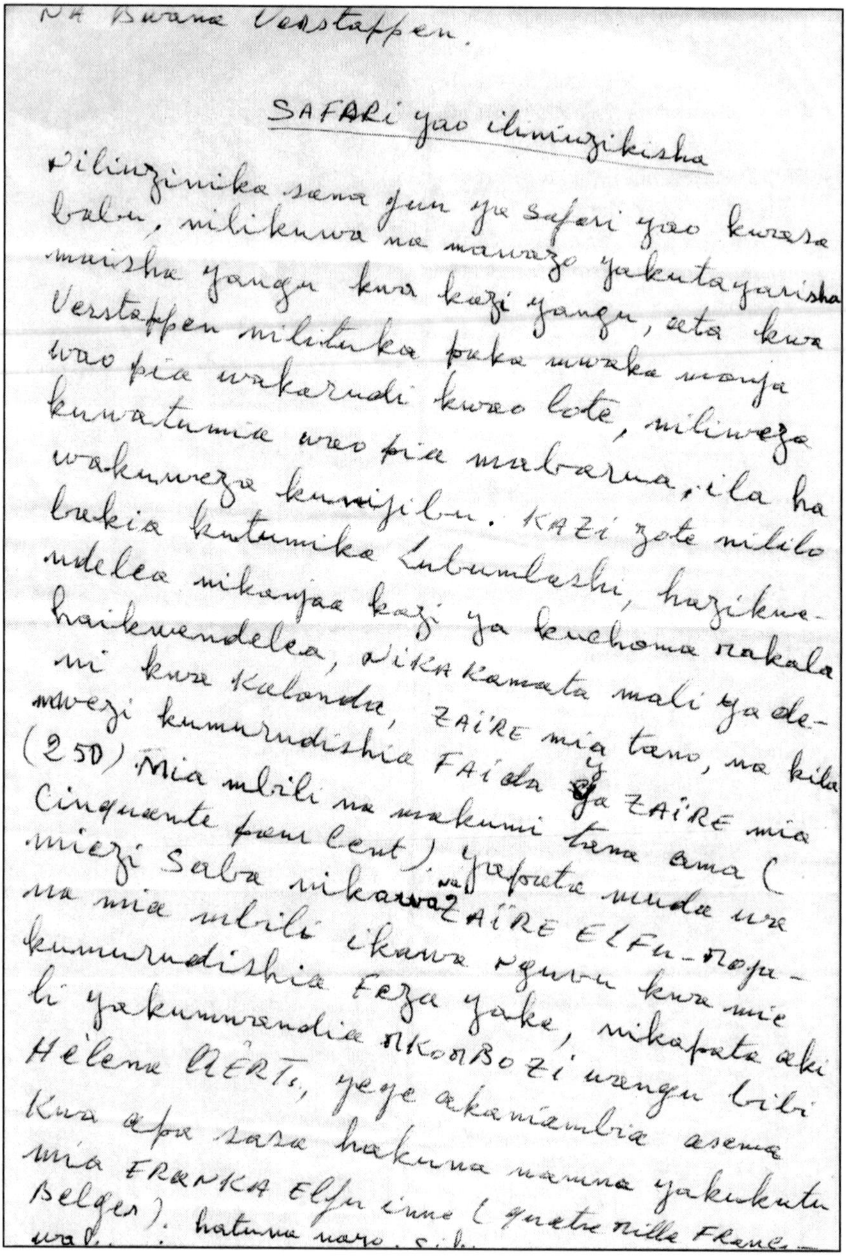

THE LIVES OF JULIEN

Na Bwana Verstappen.

SAFARi yao ilimuzikisha

Vilinzinika sawa jua ya safari yao kwasa balo, niliikuwa na mawazo yakutayarisha muisha yangu kwa kazi yangu, seta kwa Verstappen militeka puka mwaka moja wao pia wakarudi kwao lote, niliweza kuwatumia wao pia mabarua, ila ha bakia kutumika Lubumbashi, huzikuu ndelea nikawjaa kazi ya kuchoma makala haikuwendelea, nika kamata mali ya de ni kwa Kalonda, ZAiRE mia tano, na kila mwezi kumurudishia FAida ya ZAiRE mia (250) Mia mbili na makumi tana ama (Cinquante feu cent) yafouta minda uwe miezi Saba nikawa ZAiRE ELFn-nopa na mia mbili ikawa nguvu kwa mie kumurudishia feza yake, nikapata aki li yakumrandia nKooBoZi wangu bili Hélene AËRTi, yeye akaniambia asema kwa apa sasa hakuna namna yakukutu mia FRANKA Elfu imo (quatre mille Franc Belger). hatuna naro. s.l.

Figure 2.1 Copy of 1/5

Many of the features of this text remind us of the police statement with which we opened this book. The most striking feature of the text is the alteration between upper and lower case, as in [3] (NiKAkamata), [5] (ZAïRE ELFu-Moja-) and [8] (FRaNKA). It is partly systematic, partly unsystematic. Julien often uses it whenever he wants to emphasise something. Thus, in [6], the word MKOMBOZI ('saviour') is written in upper case, as well as the names of the protagonists, ARÈNS in [7] and KOLONDA in [9]. The latter, however, is previously mentioned in the fragment, and his name is written in lower case. There is little systematicity in FRaNKA [8] where an upper-case word contains one lower-case symbol. Julien also writes different versions of the same words. In our example, we see that 'KOLONDA' is elsewhere named 'Kalonda' (including in the other versions of the text), and the spelling of his main benefactor's name carries French *accents graves* that do not apply here ('Hèlena ARÈNs' instead of Helena Arens); elsewhere in the corpus her name is spelled in a variety of ways. As for punctuation, observe that the first part of the fragment contains only commas and no periods. In several places, the sentence period is not followed by a capitalised word. Other symbols, such as hyphens, also occur erratically. Compare [1], [2] and [3]. In [1], the verb form 'ha/wakuweza' is split over two lines without hyphen; in [2] and [3], in contrast, there is accuracy in the use of the hyphen. The hyphen occurs awkwardly in [5] (ELFu-Moja-) and [8] (FRancs -) and elsewhere in the texts we would find hyphens in frequently used words such as 'Helena-Arens'. In [4], we see how the placing of brackets is done, another graphic symbol the use of which appears to be less than perfectly mastered. [4] as well as [8] also illustrate Julien's unusual glossing, to which we will return further on.

These are recurrent graphic features of the Shaba Swahili parts. In addition to these, we see reflections of the pronunciation in the written form. This transpires in the absence of punctuation in the first part of the fragment, in the different written forms of the same words ('ata' and 'hata' in the example, or the different spelling of the names) and in the intuitive connecting of particles and verbs, as in 'aki/li yakumwandia' (='akili ya kumwandia': 'the wisdom to write to her'). Such traces are also prominent in the French parts of the text, where homophony in spoken language leads to errors in writing. Consider the following fragment, part of 2/16:

> on Fait des cooperatives que par les NOMS, on s'appele   ←[1]
> r FÉRMiers sans FERME, L'aide reçu ce n'est pas
> pour Faire des champs, ᴰDans d'autre pays d'afrique
> si les gouvernement veulent accordent des credits   ←[2]
> agricoles, ce sont des ministres, des riches et ceux
> qui dominent qui recevez ces credits les tracteurs   ←[3]
> restent dans leurs parcelles, les camions donnent   ←[4]
> aux Frères pour faire les transports et acheter
> peu des Maïs et Manioc soit disant que nous

THE LIVES OF JULIEN

avons des FÈRMES. D'autres gens se plaignent
ils ont vu les gens les inscrivent avec leurs enfants
parce-que ils sont pauvres et à leurs disant que
la VISION-MONDIAL va vous envoyez des aides   ←[5]

Translation:

they make cooperatives only by name, they call
themselves farmers without a farm, The help they receive is not
to cultivate fields, In other countries of Africa
if the government want to grant agricultural
credits, it is the ministers, the rich and those
who dominate who receive the credits the tractors
remain in their lots, the trucks giving
to brothers to do transport and to buy
a bit maize and manioc so-called that we
have farms. Other people complain
they have seen people enrol with their children
because they are poor and telling them that
the VISION-MONDIAL will send you aid

In this fragment, many of the features previously encountered also occur: the alteration of upper and lower case, the erratic use of punctuation symbols, problems with hyphenation, and so on. In [1], we see how Julien writes 'appele/r' without hyphen and he writes the infinitive rather than the inflected 's'appelle'. In [2], the pluralisation of 'gouvernement' is missing; in [3], he writes the 2nd plural 'recevez' instead of the 3rd plural 'reçoivent'; in [4] the expression should probably be 'les camions donnés aux frères'; and in [5] we see homophony in spoken language resulting in the wrong choice in spelling: 'envoyez' instead of 'envoyer'.

The transfer from spoken word to literacy is not predicated on a mastery of differential conventions for spoken and written codes. Yet, and remarkably at first sight, Julien does not seem to have more problems with writing French than with writing Swahili. This puzzle is complex and will take up some of the analysis I will offer further on. But part of the answer, *prima facie*, is that Shaba Swahili has no orthography, nor is the language in any significant sense standardised. The term 'Shaba Swahili' effectively covers a whole range of regional *spoken* varieties, the most prominent (and best known) of which is the Lubumbashi variety (see Schicho 1980, 1982, 1990; de Rooij 1996). Public writing would typically be in French or in so-called 'Swahili Bora', 'pure Swahili'. Since all of this raises rather complex questions, I will come back to the issue of language and code in Chapter 3.

The multilingualism of the texts reflects the multilingual environment in which Julien dwells. He is likely to have varying degrees of competence in Shaba Swahili varieties, local vernacular French, probably one or more Luba-languages (several are widespread in Shaba/Katanga and Kasai), and, given the dominance of that language in the Mobutu era in the Congo, probably also some proficiency in Lingala. As for writing, we have evidence of writing skills in Shaba Swahili and French, but not in the other languages. And the use of such languages is probably also context-specific, resulting in specific degrees of proficiency and register development in different languages. When Julien travels to Lubumbashi, he is likely to use Shaba Swahili; when he travels to Mbuji-Mayi, he finds himself in a Luba-speaking environment. When he visits Belgian missionaries, he would probably speak French, Luba and/or Shaba Swahili. Since he married a woman in Kinshasa, some Lingala could be part of the family code, although the area where he locates his family would be Luba and Swahili-speaking. Code-switching would, of course, be the rule rather than the exception, and on this as well I shall have to say a few things later.

Julien's life: a storyline

Julien was born in Manono, Northern Shaba (now Katanga), on December 10, 1946 (see the maps on pages 25–6). He finished primary school as well as a few years of secondary school. In 1965 he moved to Lubumbashi where he joined his uncle, who was employed as a cook with Belgian expatriates. In 1966 or late 1967 he got a job as a houseboy with the Degueldre family, a job which he kept until May 1969. In 1967 he married a girl named Jacqueline. When he lost his job with the Degueldre family in May 1969, his in-laws took Jacqueline away from him and married her to someone else. The couple had no children. On September 27, 1969 he became employed as a houseboy with the Arens family. When the Arens family returned to Belgium for a holiday in June 1970, Julien went to Kinshasa where he married a girl called Julienne. A first child was born in June 1971, a second in August 1972. Altogether they had six children. In June 1973, the Arens family announced their return to Belgium and when they left in September 1973, Julien got a job as a houseboy with the Verstappen family. In June 1974, they too left for Belgium, and Julien started a charcoal and firewood business. This he did until 1979, when he found himself in debt with a loan shark called Kalonda. Julien left for Kabinda and wrote a letter to Mrs Arens asking for support. She sent money and Julien was able to pay his debt to Kalonda in July 1980 or in 1981. With the rest of the money, he bought sheep and goats and sold them. In October 1981 he was in Kabinda again, where he became employed as a shopkeeper. In 1983–4 he was a farmer in Kashilangie (a somewhat unclear period), and in 1984 his wife joined him in Kabinda. In 1986 he started a farm in Malemba-Nkulu, but almost immediately he got into problems with local people and the authorities (*'agronomes'* – agricultural engineers). His younger brother died in 1986 and Julien adopted his eight children. Jealous of his success and of the support he received from Mrs Arens, villagers used witchcraft against Julien, and he was ill from 1987 until 1988. He

THE LIVES OF JULIEN

left Malemba-Nkulu and returned in 1989. In April 1990, while in Kabinda, he received a letter from his wife saying that she was in debt. In order to write to Mrs Arens for support, Julien travelled to the diamond mining town of Mbuji-Mayi in Kasai, and he became employed as a diamond digger in the adjacent town of Bakwa-Mulumba. Intense political trouble and ethnic strife (the product of 'democracy in Zaire', in Julien's terms), resulting in attempts on his life caused him to escape back to the Shaba province in January 1991, to Kabinda or to Mwambayi, a mission town, where he was helped by 'other Christians'. In the meantime, his farm in Malemba-Nkulu had been all but destroyed by villagers and animals, and its ownership was the subject of endless conflicts. Julien left on foot to Malemba-Nkulu in October 1992. In July 1993 his wife followed him to Malemba-Nkulu, suspecting adultery, and he met her in the town of Lusaka. He intended to write to Mrs Arens, and therefore he travelled to Lubumbashi, where he stayed for six months. In May 1994 he returned to the farm in Malemba-Nkulu with the money he received from Mrs Arens, and again found himself in a battle over ownership of the farm with the local authorities. In January 1995 he travelled to his birthplace Manono. And in March 1996, a second court case was initiated over the (now run-down) farm.

The life trajectory described in the texts is one of gradual but irreversible *déclassement*. Julien is a houseboy while living in Lubumbashi: not a fabulous job, but a job that offers a decent and reliable salary, housing and other benefits, as well as some measure of local prestige (see Fabian 1990a). He subsequently tries to set up a business as a charcoal and firewood seller, but catastrophic financial problems make him descend to the bottom of the labour market, selling goats, peanuts and other small goods. He has to resume life as a farmer in Malemba-Nkulu, and even if he has some ambition to transcend the level of subsistence farming, that is more or less where he stands at the end of the story. For a while he works as a diamond digger in Kasai, work characterised by brutal exploitation and physical hardship, or in Julien's own words 'slavery'. His gradual impoverishment is punctuated by periods of acute poverty and hardship. He lands himself with a substantial debt which he can only repay with Mrs Arens' financial assistance, he is poisoned by villagers, his farm runs into the ground, he has to run for his life when ethnic troubles erupt in Kasai, the death of his brother adds another eight children to his family, he has to live long periods away from home and family. Consequently, the support he receives from Mrs Arens is a constant frame for the story. There are frequent references to money and goods received from Belgium, requests for support sent to Belgium, money and goods being sent but never reaching him. Increasingly through the three versions, we also see references to religion. When he has to save himself from pogroms in Kasai, Julien receives the support of fellow Christians. From the second version onwards, he frequently refers to prayer, in particular to prayer for his saviour Mrs Arens, and he entitles a section of that version with reference to the scriptures: 'According to the Bible, the true cult is to visit the poor'. Clearly, religion (or at least religious networks of support) has become more and more prominent in his life.

36

Writing (as) a (way of) life

The storyline I have just sketched is a reconstruction made on the basis of a careful reading of the three versions written by Julien. None of the texts provides the full story, and the next chapters will address this issue: Julien painstakingly constructs a life while writing it. As a way of introducing that analysis, I need to draw attention to some particularly striking features of the texts. I will list six of them and will turn to a discusion on the last one – the fact that writing, for Julien, requires tremendous efforts. The five others will be examined in subsequent chapters.

1   The three texts are almost certainly *single and unique* copies. They were written on cheap airmail paper with ballpoint, and given the significant differences between the texts I suggest that Julien did not keep copies of the texts himself. He did not, in other words, keep an archive of his autobiography, and this has an influence on how he constructs this autobiography. I will come back to this in Chapter 4.

2   The texts are also *globalised texts*: they were written in Central Africa for an addressee in Belgium. The texts are written to be sent, they are not designed for local circulation. They are texts designed for mobility across continents.

3   The texts clearly belong to, and fit into, a *tradition of communication* developed between Mrs Arens and Julien since the late 1960s, part of which was oral and face-to-face, part of which was written. This tradition of communication was friendly and warm: intense feelings of sympathy are articulated by Julien and Mrs Arens alike. Yet, it bore traces of a neo-colonial order. Julien was a Congolese houseboy working for a well-to-do Belgian expatriate family: a labour relationship that had its feet firmly planted in the colonial social order. It was also not disinterested: money and other material goods (notably clothes) were a constant topic in the correspondence between Julien and Mrs Arens. The texts, consequently, are not standalones but clearly *targeted* and *intertextual* documents. They are explicitly other-directed, they are written for Mrs Arens and not for himself. This, too, will prove to be an important feature of Julien's autobiography.

4   Note that, in this context of intertextuality, the *code in which the text is written is quite peculiar*. Mrs Arens told me in one of the interviews that she had suggested that Julien write the story of his life in 'his own language', 'so as to be able to express himself freely and fully'. She assumed that his native language would be Shaba Swahili, the lingua franca of the Lubumbashi area and the language in which she had heard Julien converse with his fellow employees. This suggestion spawned texts in Shaba Swahili, a language which was clearly *not* Julien's native language, which was *not* understandable to Mrs Arens (hence her request to translate the texts), and which, in addition, *broke their communicative tradition*. The letters Julien wrote to Mrs Arens were invariably in French, not Swahili.[2]

5   In spite of this, a remarkable feature of the texts is that they are *monoglossic*.

THE LIVES OF JULIEN

The Shaba Swahili parts as well as the French parts are relatively 'pure' and reveal attempts at producing 'standard' varieties of language. This is remarkable because we know that the 'normal' form of use of Shaba Swahili as a lingua franca is *not* 'pure': everyday spoken language use in this area is marked by a considerable degree of language mixing and switching (de Rooij 1996). Hence, the monoglossic shape of the text must be the product of an effort to write a *special text*, a text whose generic features deviate from those of everyday speech. The monoglossic character of the texts, in other words, is an index of attempts to construct a particular genre.

A sixth feature, which I would like to look at in more detail here, is the fact that the texts represent *a massive effort*, requiring material, time and intellectual investments the magnitude of which is hard to comprehend for people travelling with laptops through the internet age.

The documents are long – 9, 17 and 20 handwritten pages respectively – and changes in the type of paper and the ballpoint shades reveal that the texts were not written in one go but piece by piece, long stretches of writing alternating with short ones. The whole writing process is also immensely long: more than six years separate the first from the third version, and during these years, quite a bit of time was spent on writing to Mrs Arens – or rather, on *getting organised for writing*.

As we have seen in the storyline above, Julien describes many long and slow itineraries. His life story is one of seemingly incessant travels between Malemba-Nkulu, Manono, Lubumbashi, Mbuji-Mayi, Kabinda, Kinshasa and other places. The geographical space in which he moves is the border area between Shaba and Kasai: not big on the map, but huge if we know that Julien does a good bit of travelling on foot or by bicycle. Here is one such itinerary (rendered in a simplified transcription format):

> After having paid the debt to Kalonda, with the money I had left I started buying goats and sold them. Every trip was as such: I left from Kabinda and went into the villages as far as the Shaba province and I returned and went to the town of Ngandazika to sell goats, from Kabinda through Shaba and returning to Ngandazika was the trip I did, walking on foot, and it was more than 620 kilometres, going out and coming back (*aller et retour*).[3]
>
> (3/6)

Julien also makes several very substantial trips *to write*. He mentions four places in relation to his correspondence with Mrs Arens: Lubumbashi, Lusaka, Kabinda and Mbuji-Mayi. Like so many people in Mobutu's Zaire, Julien relied on the services of Catholic missionaries for sending and receiving mail and parcels, and the four towns are each time connected to the presence of Catholic missionaries. These are the places where Julien wrote his letters as well as the versions of his autobiography.

38

THREE LIVES FOR MRS ARENS

Here, too, the distances are huge. From Malemba-Nkulu to Lubumbashi is about 650 kilometres; Lusaka is 300 kilometres from Malemba-Nkulu, Kabinda about 350 kilometres, and Mbuji-Mayi is 420 kilometres away. He makes these trips on foot, by bicycle and hitch-hiking, and one can imagine that such expeditions take time. He mentions that he does 'twenty-five kilometres (25) or 30, or with some effort 40 per day' (3/12). Writing letters thus involves absences of several months: the time to travel to one of these places, to write the letters and the versions of his life story, to send them and wait for a reply from Belgium. While he is absent from his farm, his family needs to survive, and he himself must find jobs and secure the assistance of missionaries and other people for an income, food and shelter. Sometimes his family is scattered over several places, and all of them need to be taken care of. The following fragment (also rendered in a simplified transcription format) captures the complexity of such writing episodes:

Lusaka – Lubumbashi 966 km

I left the village of Lusaka in the month of November 1993 in the direction of Lubumbashi. It was a 13-day journey before I arrived in Lubumbashi. In order to get money, someone with a bicycle asked me to sell him parts of my bicycle. In Lubumbashi, I wrote to Mrs Helena whether she could help me with some money to pay for a car [ride], so that I, my wife and children could go to Malemba-Nkulu and that I could pay my friends who had helped me with the work on the field at the farm. She agreed and sent me the money. I stayed for six months in Lubumbashi, because I cancelled my trip to Ndola in Zambia in order to write to Mrs Helena. I returned to Malemba-Nkulu in the Month of May [1994] and I met the 4 children who had stayed behind in Lusaka with a brother. A child of an uncle had gone to fetch them in March, and my wife too had gone to Malemba-Nkulu on their recommendation. They thought that since I had [previously] gone to Lubumbashi for several years, I would again stay in Lubumbashi for several years. I arrived in Malemba-Nkulu with that money in May.[4]

(2/12–13)

These long and tumultuous writing trips teach us something about the literacy world in which Julien lives, as well as something rather elementary about literacy: the fact that *literacy practices require an infrastructure for literacy*, and that in Julien's world *this infrastructure is concentrated in certain places*. These places are towns where there are Catholic missionaries who can reliably handle mail to and from Belgium. Malemba-Nkulu is clearly *not* a place where Julien can write from. He has to take his literacy skills to one of the towns, and only there can they be deployed with some effect. The fact that such trips are perilous and generate all sorts of problems, family as well as material, demonstrates the importance this correspondence with Mrs Arens has acquired in Julien's life. Being able to write to her is a matter of very sizeable importance, it is worth an astonishing amount of investment.

As for a literacy infrastructure: it is easy to overlook this fact when one lives in a fully integrated, connected and literacy-saturated society where postal and internet services can be found in the smallest and most remote corners. A village such as Malemba-Nkulu, however, is not a place to write. There may be paper and ballpoints, but writing is about more than that: it is about mobilising an intricate mechanism of material transfer across space. Such mechanisms can only be set in motion in particular places, where the means for mobilising them are concentrated and accessible for someone like Julien. In societies such as Julien's, such places are few and far between, and it is good to remember that this pattern is not exceptional. Many if not most people in the world face literacy obstacles that have nothing to do with the capability to produce writing, but that have to do with the unequal distribution and restricted accessibility of a material infrastructure for effective literacy. In that sense, Julien's writing practices rub our noses in the realities of structural inequalities in the world system. Writing is definitely not a simple and straightforward practice for Julien. It is difficult, complex and extraordinarily demanding. But doing it also has real benefits, and when everything works well the investment is not wasted.

Julien obviously *knows* about this literacy infrastructure. He knows that he has to travel to certain places, that missionaries are often efficient and reliable middlemen for letters and parcels, and he knows how to go about his writing business. This, too, raises issues. We must imagine Julien's world as one in which literacy opportunities are concentrated in particular places, but where knowledge of such places and opportunities appears to be known to people such as Julien, who definitely does not belong to the elite. *Knowledge of* the literacy environment thus seems to be far more democratically distributed than *accessibility* and *use* of the literacy environment: again an elementary truth about literacy which is often overlooked or taken for granted. Julien is not ignorant of the mechanisms of intercontinental literacy exchanges; getting into such exchanges, however, imposes severe demands on him and his family. And it involves a complex organisation in which all kinds of non-literacy related activities need to be deployed. Travelling, finding money and jobs, making sure his family is secure, contacting people – all of this is required in order to perform the task of writing. Writing is part of his life, and when he decides to write, it starts dominating his life and that of his family.

Context and pretext

We now should have an idea of the particular social, economic and cultural context in which Julien produces his texts. Summarised in one term, this context is the margin of the contemporary world-system. Julien lives in poverty in the border area between the provinces of Shaba/Katanga and Kasai in the Congo.

THREE LIVES FOR MRS ARENS

From what we read in his texts, he lives from what his farm produces and is to a certain extent dependent on what Mrs Arens sends him. Economically, he struggles. He has a very large family, and his family life is not trouble-free. Neither is his life at large: he finds himself in trouble with other farmers and state officials, attempts were made on his life, and he is involved in court cases over his farm. He has to travel immense distances with the most elementary means of transport in order to find economic opportunities, usually combining writing to Mrs Arens for financial assistance with finding jobs. He finds solace and support among that most basic of support networks: people sharing the same religion.

The area where he lives is located in one of the world's poorest countries, the Congo (or, as it was called under Mobutu, Zaire). It is a multilingual area where different languages and language varieties occur in layered patterns of use, and in which people have the sort of 'truncated multilingualism' skills documented elsewhere (Blommaert & Dong 2007). Julien went to primary school and took a few years of secondary education. He didn't finish the full cycle because of financial problems, and started working while a teenager, first in the service of European expatriates and afterwards in a range of occasional menial jobs and farming. His few years of schooling have given him some literacy skills, which he practices – in French – in a protracted correspondence with his patron Mrs Arens. This correspondence with someone overseas probably marks him as a rather exceptional figure in his environment. We can assume that he is seen as a bit of an eccentric in his milieu: he refers to jealousy from other farmers in his village, and suggests that the jealousy is the result of his ambition to do better than the others. The relative intensity of his writing practice, however, did not result in a mastery of the normative ortho-graphic codes of French, and his Swahili writing shows that he has an even more restricted command of writing skills in that language.

With these characterisations in place, we can have a closer look at the texts. The canvas is painted. But it is painted in such a way that the term 'context' is no longer an adequate denominator. The 'context' that characterises Julien's writing is also a *pretext*, something that *precedes* the act of writing and operates at a higher, more stable and systemic 'contextual' level. It determines what he can use in writing, how he can use it, and for what purposes he can use it. It is a series of conditions (or what Bourdieu would call 'predispositions') that appear as *constraints* on what Julien can be as a writer. His sociolinguistic 'baggage', so to speak, only enables him to perform certain forms of communication and not others, and this 'baggage' is not just an individual feature, it is to a large extent a structural feature that reflects his position in the world. Keeping in mind the fact that his texts are sent to someone far away, living in a very different 'pretextual' surrounding, we can expect *pretextual gaps*: differences between expectations and effects, between what people are expected to do and what they effectively can achieve (Maryns & Blommaert 2002). We can now turn to this and other questions.

3

GENRES AND REPERTOIRES

Resources

When Mrs Arens asked Julien to write his life history, she did it with a purpose in mind. She had plans to write a book about her life in the Congo, and Julien's autobiography could be an important piece of documentation for preparing the book. When I sent her the translation of the second version, she responded with disappointment: there was little of value in this text. She had clearly expected something different. Mrs Arens and Julien were involved in a similar exercise: both were attempting to construct an autobiography. Julien's autobiography, however, appeared to diverge significantly from Mrs Arens' expectations. There was, thus, a pretextual gap between expectations and actual performance. The question here is: why?

The autobiography is an old and well-known genre. As we have seen in the previous chapter, Julien writes three versions of his autobiography, and he does this from within a particular pretext, one that imposes severe constraints on what he can achieve with his writing skills. This pretext requires further examination, because it conditions the perceived *affordances* of writing: particular things that can be done with signifiers – with written symbols and language varieties, in this case. In a discussion of the use of colour in imaging, Kress and van Leeuwen (1996: 232–3) specify two types of affordances. The first one is 'provenance', where things come from. This is a *historical* affordance, something that anchors synchronic sign-use in histories of use and evaluation. The second one is the *synchronic* capacity to create meaningful patterns and contrasts in the use of signs. Both types of affordance create a paradigmatic-syntagmatic axis, and each instance of sign-use, i.e. the deployment and use of communicative resources, needs to be seen as a combination of the historical and the synchronic affordances of the resources. The effect of such use is maximal when the producer and the consumer of such signs are fully competent, so to speak, and familiar with the historical (intertextual) affordances of the sign, with the cultural codes and frames that make sign use understandable.

So far, so good. But what if the producer and/or consumer are *not* thoroughly familiar with the cultural codes and frames that organise the use of signs? Or what if, in the context of globalisation, a sign that is fully in line with cultural codes and frames valid in one place is transferred to another place, where that sign is understood in different cultural codes and frames? The shift from one such space into another then involves relocations of referential and indexical meanings attached to signs – a process of re-entextualisation, in Silverstein and Urban's (1996) terms. But this form of relocation is to a large extent a non-arbitrary, pretextual phenomenon that needs to be addressed sociolinguistically. One is reminded at this point of Hymes' 'second type of linguistic relativity' (Hymes 1966). Whereas the first, Whorfian, type of relativity pertained to different structures having similar functions (organising world views), Hymes suggested 'that the role of language may differ from community to community; that in general the functions of language in society are a problem for investigation, not postulation' (1966: 116). Similar structures, in other words, can prove to have very different functions depending on the particular 'cultural reality' (ibid.) in which they are used. This cultural reality, I take it, includes patterns of speech, repertoires and ways of organising them, linguistic hierarchies and ideologies; and the particular function of speech forms will depend on how these speech forms relate to the larger whole. 'Placement among some other aspects of culture implies some degree of fit for the linguistic traits' (1966: 119; cf. also Blommaert 2005a, Chapter 4).

It is this awareness of second linguistic relativity that compels me to inspect the textual, stylistic and linguistic material that Julien deploys and uses in his texts: the genres he attempts to construct, and the linguistic and literacy repertoires he uses for that purpose. We need to understand Julien's resources before we can move on. To return to the phrase with which I opened this book: we need to understand Julien's *'can write'*.

On genre

The first issue I need to address is that of genre, and before entering into the particulars of genre in Julien's writings, some theoretical observations need to be made. In its most general sense, genre is *a complex of communicative-formal features that makes a particular communicative event recognisable as an instance of a type.* You hear a particular type of speech and you understand it as a 'joke', a 'lecture', a 'quarrel'; or you read something and understand it as a 'newspaper article', an 'academic paper', a 'poem'. Or you see something and you understand it as an 'advertisement', a publicly displayed 'menu', a 'map', etc.

Genres, thus, guide us through the social world of communication: they allow us to distinguish between very different communicative events, create expectations for each of them, and adjust our own communicative behaviour accordingly. To stick to the latter: when we recognise something as a 'joke', we adopt a 'joke-listening' posture – a posture which is different, for instance, from a 'lecture-listening' posture or a 'conversational involvement' posture. And reading a poem is a different activity from reading a newspaper article or an academic paper.[1] Three features, therefore, should be kept in

43

THE LIVES OF JULIEN

mind when thinking about genre: (i) formal characteristics of communicative events; (ii) the expectations they generate and (iii) the responsive behaviour they suggest.

This general sense is the one used, for instance, in Bakhtin's work (1986). According to Bakhtin, genres can best be defined as relatively stable utterances that belong to, or fit into, a particular 'sphere' of communication: 'each separate utterance is individual, of course, but each sphere in which language is used develops its own relatively stable types of these utterances. These we call speech genres' (1986: 60). The social 'sphere' in which communication evolves – we would now say 'context' or 'domain' – *determines* the utterance: there is a compelling link between an utterance and the 'sphere' in which it occurs, in the sense that the utterance will be interpreted *from within the context* in which it occurs. When we find ourselves in a social 'sphere' such as, for example, a job interview, we will interpret utterances occurring in that context in relation to that context. Simply put: we will *contextualise* utterances in a search for ways in which they fit into the genre expectations we have. If a candidate walks into the job interview room and greets the interviewers with 'hey guys, what's up?' there is a chance that this utterance will be understood as not fitting into the context, that is, as not being the right genre for that 'sphere'.

This Bakhtinian definition has been influential, and it has spurred developments in research over the last couple of decades. One effect has been that the notion of 'genre' has left the very narrow confines in which it was previously locked: a 'genre' was an *artistic* concept that referred to literary forms (the novel, poetry, drama, etc.) and the study of genres was the study of such organised forms of written text. A more mature notion of genre covers any form of communication – spoken, written, verbal, nonverbal, linguistic, nonlinguistic.

Issues of genre have been central to the Boasian anthropological tradition, and one of the reasons is the fundamental view of culture as 'transmission' in that tradition. Culture is seen as an endless sequence of repetition-and-change of behaviour, material practices, and symbolic practices. Genres are important units for such transmission. The emphasis in this tradition (in contrast to, for instance, applied-linguistic approaches) is more on the *stuff* than on the particular forms it takes, though, of course, a lot of attention has gone to forms of genres as well. Attention to form has often taken the shape of attention to *performance*, because performance (of ritual, narrative, social practices in general) is the observable side of transmission – the moments where existing stuff is repeated and changed (cf. Bauman 1986; Bauman & Briggs 1990). And rather than treating a performance as a momentary instance of a type, it is seen as a contextualised action that requires ethnographic inspection. Thus, notions of 'text' and 'context' are dynamic: we speak of 'textualisation' and 'contextualisation' (Bauman & Briggs 1990), and the central issue is how such actions encode and transmit cultural material. Changes in culture trigger changes in genres, and vice versa (Fabian 1974, 1990b).

44

GENRES AND REPERTOIRES

The effect of this emphasis on action and transmission is a much greater flexibility in what can count as a genre (or, in a more negative expression, less clarity about what constitutes a genre). From an anthropological viewpoint, *we always communicate in genres*; every aspect of social life develops within patterns that are 'generic', i.e. culturally organised and thus culturally recognisable. There is no non-social or non-cultural communication, and therefore there is no communication that is genre-free. *Everything* is genre, and shifting, mixing, layering and overlapping of genres is the norm, not the exception. The way in which such shifts occur was brilliantly described by Hymes in 'Breakthrough into performance' (1975). A shift from conversation into narrative was a shift into 'full performance': the dense clustering of stylistic features such as pitch, gesture, intonation, lexis and grammatical patterns. But it also marked the introduction of a different epistemic frame, a different range of identity (the interlocutor, e.g., shifted from 'conversational partner' to 'audience') and so on. In other words, shifts in genre involved a radical shift in the whole of the communicative environment, and the continuous shifting in and out of genres (with the more encompassing shifts in communicative environment attached to them) is at the heart of our life as social and cultural beings.

In a more theoretical vocabulary, such patterns of general shifting, with form, epistemic/affective orientations, identity and other dimensions tied together, have been described in terms of 'register' (Agha 2005, 2007). Register is the 'stuff' that organises genres: the organised, patterned and regimented semiotic forms we deploy when we talk about particular topics or in particular domains. The terms and communicative forms that belong to the register are indexical of the things the register is supposed to articulate: a particular identity, a particular epistemic/affective orientation, a particular mutual position between the participants to the speech event. A serious topic normally is dealt with by means of a serious register; a funny topic by means of a funny one; an expert topic by an expert register, and so on (cf. also Silverstein 2006). Thus register is part of the generic organisation of communication. Observe that the notion of register (and its connections to indexicality) obviously connects this approach to the basic anthropological idea of cultural transmission (Silverstein 2004). So again, rather than an operational and institutional object, genre here is a cultural object.

As mentioned above, Hymes (1975) showed us that in everyday interaction, genres can be locked into one another, be organised as genres-within-genres. For instance, in a conversation we can shift into telling an anecdote without breaking the conversational pattern, and in the anecdote itself we can insert a recounted conversation. Goffman (1975, 1981) defined such moves and shifts as shifts in 'footing': delicate moves in which we reorder the communicative organisation, redefining the mutual roles, expectations and codes of conduct. Shifts in footing are indexical shifts, often intrinsically connected to register shifts, and so to genre shifts (Agha 2005). The question here is a terminological one: what scope of what would in other traditions be called 'genre' is here covered by concepts such as register and footing? The shifts in footing (i.e. in register and

45

genre) are instances of that other crucial point made by Bakhtin: the 'hetero-glossia', the multi-vocality of every discourse, the fact that every utterance is a compilation of different 'voices', different bits of discourse that reflect social positions, orientations towards what is being said, articulations of expected and desired role relationships in the interaction.

In a similar vein, the *transmission* of texts has been addressed as a sequence in which the text tumbles from one genre into another – it gets re-entextualised over and over again in a 'text trajectory' (Bauman & Briggs 1990; Silverstein & Urban 1996; Briggs 1997; Blommaert 2001a). Fabian (1990b) described how a fully formed genre – a theatre play – gradually evolved out of conversations and ethnographic interviews, then moved through a phase of writing, rehearsal, per-formance and re-performance, even on TV. Each time, the play (the 'cultural stuff' in anthropological approaches) changed and got reorganised in relation to means, modalities, audiences, purposes, etc. Parts of the genre remained stable, other parts changed radically, and there was no single stage at which one could call the genre 'finished' or 'complete'. Thus, in anthropological approaches, we see that the notion of genre is less unified and stable. Its scope is spread over a range of other notions – register, indexicality, footing, entextualisation. In addi-tion, the focus is on how cultural material is transmitted through and by means of particular clusters of semiotic form.

Genre, to almost any author, still refers to a cluster of formal communicative/semiotic characteristics that make a particular chunk of communication recog-nisable in terms of social and cultural categories of communication. The concept refers essentially to a congruence – a non-arbitrary congruence – between form and social context, and it suggests that such congruence means something, that a particular form of communication actually conveys 'genre'-meanings. That is: when we hear or see a particular linguistic form, we immediately tune into a complex of expectations, attitudes and behaviours. If it is a poem, we will contex-tually infer 'poetic' meanings from it; if it is an academic lecture, we will tune into that set of expectations accordingly. That such patterns of normative expectations and response behaviour are compelling was nicely illustrated by Dennis Tedlock (1983: 109), who converted his academic prose into a poetic graphical ordering:

SECOND
conversational narratives THEMSELVES
Traditionally classified as PROSE
Turn out, when listened to CLOSELY
To have poetical qualities of their OWN

Tedlock here demonstrates the 'determining' force of the 'sphere' in Bakhtin's terms: in a particular context, we *need* a particular kind of text, because only a limited set of specifically organised texts makes sense in a particular context.

This is perhaps one line of inquiry that could be taken further: the connec-tion between genre and normativity. There is a case to be made that 'standard' (as in 'Standard English' or 'Swahili Bora') does not operate at the level of language, but at the level of genre or register (Silverstein 1996), and I will develop that case further on. Given that we never just use a language, but always do so within generically organised patterns, statements about what would be 'good' language in *all* social contexts would be hard to support. Normative expectations are far more specific than that, and they operate within the scope of generically regimented language use. Such reformulations would probably have an effect on discussions on language pedagogy and language policy – where currently, issues of normativity seem to be connected only to the level of 'language', not of genre.

Another very fertile line of inquiry could be the layered nature of different genres co-occurring (in a Bakhtinian heteroglossia) in real communicative events. A job interview can be seen as one genre. But within such a genre, we see conversational bits, question-answer sequences, narratives, reading and writing moments, presentations, and so on: all of them are genres in their own right and have to be executed according to the normative expectations for these genres, and doing *all of that* fulfils the normative expectations of the job interview. The interplay of genres there is not just sequential, it is layered, because the genres stand in a hierarchical relationship to one another. The 'job interview' is the superordinate or 'dominant' genre, the other genres are subordinate but crucial to realise the superordinate one. Appraisals afterwards would take the shape of appraisals of the highest level – 'you did very well during the interview' (not 'you did very well during the conversation, question-answer, narrative, etc.'). Such complex and layered polygeneric structures are very widespread. Reducing them to their constituent parts is not helpful.

Emerging genres in an emerging tradition

Let us now come back to the point about genres and processes of cultural transmission. In an article called 'Genres in an emerging tradition', Johannes Fabian (1974) elaborated on the issue of genres in the development of a new religious movement in Katanga, the so-called Jamaa movement. The paper is of significance for capturing the role of textual practices in cultural innovation and change, in the constitution of *new* cultural forms.[2] It shows how genres – regimented textual work – help and guide people to navigate uncharted cultural waters, to develop recognisable patterns that identify their community and identities.

Fabian starts from an epistemological take-off point: the fact that ethnographic objectivity requires a critical and reflexive stance towards the use of language in the constitution of ethnographic knowledge. Ethnography, he maintains, stands out from many other scientific endeavours by its almost complete reliance on processes of communication – fieldwork, notably, is seen as a complex of communicative events in which inter-subjective knowledge is generated. Consequently, the status of linguistic data – e.g. texts collected in the field –

THE LIVES OF JULIEN

requires substantial revision. Texts are products of historical processes and events and need to be seen and examined as such. Consequently:

> It appears that a study of religious thought and action must be carried out on the *level of texts*, rather than on that of discrete terms or even propositions. More concretely, we may say that the transformation of a prophetic vision in a tradition of knowledge and communal action [. . .] is dependent on the emergence of a textual dimension of communication. Conversely, an understanding of the Jamaa movement will depend on our ability to translate features of text production into historical process. Such translation we regard as the essence of an interpretive approach.
>
> (Fabian 1974: 47, italics in the original)

Fabian reacts here against the then-dominant tradition of formal and structuralist genre analysis, and what he advocates shows affinities with both Marxism and the hermeneutic historicism of e.g. Ricoeur: there is the assumption that products are best understood by looking at the *praxis* – the socially, ideologically and historically determined practices – that produced them, and there is the assumption that texts need to be understood through their origins and sources (see Fabian 1990a: 163–5). The point he makes is largely theoretical; but while making it, Fabian demonstrates how regimented textual practices *co-create* the tradition, that is, the social processes and structures. The textual practices, in sum, are not a result of social processes, nor are they something that fits neatly in pre-existing structures, they form and shape new social processes. In doing that, people draw on and borrow from existing genres, some of which are known and have their function relocated to fit the new social processes (as when the 'confession' genre is relocated from Catholic ritual to psychotherapy – Foucault 2003a), while others only exist as a distant image or memory. This point, of genre models and memories, is further developed in Fabian (1990a), and I shall have to come back to it on several occasions. For now I must emphasise the fundamental point: that the use of genres does *not* presuppose stable or solid social and cultural patterns, but that genres must rather be seen as flexible and multi-purpose resources by means of which social processes can be given a firmer, more stable and more solid shape. Genres, in other word, can be and often are tools for cultural innovation.[3]

Let us now turn to Julien. From what we have seen in the previous chapter, his texts are exceptional, but at the same time they fit into an already developed tradition of correspondence with Mrs Arens. They are exceptional, though, for two reasons. One: the versions of his life story came about in response to an explicit request from Mrs Arens. She gave him a specific writing assignment, to write 'the story of his life'. Prior to that request, they had exchanged letters, and naturally such letters contained autobiographical narratives. The request from Mrs Arens, however, changed the generic frame: he now needed to write *a different genre*, not a 'letter', but a 'story'. Two: the life histories quickly started leading a life of their own, as we shall see later. They turned into an oeuvre in their own right, connected, of course, to the tradition of correspondence with Mrs Arens, but also becoming a new and specific genre-writing project.

Note (and I stress the importance of this point) that this genre-writing project was prompted by *a projected new type of relationship* between Julien and Mrs Arens. Whereas previously their relationship was one in which Julien asked for things, in this particular case it was Mrs Arens who wanted something from Julien. It was, as mentioned before, a form of symbolic (but also material) repayment for the support previously received by Julien. Thus, we see both an 'emerging genre' as well as an 'emerging tradition' in Fabian's sense. The emergent genre develops within, *but at the same time shapes*, the emergent relationship in which Julien and Mrs Arens now find themselves. Realising the kind of life history that (Julien believes) Mrs Arens wants will complete the process of repayment and wipe out the debt he has incurred with her. This re-shaped relationship is new territory for Julien, who still signs his versions with an identification that anchors him and his addressee in the past: *'votre ancient boy – Julien'* ('your former houseboy – Julien').[4]

Histories and letters

In Chapter 2, I pointed towards the fact that Julien's texts were monoglossic. In spite of widespread language mixing and shifting in the everyday use of language in the area where he lives, he made a considerable effort to avoid language mixing and code-switching in his text. This is, thus, a special, remarkable feature, a contrast between this particular act of communication and other patterns of communication: it is the *literate* code, not the spoken one. And it is not the only special feature. The texts are long, there are three versions of them, and we see significant differences between the versions. The texts are divided into chapters, and the two later ones carry a genre label: *'Récits'*, 'stories'. Let us now examine what is meant by 'Récits'.

The perception of genre

We must take two observations as our point of departure. One: Julien writes different versions. The second version arrived with a letter in which he dismissed the first version, and the third version was entitled '*2° partie*' ('second part'). There seems to be a process of critical revision and improvement based on an awareness that the previous version was 'not good'. Two: the appearance of the genre label 'Récits' points towards *the perception of an identifiable genre*. If we combine the two observations, we can see that this genre must have been experienced as inadequately realised in each of the versions, prompting Julien to produce a new one. The point was already clear and I reiterate it: in crafting his life history, Julien *tries to write a special text*, or in other words, he *tries to write in*

49

THE LIVES OF JULIEN

a particular genre. The resources he mobilises must now be seen as resources that are deployed, ordered and patterned in view of the realisation of that genre.

But what exactly is that genre? In *History from Below*, Fabian (1990a: 169ff) comments on the genre label of the document he examines, the *Vocabulaire de Ville de Elisabethville*. The *Vocabulaire* is a history of Elisabethville (now Lubumbashi), written in Shaba Swahili by a former houseboy named André Yav on behalf of an association of former houseboys, the *waboyi*. It is a genuine attempt at grassroots historiography, not a word list of any sort, and so the genre label 'vocabulary' is puzzling. One suggestion made by Fabian is that the name 'vocabulaire' carries authority and prestige within a local, late-colonial social and semiotic order. It may have been used by Yav 'to get the attention of readers who, in the elementary sort of initiation into literacy to which most Africans were limited during colonial times, had experienced various *vocabularies* as authoritative texts' (Fabian 1990a: 170, italics in original). But Fabian also stresses the way in which such a (superficially experienced) genre can be taken into other culturally significant domains – how the genre, now detached from its normative and formal features, can be redeployed in order to make sense of new things. Thus, '[t]he Vocabulaire contains numerous indications suggesting that to write history is conceived here as giving 'meaning' to names, appellations, and terms, and that is of course what vocabularies do' (1990a: 171). It carries prestige: 'colonial writings are authoritative because they contain the meaning of names, persons, places and events' (175). Colonial writings were, to use a neologism, 'vocabularesque', writings that defined and decided how things were, and discourses of truth and power were discourses that proceeded within this vocabularesque frame.

The colonial development of the city was described by this late-colonial subject by taking a distant image of a previously experienced genre and reapplying it to achieve the 'degree of fit' that Hymes (1966: 199) alluded to: it was redeployed in an attempt to construct a factual, objective, serious and authoritative text. Note that the genre is *distant*, it is *borrowed* and *redeployed* using very different codes and patterns. Hence, the perceived use of a genre should never rest on an a priori assumption of *full competence* in that genre, and neither should we presuppose extensive exposure to that genre as a prerequisite for using it.

Julien was born in 1946. The Congo became independent in 1960, and so Julien was exposed to very much the same 'elementary sort of initiation into literacy' as Yav and, given this largely shared background, Fabian's explanations may also be applicable to Julien's text.[5] He, too, may have used a genre label and genre features on the basis of a distant similarity with what he believed the genre was. The existence of different versions points towards that: he clearly did not feel fully confident in the genre, and so he produced new versions, each time longer and more elaborate in structure and style. He, too, like Yav, appears to have invested tremendous efforts in writing a factual and formal, serious, historiographic text. He tries to write a text that allows him to go on record, a text that tells the truth.

50

GENRES AND REPERTOIRES

Distant genres

The distant genre is unfamiliar, and its realisation is therefore 'a long, pain-fully combative process' (Mayer & Woolf 1995: 7). This becomes clear when we survey the three versions.

Version one

The first version is nine pages long and completely in Swahili. It has no title. Julien opens abruptly with a prelude to his employment with the Arens family:

> Katika **m**gi wa Lubumbashi, wakati
> nilio kuwa ku masomo, zo**e**zi langu
> lilikuwa ya kusaidia mjomba, kati-
> ka kazi yake ya Mpishi. (1/1)

Translation:

> In the city of Lubumbashi, at the time
> when I was at school [was in classes], my exercise
> was to help [my] uncle, in
> his job as a cook.

This sentence is remarkable in its linguistic, stylistic and ortho-graphic elabora-tion. Julien uses complex inflected verbs, punctuation and hyphenation. This is not a constant feature of the text, as we shall see shortly. But in general, the first half of the text is written with a degree of fluency that betrays one rather long writing effort. This is also noticeable from the contents. In a kind of stream of consciousness, Julien covers the period of his employment with the Arens family and afterwards with other expatriate families. There are anecdotes, such as an event in which Julien makes pancakes for everyone, and the anecdotal gaze shines through in fragments like this one (1/3):

> Nawakati wakula na walikwa wote
> walifurahi, na kusema hii krepi ni
> Zuri sana; ila mu moja wa wale wali
> o alikwa, bibi yake alibakiaka akapa
> ta paka habari yakama krepi ilikuwa
> Zuri, huyu mwalikiwa sikufamia ji
> na lake, alikuwa murefu tena munene

Translation:

> and at the time of eating and all
> were happy, and said that this pancake is

51

THE LIVES OF JULIEN

very good; except one of those present,
his wife had remained [at home] and got
the news that the pancake was
good, this one (who was there?) I didn't know
his name, he was tall and fat.

He also expatiates on the flour and meat that he received as part of his wage, and on some difficulties he had with another houseboy named Kalume. He then mentions the support he has received from Mrs Arens since 1973, and he notes that until 1991 he has received a total of 50,000 Belgian Francs as well as bags with clothes. This rather factual statement is followed by this one:

Nakumbuka tena wa
Kati niliendaka kuwapikia wakati wali
endaka[6] kuvua samaki, katika mtoni
mu monja ya inchii ya ZAMBIA (1/4)

Translation:

I also remember the
Time I went to cook for them when they
went fishing in a certain
river in the country of ZAMBIA.

Clearly, Julien is writing while he remembers things; the memories are as yet rather unstructured and not yet put in a coherent narrative. This stream of consciousness continues until page 5. Then, suddenly, a chapter title appears: 'SAFARi yao iliniuzikisha' ('Their trip made me sad'). The storyline simply continues. Julien had mentioned his employment with the Verstappen family, and this episode spills over into the new chapter. He then tells how he started his charcoal business and got into debt with Kalonda; he decided to write to Mrs Arens, but she replied that she could not afford to send him the money required.

The chapter title here is somewhat awkwardly placed. It enters in the middle of an episode, and it does not cover the stories told in the chapter. From page 6 onwards, however, the chapter titles correspond to the chronological unfolding of events. Two titles appear on page 6: 'The escape to Kasai' and 'After paying the debt'. Two more titles appear on page 7, 'Farming the fields' and 'In 1986 fields in the town of Katondo'. A final one appears on page 8, 'The illness of witchcraft'. In that final chapter, he describes the various crises that have punctuated his life since 1986. He talks about the writing journey to Mbuji-Mayi, about the dreadful labour conditions in the diamond mines and the widespread abuse of drugs and alcohol they entail. He ends his story with thanks for the support he received from Mr and Mrs Arens and an expression of optimism about the future.

GENRES AND REPERTOIRES

As we can see, this text contains numerous features that point towards a struggle with genre. Julien tells his story in monoglossic Swahili – this is not *spoken* language but *the language of writing*. He also tells the story in the first person singular, and his addressee Mrs Arens is mentioned in the third person. It is an auto-narrative in which Mrs Arens is a character. This leads to rather complex positional constructions, in which Julien addresses Mrs Arens in the third person singular, as in 'fortunately my SAVIOUR Hèlena aRENS arrived, she sent me MONEY' (1/9). Or, as in the final sentence of version one, addressed to the Arens couple: 'what they sent me from Belgium was even a lot more, therefore I want to express my extreme gratitude to them' (1/9). He ends his text with the oblique 'aksanti', 'thank you' – a direct call but without an identified addressee. We have also seen how he appears to discover the chronological function of chapters and chapter titles, but he does so only gradually. This story is not 'fully formed' in the sense of Hymes (1998), it does not show an adequate mapping of stylistic resources onto narrative contents, with recognisable structure as a result. This is different when we look at version two.

Version two

Julien sent this version a couple of years after the first one, together with a letter in which he dismissed the first version. This version is significantly longer, a total of 17 pages. It also carries the genre label 'Récits', and the text is divided into chapters throughout. Note, however, that 'Récits' is penned in the top left corner of the first page, at a diagonal angle and underscored. It is very likely that it was added afterwards, perhaps after finishing the writing process, or at least after having written his main title, neatly centred on the page: 'MaiSHA YANgu', 'My life'. Clearly, Julien now had come to terms with the idea of a genre ('Récits') and the thematic domain he needed to cover ('my life'). He also seems to have come to terms with the particular literate format of such a genre: the text is again monoglossic, and chapter titles are used throughout. Experience with the process of thinking about his life (the result of having written one version) has influenced the outcome.

Under the title 'My life', Julien starts with the typical opening line of an autobiography: 'NiliZALiKiwa MANONO tarehe 10–12–1946 KATIKA jamaa ya baba na mama wa Kristu Katika dini ya KatoLiKA', 'I was born in Manono on 10–12–1946 in a family of father and mother [who were] Christians in the Catholic faith'. He reports a miserable childhood that forced him to leave school and to start working in Lubumbashi in 1965 and he mentions his marriage to a woman named Jacqueline. From there onwards, more specific chapter titles occur:

'My work with Mr and Mrs André Deprins Arens' (page 2)
'My work with Madame and Mister Verstappen' (page 3)
'Difficulties begin in my house' (page 3)

53

THE LIVES OF JULIEN

'The journey to Mbuji-Mayi' (page 7)
'Labour or slavery (*esclavage*)?' (page 8)
'Trouble (*trouble*) between Katanga and Kasai' (page 10)
'Lusaka-Lubumbashi 966 km' (page 12)

All the chapter titles, albeit to different extents, cover the period and events they announce. But we see that while some chapters are very short, others are quite long. In contrast to the first version, where several pages were devoted to Julien's time as houseboy with the Arens family, this period is quickly dealt with in the second version: a few lines of text, to which he adds an account of the end of his first marriage and the beginning of his second. The issues of extra meat as part of the salary are mentioned, but they are now framed as part of a happy period in his life. Far more effort is spent on describing the period of decline in his life. The chapter 'Trouble starts in my house' covers four dense pages of text, and the four subsequent chapters all further document the difficulties that have marked his life since the Arens family left Lubumbashi. This storyline extends from page 3 to page 14, and the second version can be characterised as a harrowing story of marginalisation and *déclassement* prefaced by brief accounts of formal employment and happy periods.

While the narrative in the first version was strictly confined to Julien's own experiences, the second version occasionally offers us a glimpse of a wider panorama of events. Consider the following fragment from the chapter 'Trouble between Katanga and Kasai' (2/10–11):

> NiKafika mwezi wa januari Kabinda laki
> ni Sikuwa na Feza ya kulipa Motokari na
> kwenda Malemba-Nkulu. watu wa Katanga
> wengi walikimbia KabiNDA na kurudia ku[7]
> Katanga, ila tulibakia wawili na David
> Sababu yeye alikuwa mwenye kuowa bibi
> wa Ku Kabinda, njoo behati yake, lakini
> mie na vile nilikataa kwi <u>waolesha wa</u>
> <u>binti wangu</u> **Mbili** (Faire Marier mes deux Filles)
> wakawa na chuki. Njoo pale mara ingine
> nikamwandikia Madame Helena D.A. ya Kama
> niko katika hatari ya kuwawa, sina FEZA
> ya kulipa na kwenda kwetu.
> Kwa Huruma yake pamoja na Bwana yake
> wakanitumia FEZA, wakati FEZA ili
> po FIKA, Fujo ilipita watoto wangu kupi-
> giwa njiani na watu wakubwa, Mie walita
> ka **ku**niuwa katika munji wa KASENG
> U, ni mgini wanachimbuaka DiaMA.
> waliwaza niko na FEZA waniuwa wabeb

GENRES AND REPERTOIRES

e FEZA, bahati yangu ni watu ya Kanisa
lakini wakanifichika kwa Sultani wa mugi
ni yeye pia alikuwa mu Kristu. (Chef du Village)
Nikapata FEZA msaada ya madame HELENA
Mwezi wa octoba 1992, na kwa bahati zuri
kulikuwa Safari ya Motokari ilikuwa ina
enda kubeba Mihindi mu province ya
Katanga mu mugini MwaMBAyi kadiri ya
Kilometri 22 na Missio KYoNDO na iliku
wa safari ya mwisho ya Motokari kwingia
katika province ya Katanga yenye kutokea
KASAI

Translation:

I arrived in Kabinda in January, but
I didn't have money to pay for a car ride and
go to Malemba-Nkulu. Many people from Katanga
were escaping from Kabinda and returned to
Katanga. We stayed behind with two, with David
because he had married a woman
from Kabinda, and that was his blessing, but
I had refused to give in marriage my
two daughters (faire marier mes deux filles)
and they hated me. There again
I wrote to Mrs Helena D.A. that
I was in danger of being murdered, that I didn't have money
to return home.
Thanks to the compassion of her and her husband
they sent me the money, when the money
arrived, trouble happened that my children were
beaten on the streets by adults, and they wanted
to kill me too in the town of Kasengu,
that is a town where people dig for diamonds.
They thought I had money, to kill me and
to take the money, my luck were the people of the Church
but (= because?) they hid me in the village Chief's [place]
who was also a Christian. (*chef du village*)
I received financial help from Mrs Helena
in October 1992, and luckily
there was a car (= lorry?) transport
delivering maize to the province of
Katanga in the village of Mwambayi,
22 km from the Kyondo Mission, and it

THE LIVES OF JULIEN

was the last transport which made
it into Katanga from
Kasai.

Starting from his own and his family's experiences – his refusal to give his
daughters in marriage, his children being beaten in the streets, his Christian
connections – Julien here tells a story of ethnic pogroms against Katangese
people in Kasai. The phrase 'and it was the last transport which made it into
Katanga from Kasai' reveals a wider world and is written in the voice of the
chronicle writer, the reporter. Elsewhere in the second version, Julien talks
about the ethnic sensitivities between Luba from Kasai and Luba from Katanga
in a way that articulates politically salient stereotypes ('the Luba-Kasai have a
way of dominating other people', 2/8). The story ends on page 14, when Julien
mentions that he is now in Lubumbashi, writing to Mrs Arens and hoping that
she will send him funds for his farm.

But of course that is not the end of the second version. Halfway down
page 14, the text – until now completely written in monoglossic Swahili – shifts
to French, and from that point until the end, the whole text is in monoglossic French, and it is divided into three chapters (see Figure 3.1). This dramatic
code-switching is not the only shift we notice. Consider the three chapter titles
in this French part:

'There are no crazy trades, there are only crazy people' (page 14)
'According to the Bible, the true cult is to visit the poor' (page 15)
'One's name has great significance in life. Helena means = light' (page 17)

The whole tone of the text changes: it becomes a mixture of general reflections
on society (in the first two chapters of this part) and of comments on himself
and on Mrs Arens (in the final chapter). Mrs Arens, who was a character in
the Swahili narrative, now becomes a second person addressee, and Julien concludes the text with a direct *captatio benevolentiae* (2/17):

Votre aide pour une ferme je suis sûr, d'ici
deux ans ça n'aura plus de quiNZE Travailleurs
je loue grandement mon Dieu à cause de vos
grandes œuvres; Madame Helèna ARÈNS et Monsieur
andré D. ARÈNS
        Votre ancien Boy
        Julien

Translation:

Your support for my farm I'm sure
two years from now it will have more than fifteen workers

14

FEZA ile nilifika mayo nalembe-nkulu
mwezi wa nei, kufika mwezi wa Ogistino
ikatemuka nguvu (devaluation) kazi
ya mashamba shikuritumika apana vile
vilivyo waza kuritumika (programe)
niliombaka madame Helena na Bwana
yake de grave wanisaidie miaka tano,
njoo sababu nilifika Hapa LubumBASHI
kuve Kupokea msaada na masaidio yao
ni pate namna ya kuishi na fun ya
maendeo ya kazi ya FERRO.

Il n'y a pas de SOT metier, il y a que le
SOT gens

les noirs riches et intellectuels preferent avoir de
domestiques, mais ils les considerent comme des gens
inferieurs, qu'ils ne peuvent pas parler longuement avec
eux, ni s'assoire ensemble autour d'une table, ni
boire dans ~~ses~~ Bar ou restaurant, même pour les pay-
ement de salaire il y en a qui disent à leurs à leur
BOYS, tu mange ici et tu n'a pas de respect pour
reclamer ton salaire. les BOYS repliquent parfois que
vos ~~nos~~ FAmilles ne viennent pas manger ici, ça aboutir souvent
au dispute ou les BOYS quittent les services.
depuis la colonisation et aujourd'hui, pendant les
crises politique et economique les boys gagnent
toujours bien leur vie par rapport, aux directeurs
commis, professeurs, mecaniciens, menuisier. à moins
que les derniers trouvez ce leurs services les

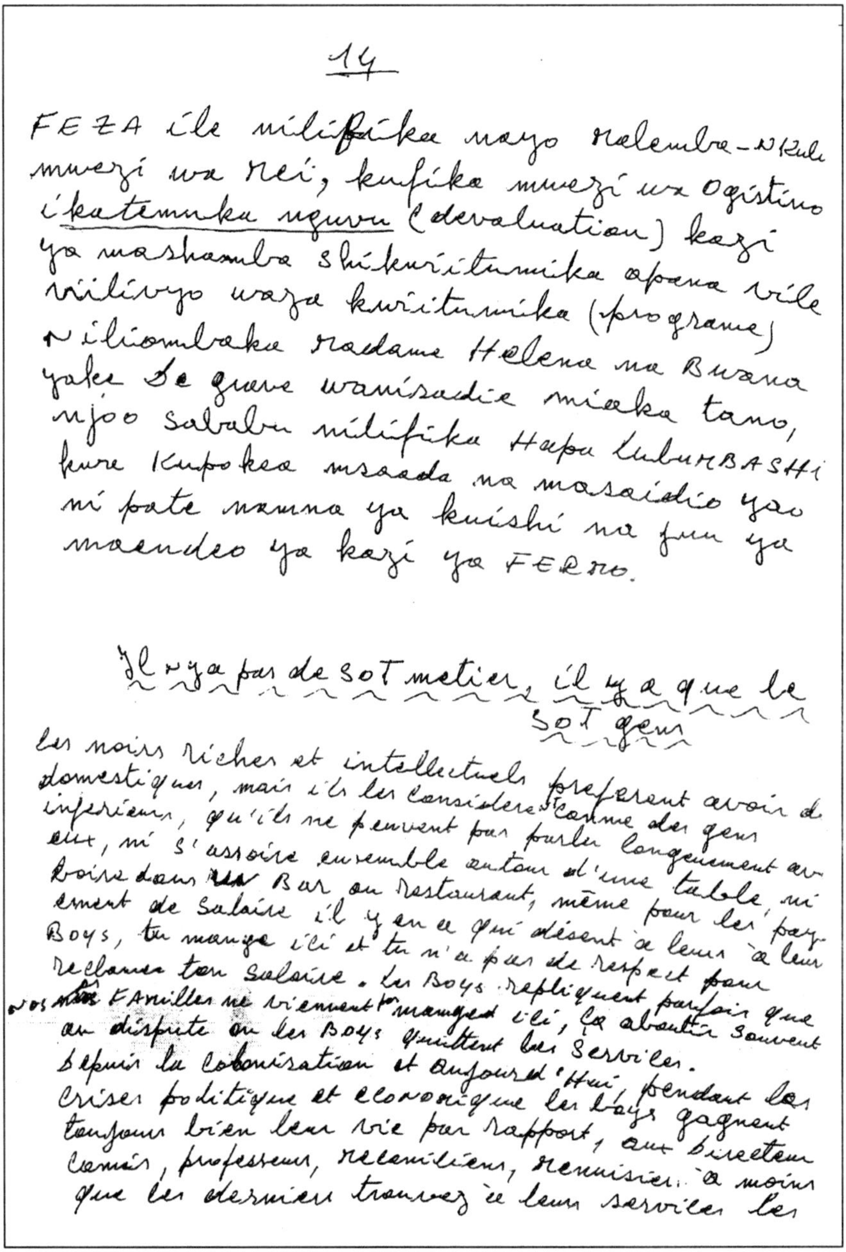

Figure 3.1 Copy of 2/14

I greatly praise my God because of your
Great works; Madame Helèna Arens and Mister
André D. Arens.
          Your former boy
               Julien

While we saw that general statements or statements reflecting on issues that transcended his own life were absent from version one and rare in the Swahili part of this version, the tone becomes sharply political in the French part of the text. Julien now criticises corruption, exploitation and fraud, not just in his country but also 'dans d'autres pays d'Afrique' ('in other African countries'). The chapter 'There are no crazy trades, there are only crazy people' (2/14) starts with a bitter critique of inequalities in his own society:

> Les noirs riches et intellectuels preferent avoir des
> domestiques, mais ils les considere[NT] comme des gens
> inferieurs, qu'ils ne peuvent pas parler longuement avec
> eux, ni s'assoire ensemble autour d'une table, ni
> boire dans **UN** Bar ou restaurant [. . .]

> *Translation:*

> Rich and intellectual blacks prefer to have
> house personnel, but they consider them as
> inferior people, with whom they can't talk long
> or sit together around a table, or
> drink in a bar or restaurant [. . .]

And a bit further, he states (2/16):

> Les dirigeants de l'Afrique recevant des
> Aides, mais ils les utilisent mal, les pasteurs
> trompent leurs communautés de l'occident en les
> envoyant des livres, des Lunettes et des medicaments
> pour aide les pauvres mais, les aides sont vendu

> *Translation:*

> The leaders of Africa receive
> Aid, but they use it wrongly, priests
> deceive their western communities who
> send books, spectacles and drugs
> to help the poor but, the donations are sold

GENRES AND REPERTOIRES

And so on. Julien sketches a world full of poverty, exploitation, abuse and evil, and contrasts this world with his own character – 'you have known me as a poor houseboy and until now I have been supported solely for that reason'. He connects his own auto-history with a broader historical complex of people, events and moral categories in the construction of a *captatio benevolentiae*. The text, as we know, is not disinterested, it is a motivated request for continued support, and is in that sense an extension in a new textual format of that genre in which he already had accumulated some experience: the letter to Mrs Arens.

Version three

The third version, 20 pages long and sent in 1997, extends this stylistic pattern. The text is in monoglossic Swahili until the end of page 18; the two final pages are in monoglossic French. The first page carries a title, 'UKARaSA wa pili (2° partie)', and Julien opens with a framing statement that defines this version as a complement to the previous one (3/1):

> Sawa vile nilivyo kufasilia mu mandiko ya kwanza
> Sasa napenda kukufasilia ngizi maisha yangu
> iko sasa. Mbele ya hiyo tafasilia mangumu yangu
> ya mwazo.

Translation:

> Like I narrated in my first writing
> I now want to tell you the way my life
> is now. Prior to that I'll tell my difficulties
> from the beginning (= my earlier difficulties).

We shall see in Chapter 4 that this 'second part' isn't really a complement to the previous version: Julien provides a new entextualisation of the whole story of his life, with attention to the recent conflicts over the ownership of his farm. Thus, this new version also provides accounts of his various jobs, travels, marriages and problems. Chapter titles are used throughout, and their use is now systematic. No less than 19 chapter titles occur, all of them more or less adequately covering the particular events or episodes they claim to cover.

The calibration of episodes is roughly similar to that of the second version. Julien opens with a very summary account of his difficult youth and his first jobs, then moves on to provide an account of his job with the Arens family. This time, a lot of emphasis is put on their departure to Belgium: two chapters are devoted to it. The first one (3/2) is entitled 'Habari ya kurudi Ubeleji' ('The news of the return to Belgium'). The second one is stylistically interesting. On page 3, the chapter title is reported speech (a stylistic echo of the proverbial title 'There are no crazy trades, there are only crazy people', 2/14),

THE LIVES OF JULIEN

part of a conversation he appears to remember, and it spills over into the narrative itself.

Tunarudi UBeleji, utatumika
Kwa Madama na Bwana VerSTAppen
Tutakuacha utumike kwa Madame Verstappen
Usinungunike, wao vilevile wako wema sawa
sisi.

Translation:

We return to Belgium, you will be employed
With Madam and Mister Verstappen
We will leave you to be employed with Madam Verstappen
Don't be disappointed, they too are good ones like
us.

This conversation initiates a brief account of his work with the Verstappen family, after which he begins the story of his problematic business ventures. From page 4 to page 14, a similar sequence of events is covered as in the second version: the different jobs, the travels, the family problems. The pages 14 to 16 are taken by a long account of the various problems he has had with his farm in Malemba-Nkulu. Local people vandalised his palm tree plantations, officials did not provide any help but sided with the opposition, police people came and stole goats and ducks, and he now plans to go to Kinshasa to initiate court proceedings. Page 16 shifts the frame from a factual account to a more general complaint:

Sasa niko na miaka 51^{ans}, Nguvu (Force) ya
kulima iko inaisha, ni sikitiko nyingi
(Tristesse) Kwangu juu ya watu hawa na
Wa ongozadi (autorités). [. . .] (3/16)

Translation:

I am now 51 years old, the force (*Force*) to
cultivate the fields has gone, it is a lot of sadness
(*Tristesse*) for me about these people and
the leaders (*autorités*).

This is an old, disappointed and worried man talking. Yet, the chapter that immediately follows this statement, 'Hectare SABA (7) ya MiHogo' ('Seven hectares of manioc'), is optimistic. Julien outlines his plans for cultivating manioc, a high-yield crop that would leave him and his family secure later in life. Then,

GENRES AND REPERTOIRES

when we turn the page, he suddenly enters into the story of his marriages, divided into two chapters, 'My marriage with Miss Jacqueline' (3/17) and 'Getting married to Miss Julienne' (3/17). The first marriage is described as happy, a marriage of 'real love' but without children and terminated by his in-laws when, in 1969, Julien was unemployed for a few months. His marriage with Julienne, in contrast, steadily became more difficult, and (3/18):

toka mwaka wa 1981 mupa
ka sasa ana vitendo mingi, Niliweza kuvuja
Ndoa yetu na bibi julienne na kira mara Madame
Helna-ARENS eko ananipa <u>adibisho</u> (CONSeil)

Translation:

Since the year 1981 until
now she has done many things, I could have
divorced Miss Julienne and each time Madam
Helna-ARENS gave me <u>advice</u> (*conseil*)

As we can see, at the end of page 18 Mrs Arens is still addressed in the third person, she is a character in the story (the same one as before: the benefactor and saviour). Page 19, however, shows the same shift as in the second version: she is addressed in the second person, and the text again becomes a letter to Mrs Arens. This time, however, the shift to monoglossic French letter writing is done without a chapter title. The storyline abruptly terminated on page 16 – the plans for planting manioc – is here resumed (3/19):

Normalement ma ferme a dix ans, le jour ou je coMMancais
a Faire les-champs de Manioc, Mais, arachides, et soja, le plantation
de palmiers c'etait en 1986 et 1988 c'est l'année ou les autorités local ont signé mon document de Fèrme.

Translation:

Normally my farm is ten years old, the day I started
cultivating the fields of manioc, maize, peanuts, and soy, the plantation
of palm trees that was in 1986 and 1988 that's the year in which the
local authorities signed the deed for my farm.

Julien recapitulates the things he said in pages 14 to 16, including the references to his age and deteriorating physical condition. It is a kind of French summary of the essence of what this '2nd part' tries to convey: that of late, things have got even worse than before, that his farm is in serious danger, and that he is now facing the challenge of growing old in poverty. And, as in the second version,

THE LIVES OF JULIEN

it leads to an extensive *captatio benevolentiae,* but note the way in which his recent concerns penetrate that statement (3/19):

Je termine en vous felicitant pour Votre argent que
vous avez voulu depensé pour que je **ne**[NE] sois pas un pau-
vre-malheureux. Il est aussi triste que les agronomes
malgre mes **dolean**ces ne sont pas inquite voir
même les cultivateurs.*par les autorites local ni eux*
avoir peur du gouverneur et des ministres, Mainte
nant je ne vois que le chemin de la justice.

Translation:

I end by congratulating you for your money
that you have wished to spend so that I wouldn't be an
unhappy-pauper. It is also sad that the agricultural experts
in spite of my complaints are not worried even
the farmers.*by the local authorities nor*
being afraid of the governor and the Ministers, now
I can only see the road of the Law.

While the whole of this text is written with a black ballpoint, the italicised parts are written in blue: a later addition to the text, probably an attempt at clarifying the 'worries' that the corrupt experts and the malicious farmers should feel at facing the authorities and the Law (*'avoir peur'*). A similar later addition can be found at the bottom of page 16, where Julien adds the phrase 'mu Mwaka wa 1997 à 1998' ('in the year 1997 to 1998') to some of his plans to cultivate manioc. In some other places we see that he corrected grammatical and orthographic mistakes in black ink (but in a different handwriting style). On the final page, Julien thanks Mr and Mrs Arens as well as their son and Mrs Arens' mother. Interestingly, the name of the mother ('uma-aNgELINa' – 'grandma-Angelina') is written in blue. Here, Julien must have left a blank slot in his text, taking time to check (or remember) the name of this person and adding it, along with the other additions in blue and the confidently underscored genre label 'Récits' (also written in blue and upside down, as if written after he folded the document), as soon as he was ready for it (see figure 3.2).

It is evidence of the fact that Julien has *reread and edited* this version. And interestingly, we now have evidence of the fact that Julien added the genre label 'Récits' *after* having written his text and after having added precision and detail to his story, as a sort of quality label reflecting satisfaction with a job well done. There is more awareness of the genre and more conscious genre work here. Similar but fewer corrections and additions were visible in version two – Julien added some dates to reported events and corrected some grammatical and ortho-graphic errors there as well. The third version, however, displays

62

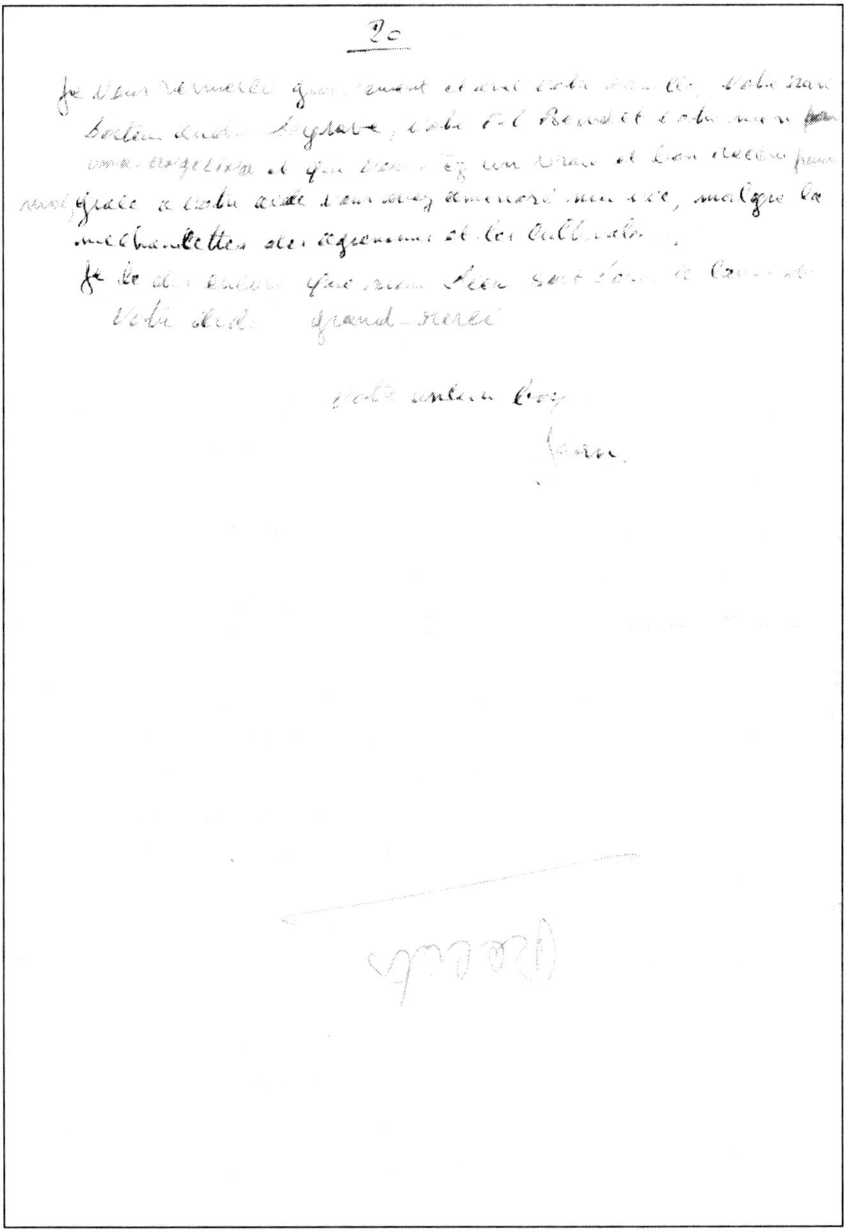

20

Je vous remercie [illegible] et avec votre [illegible], votre [illegible]
[illegible]
[illegible]
[illegible] grâce à votre aide [illegible], malgré les
méchancetés [illegible]
Je [illegible] que [illegible]
Votre [illegible] grand-merci

votre [illegible]

Jean

Figure 3.2 Copy of 3/20

THE LIVES OF JULIEN

more such features and more sophistication in the technique of using them. The fact that he made additions and corrections both in black and blue ink suggests at least *two rounds* of textual revisions; and when he left the blank slot in his final paragraph, he was actually *anticipating and planning* the revision and editing. There is no evidence in the second version of such conscious planning and rigour of textual revision.

At the same time, this work of revision left many things unaltered. Thus on page 10, the chapter title 'SAFARI ya kwenda Lubumbashi' ('The trip to Lubumbashi') appears halfway down the page. The remainder of the page, however, is left blank, and page 11 opens with the title 'Katika magumu hii niko **na**[NA] Bibi Julienne, watoto 6 na watoto 8 wa dugu yangu' ('In these troubles I was with my wife Julienne, six children and eight children of my brother'), in which he tells about the expansion of his family after the death of his younger brother, which increased his economic needs as well as his gratitude for Mrs Arens' support. The next page then recapitulates, in identical orthography, the title from page 10: 'SAFARI ya kwenda Lubumbashi'. It looks as if Julien realised, as he was about to report on the trip to Lubumbashi, that the contextual circumstances for that trip needed to be clarified: the increasing pressure on his family, now more than doubled in size, which compelled him again to appeal for help to Mrs Arens by writing another version of his life story.

In contrast to the second version, Julien's third version is (like the first version) very much an auto-history with very rare references to the wider historical and social context. Julien does not engage in the strident criticism of corruption, fraud and abuse we encountered in the second version. This criticism is brought home, so to speak, and takes the shape of accounts of his battle with the 'agronomes', and their insolence and temerity in the face of his threats to appeal to the highest authorities. The failure of Mobutu's system of governance has become immediately palpable in his own life, and that is what he focuses on now. There is one intriguing instance, however, where Julien opens a window onto bigger historical and political processes. As in version two, it appears when he discusses the crisis that erupts between Kasai and Katanga (3/9):

Democratie mu ZAIRe en 1990
Mwisho wa 1991 Fujo (Trouble) ikaza kati ya
Kasaï na province ya Shaba, watu wa jiMBo (province)
yote mbili wakaza kuuwana, mie sikuwa na Feza
yakulipa gari (Vehucule) nipate kukimbilia katika
jimbo letu, mie, bibi na watoto munane (8) . . .

Translation:

Democracy in Zaire in 1990
In the beginning of 1991, trouble (*Trouble*) begun between
Kasai and the province of Shaba, people of both

GENRES AND REPERTOIRES

provinces (*province*) started murdering each other, and I didn't have
   money
to pay for a car (*vehucule*) to escape into
our province, me, [my] wife and eight (8) children . . .

The troubles between both provinces are seen as an effect of 'democracy in Zaire'. In 1990, President Mobutu announced the first multi-party elections since independence, and allowed other political parties. This modest 'democratisation' (which, unsurprisingly, led to nothing) triggered civil unrest, and it is this bit of historical context that Julien invokes here in a couple of lines.[8] We see, however, how he immediately takes this episode into his own life, and we know the further sequence: he wrote for support to Mrs Arens and was able to escape to Katanga.

Increasing tightness

Having surveyed the three versions, it is clear why Julien dismissed his first version. In comparison with the two later ones, it was anecdotal, confused, and unstructured. It did not satisfy the genre requirements he had gradually constructed as a target for his writing. The question as to what the third version represents in relation to the second is more complex and will be addressed in Chapter 4. But we clearly see how the three versions display increasing degrees of genre formalisation. Each text shows an increase in text-structuring devices, improvements in the mapping of textual and stylistic resources onto narrative contents. This increasing structural tightness of the texts is reflected in several features. From the second version onwards, Julien confidently qualifies his texts, in an act of reflexive categorisation, as 'Récits': they now *belong to a genre*. And features of that genre are features of *gravitas*: monoglossic language, more careful editing and fine-tuning of the text, and, most visibly, the division of the long and complex story into narrative units – chapters.

Consider the table below, in which I provide the distribution of chapter titles. I also mark the place in the texts where a shift to French occurs, and French titles and glosses are given in italics. I also include the closing formulae of the texts.

p.	*Version one*	*Version two*	*Version three*
1		'Récits' 'My life'	'Second page (*2° partie*)'
2		'My work with Madam and Mister Andre Deprins Arens'	'The news of the return to Belgium'
3		'My work with Madam and Mister Verstappen' 'Difficulties begin in my house'	'We will return to Belgium, you will be employed with Madam and Mister Verstappen'

THE LIVES OF JULIEN

p.	Version one	Version two	Version three
4			'The work of cutting firewood and selling charcoal' 'In order to make progress in the charcoal business I incur a debt from Theo Kalonda'
5	'Their trip made me sad'		'A letter to Mrs Arens'
6	'The escape to Kasai' 'After paying the debt'		'buying and selling goats'
7	'Farming the fields' 'In 1986 fields in the town of Katondo'	'The journey to Mbuji-Mayi'	'The idea (*idée*) to start a farm in 1986'
8	'The illness of witchcraft'	'Labour or slavery (*esclavage*)?'	'The letter from my wife Julienne in 1990' 'The work of diamond digging in Bakwa-Mulumba'
9	'thank you'		'Democracy in Zaire in 1990'
10		'Trouble (*trouble*) between Katanga and Kasai'	'The trip to Lubumbashi'
11			'In these troubles I was with my wife Julienne, six children and eight children of my brother'
12		'Lusaka-Lubumbashi 966 km'	'The trip to Lubumbashi'
13			
14		*FRENCH* 'There are no crazy trades, there are only crazy people'	'1986 to 1996 the farm will be ten (10) years old'
15		'According to the Bible, the true cult is to visit the poor'	'The destruction (*destruction*) of the farm'
16			'Seven (7) hectares of manioc'
17		'One's name has great significance in life. Helena means = light' '*Your former Boy, Julien*'	'My marriage with Miss Jacqueline' 'My marriage with Miss Julienne'
18			
19			*FRENCH*
20			'*Your former Boy, Julien*'

GENRES AND REPERTOIRES

While the quantitative difference in occurrence of chapter titles between versions 1 and 2 is not dramatic (7 against 12 respectively, but version two was almost double the length of version one) the difference between versions 2 and 3 is quite significant: 12 against 19 titles respectively. In his third version, Julien uses chapter divisions as one of his main text-structuring tools. The way in which chapters are spread over the text – a qualitative measure – is even more telling. While we saw that the first five pages of version one were chapter-less (and that the text itself bore no title or genre label), a sequence of very short chapters emerges between pages 5 and 8. Chapters occur far more systematically in the second version, even if we see very short chapters being followed by excessively long ones. In the third version, chapter titles occur on almost every page of the document. The life story has by then been textually organised in relatively well-balanced units. Julien has realised a genre *that is characterised by the division of the text into episodic chapters.*

Having said this, this division into chapters still very much looks like an unfinished project, even in version three. The genre is approximated, not fully realised. I have noted several strange features in the preceding section: the curious relationship between the chapters 'The news of the return to Belgium' and 'We will return to Belgium, you will be employed with Madam and Mister Verstappen' (in which the storyline is interrupted by a chapter title that seems to be borrowed from the conversation reported in that episode), and the empty chapter 'The trip to Lubumbashi', reiterated after an interspersed contextual narrative about Julien's expanded family. The genre is distant: it is an image of how the text should be organised. For this kind of organisation certain resources are required, and Julien makes three attempts at developing such resources. He does so with increasing success, but some shortcomings still remain. Consequently, the text acquires *some* structural tightness, *some* resources are developed and applied – chapter titles, for instance – but others remain undeveloped. The texts are *essais* – exercises to develop a generically regimented statement, a statement the generic structure of which indexes the truth about his life, his subjectivity.

The genre is distant also in the sense that it seems to interfere with (or be interfered with by) a clearer and more familiar genre: that of the letter to Mrs Arens. We have seen how versions 2 and 3 suddenly shift from a Swahili 'story' to a French 'letter'. The letter carries a *renvoi* and a signature, while the narrative did not carry a formula of address such as 'Dear Mrs Arens'. The 'letter' starts *in* the story, and this start is most clearly marked by the code-shift from Swahili into French. That it starts in the story is clear in both versions. In version two, we see how the main structuring tool of the 'story' – chapter titles – simply continues into the 'letter'. In version three, the line of argument developed at the end of the Swahili 'story' continues and is summarised in the French 'letter' part. The shift appears abrupt and dramatic linguistically because of the shift in code; stylistically, however, it is far more gradual and gentle.

The end product is what it is: an example of the emergence of genre features on the basis of a distant image of what the genre ideally should look like, and

67

with leaky boundaries between the target genre and another, more familiar one. It is a genre under construction, and the construction work is done by someone who 'uses all there is to use' (Hymes 2003), his best possible resources and skills as well as some new ones that he manufactures on the spot. The work is pre-textual: the genre construction develops in a field of tension between perceived norms and expectations, and available and possible resources; between what Julien believes he *should* write, and how he *can* write.

The repertoire

We must slightly change the decor now and briefly consider the linguistic resources that Julien deploys in his texts. The genre work described here develops within the constraints of language varieties, language forms and literacy skills. These are relevant: I have repeatedly pointed towards the monoglossic character of the writings, saying that this monoglossia is a constant feature and that it instantiates the preferred literate 'code'. I made this claim on the basis of what we know about spoken vernacular Swahili in Julien's region: it is replete with borrowings from and code-switching into French, and it is influenced by other locally used languages, notably of the Luba-group (Fabian 1982; de Rooij 1996).

What I mean by monoglossic is not 'monolingual'. The texts, as we have seen, are manifestly *not* monolingual. 'Monoglossia' identifies a language-ideological stance of language 'purity' and 'standard' (Silverstein 1996). The realisation of such a stance may well be very polylingual, 'impure' and 'sub-standard'; the point is that a conscious attempt is made to produce 'pure' and 'standard' language. The texts provide us with plenty of evidence that Julien consciously attempts to produce a 'pure' and 'standard' narrative. The evidence, paradoxically, is in code mixing.

The French glosses

Several of the textual examples I gave earlier already showed the frequency with which Julien provides French glosses for Swahili expressions. He often does this by underscoring the Swahili word, and then following it with a bracketed French translation. Fabian noticed similar patterns of glossing in the *Vocabulaire* (1990a: 173–5). He suggested that such 'doublets' (as he calls them) have a primarily rhetorical and stylistic function: '[d]isplay of foreign terms shows that an author commands knowledge about the world to which these terms belong' (1990a: 174). While this might surely be one aspect of their occurrence, there is far more to be said about them. Let us recall one example, a particularly interesting one because it also contains independently used French loanwords:

Democratie mu ZAIRe en 1990
Mwisho wa 1991 Fujo (Trouble) ikaza kati ya

GENRES AND REPERTOIRES

Kasaï na province ya Shaba, watu wa jiMBo (province)
yote mbili wakaza kuuwana, mie sikuwa na Feza
yakulip**a** gari (Vehucule) nipate kukimbilia katika
jimbo letu, mie, bibi na watoto munane (8) . . .

Translation:

Democracy in Zaire in 1990
In the beginning of 1991, trouble (*Trouble*) begun between
Kasai and the province of Shaba, people of both
provinces (*province*) started murdering each other, and I didn't have
   money
to pay for a car (*vehucule*) to escape into
our province, me, [my] wife and eight (8) children . . .

We see that Julien glosses three Swahili words: 'fujo' is glossed as 'trouble',
'jimbo' is glossed as 'province', and 'gari' is glossed as 'vehucule'. The glosses
in his texts quite systematically occur after words that have a certain register-
dimension: that of Standard Swahili, or Swahili Bora. Thus in version three
for example, terms such as 'mushahara' (elsewhere written as 'mshahara',
3/9) is glossed ('salaire', 3/1), 'kartasi' ('papiers' – documents, 3/7), 'anuani'
('addresse', 3/10), 'uharibifu' ('destriction', 3/15) and 'msaada' ('aide, cadeau',
3/18), all of which have a distinct East-Coast Standard Swahili ring to them
and belong to the large stock of Arabic loanwords in the Swahili of Zanzi-
bar, Mombasa and the coastal strip of Tanzania.[9] He also glosses expressions
that have some cultural opacity, like 'Mdogo yangu' ('petit-frère' – a younger
brother, literally 'my little one', 3/11) or 'wa Zungu wema' ('Blancs de bon
caracteur' – white people of good character, 3/2), or expressions the bearings
of which may not immediately be comprehended by Mrs Arens, like 'Mungu
Jehova aliyeumba mbingu na dunia' ('Dieu Jehov qui à crèe le ciel et la terre'
– the Lord Jehovah who has created heaven and earth, 3/11).[10] To that extent,
he glosses 'strange' words and phrases, things that do not belong to 'normal',
vernacular Swahili.

But the glossing is not systematic, and neither is the use of these 'strange'
words. In the example above, we saw that Julien glossed the term 'jimbo' as
'province', after having used the French term 'province' himself in the previous
line. It is not the only direct borrowing in that example, he also uses 'democratie' in the chapter title. Elsewhere in version three, he uses 'adresse' instead
of 'anuani' (3/5), while a frequently occurring term, usually employed without a gloss, suddenly receives a French equivalent: 'magumu' ('difficulté'). In
fact, 'magumu' is in many ways a *Leitmotiv* in the story of his life, and the term
appears un-glossed in two chapter titles (one in version two and one in version
three). We also see that he provides French translations for rather mundane
terms belonging to the contextual universe of his former employment as a

THE LIVES OF JULIEN

houseboy: 'Mpishi' ('Boy', literally 'cook', 3/1), 'ma pumziko' ('vacance' – holiday, 3/1), 'mingazi' ('palmiers' – palm trees, 3/7), 'mavazi dani ya sanduku' ('Habits dans les malles' – clothes in suitcases, 3/11), 'mihigo' ('manioc', 3/15), 'mbuzi na bata' ('chevre et canard' – a goat and a duck, 3/15), 'mafuta' ('huile', 3/15) and 'ngombe' ('bovins' – cows, 3/16). And he also provides glosses for words that, even in their Swahili form, would not cause too many difficulties to understand: 'Ubeleji' (Belgique, 3/2, this gloss occurs after he had used 'Ubeleji', un-glossed, in the chapter title), 'padri' ('père' – a priest, 3/9), 'wa Kristu' ('Chretiens' – Christians, 3/10) or 'dispenseri' ('dispensaire', 3/11). Finally, he sometimes provides French terms when the Swahili expression doesn't appear to be adequate or comfortable. Thus in describing his attempt to escape from Kasai, he writes 'sikuwa na feza yakulipa gari': 'I didn't have money to pay for a car' (3/8). This is followed by a bracketed gloss: 'Transport Bus ou camion' – 'transport by bus or lorry'. The French here is not a translation but a clarification. Similarly, on 3/15 we read: 'wakaangusha na Hagar (volotairement)'. 'Hagar' is a French loan, 'hangar' ('shed'), so the translation would read 'they also destroyed the shed'. The 'volontairement' ('on purpose') here seems to be more of an added qualifier than a gloss.

The bottom line, I believe, is: *Julien performs code-switching throughout his texts.* He switches from Swahili into French, as in the last couple of examples where the French was not really a gloss, or as in the use of 'province' and 'democratie' in the example above. But some of it – a lot more interesting – works the other way round: from French into Swahili, or rather, *from a mixed Swahili-French code into 'pure', monoglossic Swahili.* It is very probable that Julien would rather use the term 'Belgique' than 'Ubeleji', 'Chrétiens' than 'wa Kristu'or 'père' than 'padri'. It is also quite likely that he would rather use 'vacance' than 'ma pumziko' or 'addresse' than 'anuani'. In sum: the French glosses probably offer us a glimpse of *the terms that Julien would have used in an everyday, informal and vernacular register of Swahili use.* They allow us to read back from a clean, purified and formal language variety to another, informal one, characterised by many 'impurities'. In that sense, they offer us a rare view on language ideologies in action: Julien *makes a conscious effort to 'purify' his language*, to create a monoglossic text, because that is part of what the genre demands. The fact that, much like the use of chapter titles, this effort results in a very unfinished product (the French, as well as the Swahili, is replete with orthographic instabilities, as when he writes 'vehucule' instead of 'vehicule' or 'destriction' instead of 'destruction') should not surprise us, nor does it deserve extensive comments. Here, too, we are facing an aspect of an emerging genre for which the available resources and skills are less than fully developed.

What is Shaba Swahili? On defining Julien's repertoire

The evidence we have of code-switching while making a conscious attempt at monoglossic textuality has a thought-provoking implication. In order to formulate it I need to take one step back and consider the issue of 'language' – what is Shaba Swahili? Or better, what is Julien's Shaba Swahili?

Let us note, first, another similarity with the *Vocabulaire*. Walter Schicho, in his linguistic remarks on the *Vocabulaire*, observes:

> The language used by the **Vocabulaire** has a somewhat formal character. We assume that is so because it was composed as a memorandum for a social group (*waboyi*). Formal varieties [. . .] tend to be nearer to standard or upper-class varieties. In the case of Shaba Swahili and Lubumbashi Swahili this formal level is referred to as *swahili bora*, meaning in a wider sense Standard Swahili and the variety taught in school by the Missions.
>
> (Schicho 1990: 35)

Shaba Swahili, Schicho also affirms, 'could be considered a creolized variety of Swahili' (1990: 33), and that creolisation process was described by Fabian (1986): it was a creolisation process 'from above', directed by the colonial authorities. Important here is that Swahili Bora – the monoglossic Swahili in Julien's texts – is seen as a 'formal level', that is, as a *register*. It is a special form of occurrence deployed for special purposes such as 'official' and 'serious' writing. This special form is assembled out of the totality of language resources, as we have seen above: it is done by weeding out certain 'impure' forms (French loans, in particular), by using certain 'special' terms that index 'purity' (the East-Coast elements such as 'mushahara', for instance), by using 'correct' grammatical inflections and correspondences and, most of all, by writing in a particular genre, the 'Récits'.

But monoglossic Swahili is not the only variety written by Julien: he also writes monoglossic French. This variety is equally 'special', and its production also proceeds by weeding out Swahili words, seeking correctness in grammar and sentence structure, and by writing in a particular genre, the 'letter to Mrs Arens'. This monoglossic French is as much part of Julien's 'Shaba Swahili' as the specialised variety Swahili Bora. It may sound somewhat counterintuitive, perhaps even provocative, but *'pure' French is part of the Shaba Swahili repertoire* used by Julien in crafting his texts. The varieties occur in a highly specialised (even almost experimental) practice of genre-writing, and the various features we previously encountered demonstrate that Julien is not a 'fully competent' user of either language: he assembles the varieties from within a repertoire that contains sufficient material for a reasonably adequate assemblage of that kind. It is therefore best to abandon notions of 'language' when we consider Julien's texts: such notions risk distorting the perception of what really happens in his writing. It is not the 'use of two languages' but the deployment of two (or more) specific *registers from his repertoire*. One of these bears resemblances to Standard French, another to Standard Swahili. But both only exist *as such* in their deployment in this highly specific act of communication, as a resource for constructing the emerging genre.

THE LIVES OF JULIEN

This implication, of course, challenges more established views, in which language variation is primarily seen as organised in dialects or (a rather less comfortable term) sociolects. The issue is, I believe, one of sociolinguistic descriptive accuracy and preciseness in ethnographic interpretation. Julien 'writes with an accent'. That accent reflects and sheds light on the structure of his repertoire. Part of that repertoire will be shared by people with similar profiles, but another part will be idiosyncratic, the product of Julien's particular trajectory as a producer of linguistic messages. This trajectory includes – no doubt a very peculiar element – the writing of three versions of his life history for someone in Europe: a genre he had no experience in and for which he needed to 'invent', so to speak, new elements of his repertoire. People invent 'language' when tasks call for such inventions. And while they do so, they also shape new social patterns and relationships. The work of organising a genre is the compass that guides them through the field of tension between what they have in the way of resources, and what they intend to achieve with them.

The misfit

I opened this chapter by referring to the peculiar communicative history of Julien's texts. When Mrs Arens first received them she was disappointed: the texts did not match her expectations. They were 'strange' and deviant, something that needed to be decoded and deciphered rather than read, reconstructed rather than translated. We may have part of the explanation for this now. In considering some formal characteristics of the way in which Julien constructs his text, we could see how, step by step and never fully comfortably, he 'wrote towards' a genre. This genre was a distant genre. He had a more or less clear idea of what it should be – it definitely needed to be a serious text with a factual, coherent and sequential account of different stages of his life, organised in textual units – chapters – and written in a code that indexes the seriousness of the affair. The text, thus, was oriented towards a genre model which is essentially auto-historiographic: a narrative of the Self organised in a sequential order in time and space, and in relation to other people.

We now begin to understand what the genre label 'Récits' means. It stands for a *formal* text, a text which is long, structured, serious and true. It is a text in which a story is organised into episodic chunks, and in a particular topical flow, a chronological and thematic one. It is also something to *recite*, that is, to reproduce from memory. The *Récits* are *recollections*, consciously remembered and narrated subjectivity.

But the construction of that genre needed to be done with resources to which Julien either had restricted access – think of normative literacy codes or a fully standardised language variety – or which he needed to assemble in the process of writing itself: the use of chapters, for instance, and the difficult exercise of manufacturing a monoglossic code in Swahili and French. Thus, while there is evidence of knowledge of the genre (even if this knowledge is basic or fragmentary), there is also evidence of the fact that the genre is just out of reach for Julien. The result is a corpus of texts which, indeed, requires significant efforts to decode and to make sense of. These are texts that do not travel well: while they may represent an exceptional and outstanding literacy achievement for Julien (and doubtless for many other people in his milieu) they quickly become a literacy *curiosum* elsewhere. It may be a champion's effort of writing in Katanga, something in which we see the mobilisation of tremendous amounts of creativity done with all the available linguistic and stylistic resources. But it failed to surrender its meanings when the addressee, Julien's *confidante* and benefactor Mrs Arens, first saw it in Belgium. The texts show us how 'placed' certain linguistic and communicative resources and skills are, how little mobility potential they have, and how their function and value is restricted to particular places in the world.

This is only part of the story, though. While I have considered the formal characteristics of Julien's writing here – his struggle with genre and linguistic and stylistic resources – another aspect of the texts is *what* they tell us. Julien tries to write 'his life'. But what exactly is 'a life'? To this we can now turn.

4

WRITING, REMEMBERING
AND BEING

Emerging genres, emerging lives

We have seen how Julien produces texts that are generically mixed, with historical narrative and letter-writing blended in different codes and styles. This could be explained, partly, by looking at the particular resources he had at his disposal. Given the pretextual constraints under which he worked, and in particular given the uneasiness generated by the task of having to construct a long text in an unfamiliar code not usually applied to such endeavours – given such constraints he produced a remarkable body of texts.

We need to take yet another look at the issue of emerging genres, however, because there is more to Julien's texts. He produced three versions, not one, and the comparison of the three versions shows a gradual evolution of structural and stylistic tightness. It shows, I argued above, the slow and painstaking development of something he believes approximates the genre he believes he has to perform: a serious auto-historical narrative, a *Récit*. This work of construction is slow and painful, because again, Julien proceeds under severely constraining circumstances. And we now see another issue emerge: the 'stuff' that needs to enter such narratives, the 'facts' of history, are not readily available. Such facts are contained in memory or in an archive – something about which Derrida (1996) said that it can be seen as an object of absolute factuality and epistemic certainty, and an object that allows individuals not to remember the facts contained in the archive. The availability of archives enables and facilitates factual and 'objective' narratives; absence of such an archive throws one back to 'subjective' memory, for which other kinds of narrative are more suited. What Julien offers us is an opportunity to have a close look at the processes of remembering in conditions where an archive is not available, as well as at their conversion in, and *through*, writing practices. The remembering, note, is autobiographic: Julien tries to remember his own life. Thus, through the processes of writing and remembering, we also see the gradual construction of the concept of a life as something that can be narrated in particular generically regimented ways. We see the step-by-step evolution of a particular narrative format that represents someone's idea of a life: a place in the world, roles and identities, forms of individual agentivity, the logic or absence thereof of events and stages in life, and views of the forces that control it.

Writing and remembering

The Récits are formal, structured and serious *remembered stories* about Julien's own existence. Being raised and bred in an affluent and highly literate society, one tends to overlook the importance of a number of basic communicative resources in social life. Having a full mastery of the material, physical, linguistic and cultural preconditions for performing the highly diversified tasks of literacy is one such resource, and the non-self-evident nature of it has been emphasised in earlier chapters. We saw how Julien had to manufacture such resources in order to satisfy the requirements of the genre he believed he had to construct; we also saw that his effort, while impressive, still resulted in an unfinished genre-product, so to speak. We saw how Julien increasingly structured his story in chapters, we saw that he used the genre label 'Récits' for his two last versions, and we saw how he started the second version with that emblematic statement of the autobiography: his date and place of birth.

Another such resource is the kind of material needed for being able to remember one's life. Most of us possess a modest sort of archive, which documents moments and phases of our life. Usually it is not perceived as an archive: it is a sometimes chaotic collection of all sorts of documents and material objects – diaries, notebooks, photographs, movie or concert tickets, *billets doux* from an early sweetheart – by means of which we are able to remember the events associated with these items or documented in them. We put them on our walls or keep them in shoe boxes. A large part of these archives is literate material, products of a literate culture, and literacy in cultures such as ours helps shape active concepts of one's life (Radley 1990).

Julien clearly did not possess such an archive when he wrote his three versions.[1] The three versions of his life history offer us a rare glimpse of how an individual's 'life' is constructed through the process of narrating it in writing – in other words, through the process of material visualisation of meaning driven by perceptions of genre. Let us recall that nearly seven years separate the first from the third version of the story. During that time, Julien formulates, so to speak, his life over and over again, each time adding detail and structure to the story. He never quotes from a previous version, every formulation is different, as we shall see. Let us also recall that perceptions of generic conventions contribute to structuring the story: Julien clearly realises that he goes on record by means of a serious, formal text. So what we witness in the three versions is a gradual structuring of a narrative format in which Julien's 'life' becomes a matter of linear chronology, referential and deictic accuracy, and precision expressed in narrative detail and attempts at filling gaps in the autobiography.

I will illustrate this process of remembering-through-writing in two ways. First I will examine the sequence of events and the chronology in the three versions; next, I will focus on the way in which one particular episode is developed in the three versions.

THE LIVES OF JULIEN

Chronology, events and linearity

One indicator of processes of remembering in the sort of formal, literate and auto-historiographic generic context sketched above, could be the way in which chronology is handled in the autobiography. Historical narrative for Julien involves chronological accuracy expressed by providing explicit chronological marking points: dates. I mentioned in the previous chapter that dates were frequently added by Julien when he revised his second and third versions. Providing accurate dates obviously mattered to him. Before moving into a more detailed discussion, however, we must remind ourselves of the relation between the three versions.

As we know, Julien wrote three versions, of which he disqualified the first while the third version was presented as an addition to the second one ('2nd part'). Surely, there must have been an impression that the first version did not fit the genre requested by Mrs Arens: the 'story of your life'. Thus he dismissed it and wrote an entirely new one. Evidence for the fact that he did not keep a copy of his versions is textual and generic. Although version three is marked as a *complement* to version two (the title '2° partie' suggests that Julien will provide additional and/or more recent information to the previous version) both versions are to a large extent overlapping in terms of narrated periods and events. Julien extends the period covered in his life history, mentioning some events in 1995 and 1996, and he inserts a chapter on a legal battle he was (and is) locked into with officials over his farm in Malemba-Nkulu. But apart from that, he tells his life once again.

So there really is not much of a 'second part' in the latest version. It is a *new* version of the same story, written again, and with one main qualitative difference: there is far *more explicit chronology* in the third version than in the second one. Let us compare the dates mentioned in the three versions (see table facing page and overleaf).

There is a considerable difference in the amount of explicit chronology. In the first version, Julien mentions 14 dates, usually years or month-year combinations. Only two day-month-year strings are mentioned: 27/9/1969 (the day on which he got his job with the Arens family) and 18/1/1986 (the death of his younger brother). In the second version we note 28 instances of explicit chronology. Day-month-year strings are still rare, but Julien mentions his date of birth (10/12/1946), the day he got his job with Arens (27/9/1969) and two precise dates for his trip from Mbuji-Mayi to Bakwa-Mulumba (15/5/1990 and 18/5/1990). We find no less than 43 instances of explicit chronology in the third version. While only one of them is a day-month-year string (27/9/1969), it is clear that in the third version, Julien has managed to accomplish a superior degree of chronological accuracy in his life history, and certain episodes of his life are now documented in considerable detail. Remarkably, one of these better documented episodes is a relatively remote one: the period between 1967 and 1974 is chronologically more precise and provides more reported events (e.g. the two holidays of the Arens family) than in the previous versions. A second episode which

76

WRITING, REMEMBERING AND BEING

	Version one	Version two	Version three
pre-1967		10/12/46 birth 1965 job with uncle 1966 job Degueldre	
1967		1967 marriage Jacqueline	late 1967: job Degueldre *1967: marriage Jacqueline* *2/1967: living with Jacqueline*
1968			
1969	27/9/69 job Arens	27/9/69 job Arens *1969–73: living with Arens*	5/1969: end job Degueldre 27/9/69 job Arens *5/1969: unemployed* *27/9/69: job Arens*
1970	6/1970: marriage Julienne	6/1970: marriage Julienne	6/1970: 1st holiday Arens 9/1970: return Arens *6/1970: marriage Julienne*
1971		6/1971: birth of child	6/1971: 2nd holiday Arens 9/1971: return Arens
1972		8/1972: birth of child	
1973	9/1973: departure Arens	6/1973: announcement of departure Arens 1973–9: support from Arens, trouble starts in 79	6/1973: announcement of departure Arens 9/1973: job Verstappen *1973–90: support from Arens*
1974			6/1974: departure Verstappen 1974–9: charcoal business
1975			
1976			
1977			
1978			1978: firewood business
1979	1979: to Kabinda		
1980		7/1980: repayment of debt to Kalonda	
1981	1981: repayment of debt to Kalonda	10/1981: arrival in Kabinda	*1981–now: problems with* *Julienne*
1982	9/1982: shopkeeper in Kabinda		
1983	1983–4: farming in Kashilangie		
1984		1984: wife arrives in Kabinda	
1985			

1986	1986: farming in Katondo (Malemba-Nkulu) 18/1/1986: death of brother 4–6/1986: start of farm in Malemba-Nkulu	1986: leaving Kabinda for farm in Malemba-Nkulu	1986: the farm in Malemba-Nkulu 1986: start of the farm *1986–96: ten years of farming in Malemba-Nkulu* *1986–8: first fields on the farm* *1986: death of brother*
1987		1987–8: illness due to witchcraft	
1988			
1989	4/1989: return to Malemba-Nkulu	1989: to Malemba-Nkulu	1989–90: growing palm trees
1990	5/1990: to Mbuji-Mayi 5/1990: Bakwa-Mulumba	4/1990: letter from Julienne 15/5/1990: from Mbuji-Mayi to Bakwa-Mulumba 18/5/1990: diamond digging job 15/5/1991–1/1991: diamond digging	1990: letter from Julienne 3/1990: letter from Julienne 6/1990–1: support from Arens 1990: democracy in Zaire *1990: first destruction of the farm* *1990: letter from the Chief re the farm* *4/1990: to Kabinda*
1991	1/1991: leaving Bakwa-Mulumba for Kabinda	1/1991: arrival in Kabinda	
1992		10/1992: escape to Mwambayi, support from Arens, to Malemba-Nkulu	*9/1992: meeting with 'agronomes'* *1992: destruction of the farm*
1993		7/1993: wife follows Julien to Malemba-Nkulu	11/1993: to Lubumbashi *1993: beginning of court case* *1993: second letter re the farm* *1993: support from Arens*
1994		5/1994: return to Malemba-Nklulu, meeting children in Lusaka 3/1994: relative fetches children 5/1994: arrival with money in Malemba-Nkulu 8/1994: devaluation of currency	*12/1994: take-over of farm by 'agronomes'* *1994: burning of palm trees on farm*
1995			1/1995: from Lubumbashi to Manono
1996			3/1996: new court case 1996: burning of coffee and palm trees
1997			1997–8: prospect of farming palm trees and coffee

WRITING, REMEMBERING AND BEING

is better documented in the third version is the period 1993–4, more specifically the legal battle over his farm. In the second version, this episode is treated obliquely; in the third version it becomes the topic of a separate chapter.

There is an increase of chronological accuracy and narrative detail through the three versions, but this does not mean that the third version is the most 'linear' chronologically and in terms of event sequences. In the scheme given above, the italicised parts were 'out-of-sequence' elements in the versions, i.e. narrated events that broke the linear-chronological sequence of narrated events. Usually the out-of-sequence elements are flashbacks: retrospective narrations of past events. And whereas we only note one out-of-sequence element in version two (a reference, in the 'letter' part of the text, to the period 1969–73 when Julien was employed by Arens), out-of-sequence elements are rather frequent in the third version. And in contrast to version two, out-of-sequence elements in version three are a clear feature of narrative structure. We get a more or less linear narration of a sequence of events until January 1995, when Julien travels from Lubumbashi to Manono. This is on pages 12–13 of the third version. The remainder of the text is of a different nature. It consists of three separate parts:

1   A long and detailed expatiation on the trouble Julien has had with his farm in Malemba-Nkulu. This part takes three full pages of text and is divided into three chapters: (i) 'From 1986 until 1996: ten years of my farm', (ii) 'The destruction of the farm', (iii) 'Seven hectares of manioc'. Julien narrates the court cases and the various forms of obstruction from the villagers that have nearly destroyed his farm; towards the end of this part, he mentions his farming plans for 1997 and 1998. This part adds detail to the second version.

2   A two-page account of his two marriages, (i) 'My marriage to Jacqueline' and (ii) 'Getting married to Julienne.' Most of the sad story of his marriage with Jacqueline had already been told in the second version of the text. Here, we learn that his marriage with Julienne was fraught with problems and that he considered getting divorced. Towards the end of the part on his married life, Julien mentions the important role of Mrs Arens in all this: she has given him advice on personal matters too.

3   This introduces the third part: on page 19 Julien shifts into French, and whereas Mrs Arens was a character in the narrative until now, she is now directly addressed by Julien. He summarises the state of his life in French and thanks her for her support. Typologically, this part of the text is identical to the last part of the second version, where a shift into French also marked the transition from historical account to direct address (letter), summary and thanks. In both versions, Julien also signs the text with 'your former houseboy – Julien.'

So what we see is that new information and new detail is on the one hand incorporated in the 'sequential' part of the text (1960s–1995), and on the other hand narrated in separate, out-of-sequence sub-narratives towards the end of the text. We do not really get a more 'harmonious', generically streamlined text in the third version; but we do get more detail and more chronological accuracy in the 'stuff' with which Julien builds his autobiography. Both projects – the 'remembering' one and the 'textual' one – are moving in separate ways, so to speak. In the third version it is clear that Julien remembers *more* and *better*, but this has not yet led to a better realisation of the genre which he seems to attempt to realise: chronologically linear historical (written) narrative. Remembering and writing are two connected activities, but the relationship between them is an uncomfortable one.

The writing transforms the remembering into something else, into 'facts' documenting someone's life story. Interestingly, the more we see genre features emerge in the writing, the less we see references to 'remembering' itself. The first version contained several statements in which Julien explicitly writes 'I remember', such as:

> Nakumbuka tena wa
> Kati niliendaka kuwapikia wakati wali
> endaka kuvua samaki, katika mtoni
> mu monja ya inchii ya ZAMBIA (1/4)

Translation:

> I also remember the
> Time I went to cook for them when they
> went fishing in a certain
> river in the country of ZAMBIA.

No such statements are encountered in the second and third version. Remembering itself is no longer a part of the story, it has been absorbed by textual genre features that represent the *result* of remembering.

The problems with Kalonda

The matter can be further illustrated by taking a closer look at one particular episode in Julien's stories: the episode in which he reports on the financial debt he has with Kalonda. This episode is mentioned in all three versions of the story and it has some importance: the problem with Kalonda in 1979 marks the end of a period of his life characterised by some happiness and relative prosperity. After the Kalonda episode, the story of his life is one of gradual impoverishment. As we shall see, Julien never quotes from his own previous texts. Each version is rather considerably different. I shall first give the three versions of this episode, after which I shall briefly compare some of the features of the versions.

WRITING, REMEMBERING AND BEING

Version one

. . . KAZi zote nililo
bakia kutumika Lubumbashi, hazikwe-
ndelea nikanjaa kazi ya kuchoma Makala
haikwendelea, NiKAkamata mali ya deni kwa Kalonda, ZAïRE mia tano, na kila
mwezi kumurudishia FAida y^{y}a ZAïRE mia
(250). *M*ia mbili na makumi tana ama (
cinquante pour Cent). yapata muda wa
miezi saba nikawa^{Na}ZAïRE ELFu-Moja-
na mia mbili ikawa Nguvu kwa mie
kumurudishia Feza yake, nikapata aki
li yakumwandia MKOMBOZI wangu bibi
Hèlena AÈRTS, yeye akaniambia asema
Kwa apa sasa hakuna namna yakukutu
mia FRaNKA Elfu innen (quatre Mille FRancs -
Belges). hatuna nayo, sikuwa na ngishi hata Mtu
wakunisaidia ao kunikopesha feza nilipe
*d*eni ya KOLONDA.

*. . . All the jobs which I was
employed in in Lubumbashi didn't
continue I started the work of burning charcoal
it didn't continue, I got a financial
debt with Kalonda, five hundred Zaire, and every
month to give him back an amount of hundred
Zaire (250). Two hundred and fifty or (
cinquante pour Cent). After a period of
seven months I had one thousand and
two hundred Zaire that was what I could get
to give him back his money, I got the
idea of writing to my guide Mrs
Helena Arens, she told me saying
that right now there is no way of sending you
four thousand francs (quatre mille Francs-
Belges). We don't have it, there was no one
to help me or to give me the money to pay
The debt to Kalonda*

KuKiMBiLia – KASAï

KaloNDA akanizuri sana sababu ya Feza
yake, nikapata kukimbilia KASAï mu
mgi wa KABiNDA, mu mwaka wa 1979,
lakini rafiki *y*a^N*gu* akanielezea yakam
a naye hana FEZA yakuweza *ku*nisaidia
nayo. Kisha hayo nikakumbuka tena
paka MwoKOZI wangu HÈLENA ARENS, nika
mwandikia akajibu, na akanitumia
Franka Elfu inne, LiKAlipa deni yangu
mu mwaka wa 1981, nilipendelea nakumwa
ndikia bwana Degrave ARENS, ila bibi
Hèlena ARENS akanijibu mimi nakutumi
a FREANKA, Njoo, ni sisi wote pamoja na
bwana degrave AÈrts. Nilikuwa na furaha
kubwa sana pakupata *f*eza hii pasipo kwiitu
mikia kazi kwao.

Fleeing – Kasai

*Kalonda was very angry with me because of his
money, I fled to Kasai
to the town of Kabinda, in the year 1979
but my friend told me that he
too didn't have money to help me
After this I remembered again
my guide Helena Arens, I
wrote her and she answered, and she sent me
four thousand francs, it paid my debt
in the year 1981, I wanted to write
Mr Degrave Arens, but Mrs
Helena Arens answered me and sent me
francs, yes, it is us together with
Mr Degrave Arens. I was very
happy to get this money without
Having to work for them.*

Version two

. . . Kazi ikandelea muzuri
Kisha mwaka moNja ma Kapuni ikakataa
Kuniuza kuni. Kwa sababu wao walipewa Ru
husa ya kukata kuni wao wenye, na pale nikawa
na deni ya FRANKA kwa THÈO-KALONDA
nilikuwa nalipa kwake 50% kila mwezi
juu ya deni yake. Kwachwa kwakuuza
Kuni KUKANILetea magumu na mateso
mengi na kuwayawaya juu ya deni ya
kulipa kwa KALONDA.
Sawa vile nilikuwa naandikia Madame

*. . . The work went on well
But then one year the companies refused
to sell firewood to me. Because they had obtained
permission to cut firewood themselves, and thus
I had a debt in Francs with Theo Kalonda
I paid him 50% every month
on top of his debt. The end of the firewood selling
job brought me lots of problems and sorrow
and they came on top of the debt I
Had to pay to Kalonda
As I had written letters (lettres) to*

HELÈNA AÈRTS ma <u>Barua</u> (Lettres) Nikwawa
na wazo la kumwandia, sababu kila
mwaka alikuwa amenitumia <u>mavazi</u> (
Habits) na FRANKA Ku <u>anwani</u> (adresse)
ya Madame na Bwana Bertos; Na Hapo
ni Tangu 1973 mupaka nakufika 1979
mwaka mateso ilinipita bwingi.
Madame HELENA-ARENS akanijibu diyo
TAKusaidia, lakini KALONDA matata
ikapita njoo pale nilimkimbilia
KABINDA mu province ya KASAI.
NIKAmwandikia Madame Helena AÈRTS
pale KabiNDA akanitumia FRaNKA, NIKA
mutumia KALONDA FRaNKA yake pale
LubuMBASHI wakati nililipa FRANK
A ilikuwa mwezi wa julai (juillet)
1980

*Madame Helena Arens I thought of
writing her, because every
year she sent me clothes (
Habits) and Francs to the address (adresse)
of Mrs and Mr Bertos, and this
was since 1973 until I came to 1979
The year great sorrow came over me
Mrs Helena Arens answered me yes
I will help you, but with Kalonda the
problems came to me and so I fled to
Kabinda in the province of Kasai
I wrote Mrs Helena Arens
there in Kabinda she sent me Francs, I
sent Kalonda his Francs there in
Lubumbashi the time I paid the money
was the month of July (juillet)
1980*

Version three

<u>Kwa kuendelesha Kazi ya kuni niK[a]twaa
[N]deni kwa THÉO-KALONda</u>

*In order to continue the work of firewood I incur
a debt from Theo-Kalonda*

NaMNA yakuendelesha kazi yakukatisha
kuni, nikatwaa ndeni kwa Kalonda.
Ile ilinilete[a] tabu ilikuwa kila mwi[sho]
wa mwezi nilikuwa namulipa kwa [Nde]ni
yake 50% pakulipa wa kazi, nilikuwa
na <u>magumu</u> (difficulté), Njoo pale nikako
sa namna yakumulipa ndeni yake, naye
akawa na wazo yakunipeleka mbele
ya <u>waamzi</u> (juges) nikapata akili ya
kukimbilia KabiNda / KASAî-oriental.

*As a way of continuing my work of cutting
firewood, I took a loan from Kalonda
This brought me the problem that every end
of the month I had to pay him for his loan
50% for paying the workers, I had
problems (difficulté), and thus I failed
to repay him his loan, and he
figured he would send me in front of
the judges (juges) I had the good sense
of fleeing to Kabinda / Kasai-oriental*

<u>Barua kwa Madame HELENA AÈRTS</u>

A letter to Mrs Helena Arens

Sababu ya ndeni hiẏo nikamwandikia
Madame Helena-AÈRTS, anisaidie na <u>msaada</u>
wake (aide, cadeau) ila yeye akanijibu ya
kama kwa Shiku hii hakuna namna.
Kwa jibu hiyo nikapata, tena wazo ya
kwenda Kabinda, nakule nikamwan[d]ikia
barua ya pil[i], na kwa mapendo yake
akanitumia [Fe]za, nikalipa Feza ya
Kalonda, tena nikabaki na Feza ingine
nikaza kununuwa MbuZi nakuuzisha.
Mbele ya kunitumia Feza ile ku mgi ya
KabiNda, nilikuwa 8[nilikuwa na pata] msaada kwa
　　Ma[d]ame
Helena AÈRTS na aliku[wa][a]naïtuma mu
adresse ya Madame na Bwana BertoS ku
Lubumbashi.

*Because of this debt I wrote to
Mrs Helena-Arens, to help me with her
support (aide, cadeau) but she replied to me that
in those days there was no possibility.
Because of this answer I thought again of
going to Kabinda, and there I wrote her
a second letter, and because of her affection
she sent me money, I paid Kalonda's
money, and even then I had some money left
and I started to buy goats and to sell them.
Before sending me this money to the city of
Kabinda, I had received help from Mrs*

*Helena Arens and she had sent to me at
the address of Mrs and Mr Bertos in
Lubumbashi*

WRITING, REMEMBERING AND BEING

In version one and three, the episode is broken into different chapters. The escape to Kasai is marked as a chapter in version one, and the whole episode is divided into two chapters in version three: the debt to Kalonda, and the letter to Mrs Arens. In version two, the Kalonda episode is part of a long chapter entitled 'Troubles start in my house'.

More relevant is the way in which these three versions relate to one another in *what* and *how* they tell us about the episode. A skeleton structure for the episode can be discerned in all three versions:

1 Julien has a charcoal business but doesn't do well
2 he takes a loan with a heavy interest rate from Kalonda
3 he writes to Mrs Arens for support
4 he flees to Kabinda in Kasai
5 Mrs Arens sends him money
6 Julien repays his debt to Kalonda

But apart from this common structure, several important differences can be observed between the three versions. Let us juxtapose the parts of the narrative in the three versions:

Version one	*Version two*	*Version three*
(1) the charcoal business is in difficulty	(1) Julien's business is OK until the companies stop buying his firewood	(1) the charcoal business is in difficulty and Julien takes a loan with an interest rate
(2) the loan and the interest rate		
	(2) the loan and the interest rate	(2) Kalonda threatens Julien with a court case
(3) a letter to Arens followed by a negative reply	(3) a letter to Arens	(3) Julien flees to Kabinda
(4) the trip to Kabinda	(4) a motivation for writing this letter: support from Arens from 1973 until 1979	(4) Letter to Arens followed by a negative reply
(5) no one can help him in Kabinda		(5) Julien goes again to Kabinda and writes a second letter
(6) A second letter to Arens, followed by a positive reply	(5) positive answer from Arens	
	(6) problems cause him to flee to Kabinda, where he writes to Arens	(6) Arens sends the money
(7) repayment of the debt in 1981		(7) repayment of the debt
(8) Julien expresses his happiness	(7) Arens sends him the money (8) repayment of the debt in July 1980	(8) Julien buys and sells goats
		(9) context to Arens' help: this money was sent to Kabinda, not Lubumbashi

When we compare version two to version one, we notice that Julien elaborates on the circumstances of the loan. His business got into trouble because his main customers stopped working with him. We also see (again in contrast to version one) that Julien does not mention the negative reply from Arens to his first letter. In fact, it is dubious whether he mentions two letters: part (6) of the narrative can also be seen as a further contextualisation of the writing of *the* letter to Arens, already mentioned in part (3). Julien also does not mention the presence of friends in Kabinda, nor that he made an appeal for help to them as well. We also see how the writing of the letter is (apologetically, one could say) contextualised and motivated: Arens had supported him from 1973 onwards. Finally, the expression of happiness and gratitude which concluded the narrative in version one is absent from the two other versions.

Looking at version three, we notice that Julien elaborates on the circumstances of his hurried escape to Kabinda: Kalonda threatened to take him to court. Julien also seems to have travelled *twice* to Kabinda, once after Kalonda's threat to take him to court and a second time after having received Arens' negative reply. This version ends with a contextual detail about Mrs Arens' help: this time, money was not sent to Lubumbashi (as had become customary, apparently), but it was sent to Kabinda.

It is unclear which of the three versions is more 'precise'. Versions 2 and 3 provide more detail, elaborating on the circumstances of Julien's financial difficulties (version two) and on his reasons for his escape to Kabinda (version three). Both also provide some background about the systematic nature of the financial support from Arens: it consisted of an annual shipment of clothes and money sent to friends in Lubumbashi. But in version two, the first letter to Arens and her negative reply are not mentioned, while in versions 2 and 3 Julien's appeal for help to his friends in Kabinda is not mentioned, and the impression we get is that Julien travels to Kabinda solely to be out of Kalonda's sight and to be able to write a letter to Arens. This is not inconsequential: writing from Kabinda to Arens is marked as unusual by Julien, and the reason for this may be the presence of friends who could give him financial assistance. So apart from an increase in narrative detail, the two later versions also contain some gaps and leave some questions unanswered.

Details such as these do matter when we investigate remembering in a context such as this one. Just as in the previous subsection, we see how the process of writing different versions produces more narrative detail without, however, culminating in a once-and-for-all 'final' version which cancels all the previous versions. The remembering is clearly done anew every time, and the previous versions are clearly not there to be re-read and corrected. We get *new* stories with every new version.

One life or three?

Julien's three versions are not cumulative. Naturally, each version is a new narrative; but more importantly it is a new text, generated without direct, archival contact with previous texts. There is intertextuality of course, but not in a literal sense because Julien did not keep copies of his texts. The versions are intertextual with a process of formulation and remembering that develops in Julien's head rather than in notebooks or drafts of parts of the narrative. The period of almost seven years which separates the three versions is a period in which Julien remembers and shapes his life. This remembering culminates in three periods in which he travels to a place from where he can write a letter, and where he effectively writes a new version of his story. These versions bear witness to the effort of remembering: there is more in each version and in particular, there is more precision in each new version. The process of remembering is influenced by the different writing efforts, and the versions 'improve' each time. But they also document the particular communicative economy, a pretext which governs Julien's writing: each time, the narrative has to be written anew, without recourse to a body of textual documentation or generically related writings which could serve as models or examples for writing the story.

This is perhaps most clearly illustrated by the qualification of 'Récits' at the end of version three. We recall how version three was entitled 'ukarasa wa pili (2° partie)' – the text was announced as a complement to version two. However, at the end of the text, and probably after having finished the writing of the text, Julien added 'Récits' to the final page of the text, perhaps in recognition of the fact that to him as well, version three was a new life history, a new *recollection* in the literal sense of 'something collected again', not just a new chapter to an earlier, archived version. So Julien's writing did not result in the literate construction of one 'life', cumulatively documented in three texts, but in three 'lives', each one of them the product of extended periods of remembering as well as of renewed efforts at writing in a particular (borrowed and distant) genre.

Who is Julien?

Writing is, of course, an act of identity. It always betrays who you are, because all of us 'write with an accent' – the different accents of our identity repertoire. Whenever I write, I write as a middle-aged middle-class man from Belgium, with an advanced educational background and experience in writing in several genres. These features will always be there. I cannot write as a woman, not as an 11-year-old, not as a poorly educated man, not as a working-class man, not as an African. But I can write as a friendly middle-aged, middle-class and so forth man, or as a mean one, as a loving man or as an angry one, in a matter-of-fact way or in an emotional way, as an academic or as a friend. I can select from my repertoire of identities those aspects I wish to articulate, and I will select resources that index them to others. The scope, breadth and depth of my resources, the skill I have in using them, and the way in which others perceive them, will determine the outcome, and I have no control over the uptake part of this process.

Writing an autobiography only differs from other acts of identity in that identity is a topic and not just an instrument. It is a reflexive act which has two aspects, a topical one (what is written) and a formal one (how it is written) working with or against one another, in harmony and confirmation or in conflict and disconfirmation. Note, therefore, that a lot of what we can get from the texts in the way of Julien's identity repertoire is derived from *formal* characteristics of the texts: the formal characteristics index their contents, they add a layer of metapragmatic interpretation to it. They allow us to see not only a cognitive subject, but also a *practical* subject, someone who works in a particular way in structuring ideas, concepts, and relations between them. We have seen how Julien *made* a story of himself, and that story can only be understood by paying attention to the ways in which he went about manufacturing it.

Several questions demand our attention now. I will first have to comment on some implications from the analysis so far, because they have epistemological and ethical import and condition what *can* be said about Julien. Next, I will look at the way in which Julien presents himself in his texts. How does Julien talk about his own character in the story and how can we understand it? After that exercise, we may have a more or less precise idea of the author of these mesmerising documents, and we can turn to a final set of remarks on the connection between genred textuality and subjectivity This latter part will take us to some general conclusions on the lives of Julien.

The archive and the storyline: 'objective' and 'subjective'

In Chapter 2, I provided a 'storyline' and I mentioned that it was the product of a careful reading of the three versions of Julien's life history. As we have seen in the preceding section, such a 'complete' story could only be constructed by means of such a comparative detour, since none of the three versions contained the full and 'complete' story. The reason for this was the absence of an archive that allowed Julien to compare for himself, to edit new versions on the basis of older ones, to copy and quote himself from earlier texts. His intertextual corpus had been sent off to Europe, and what was left was the process of remembering and of genre construction. Both exercises, as we have seen, had their problems.

The storyline I have constructed raises epistemological issues, issues that revolve around what Derrida (1996) called 'archontic power': the power to construct an archive and to decide what belongs to it and what not. Given the status of absolute epistemic certainty which Derrida ascribes to the archive – it is a place of facts and 'evidence' – archontic power also means the power to define what are or are not 'facts'. It thus becomes a regime of Truth, a system in which that which belongs to an archive (defined through archontic power) is potentially truthful, and that which does not belong to an archive is potentially doubtful. I say potentially, because the Truth must still be established by means of methodology; the point is that 'facts' from an archive would more rapidly and easily become Truth than things that do not belong to an archive. In the absence of an archive, consequently, we need to proceed 'subjectively', that is on the basis of things we call 'impressions', 'experiences', 'intuitions' or even *recollections* (rather than, e.g. 'histories' or 'memoirs'): distinctly non-scientific things if one assumes a positivistic posture. Julien, who proceeded without the help of an archive, thus proceeded 'subjectively'. For us this offers a privileged window onto his 'subjectivity' and the way in which he textually 'objectified' his subjectivity by means of an emerging genre format. It is precisely the absence of 'objectivity' in Julien's account that allows us to catch the sense and direction of his subjectively constructed stories, and to see his subjectivity at work, so to speak.

I could be content with this 'objective' ethnographic statement, were it not for the fact that it begs the question about *my own* objectivity and subjectivity, and I must go back to Fabian's statements on ethnography as communication for a more precise formulation of that question. Fabian (1974) emphasised the fact that ethnographic knowledge emerges out of a language-based communication process, an *inter-subjective* process that does not yield (positive) 'facts' and assertions, but something we could best describe as re-positioned (and thus re-theorised) descriptive statements. We provide theory-saturated accounts of communication with others, and the relationship between our capacity to formulate statements and that of others needs to be critically questioned. Traditionally, such relationships were quite simply put. There was a clear and rigid hierarchical relationship between the researcher and the 'informant' and while the informant naturally provided the 'information', the 'interpretation' was done by the researcher. Fabian (2001: 25; also 1983) cautions us against this hierarchical assumption, which is an axiom that makes life easy for an ethnographer. It deletes a vast range of difficult issues from consideration and we can now comfortably focus on providing objective, factual descriptions.

Of course, this is exactly what Julien tried to do in his genring of the story of his life. This painful epistemological loop is hard to avoid; but we can start by acknowledging that '[i]n ethnography [. . .] the knowledge process must be initiated by confrontation that becomes productive through communication' (Fabian 2001: 25). 'Confrontation' here means that the communication process is not 'anodyne, apolitical, conciliatory' but based on a dialectic between real positions in a real world. It is also not neutral, smooth or glib, but it contains 'incomprehension, denial, rejection or [. . .] simply Otherness' (ibid.). In fact, the process becomes *productive of ethnographic knowledge* only when it encounters such forms of confrontation. These confrontations are, in a way, theoretical: they confront the logic of one regime of knowledge with that of another.

One is clearly reminded here of Pierre Bourdieu's views of ethnographic epistemology (articulated clearly in e.g. Bourdieu 1984, 1990, 2000; see Wacquant 2004 and Blommaert 2005b for a discussion). Bourdieu systematically emphasised the fact that his 'reflexive sociology' rested on the assumption of epistemic positioning: the fact that particular forms of knowledge are determined by one's position in society – one's habitus – in contrast to that of others. This is how he described this epistemological issue in a paper reflecting on his work on the economic habitus in Algeria:

THE LIVES OF JULIEN

> [. . .] nothing had prepared me to understand the economy, especially my own, as a *system of embodied beliefs*, I had to learn, step by step, through ethnographic observation later corroborated by statistical analysis, the practical logic of the precapitalist economy, at the same time as I was trying as best as I could to figure out its grammar.
>
> (Bourdieu 2000: 24)

Bourdieu, like Fabian, starts from an acute awareness of 'framing' in research (see Wacquant 2004 for extensive discussions). We all enter our research under particular sociohistorical conditions and they have an effect on what we see and perceive and understand. Bourdieu was aware of this during his 1960s fieldwork in Algeria. The country had just passed through a traumatic war of liberation, and the impact on his fieldwork was considerable. (A wonderful vignette he uses to illustrate is this: he had recently looked at a photo taken in a house in Kabylia during fieldwork and he was surprised to see how well lit the indoors image was, despite the fact that Bourdieu did not have a flash on his camera. The reason was that the roof of the house had been blown off by a French grenade during the war.) In order to escape this bias, Bourdieu explored two measures. First, he emphasised the importance of revisiting the same object over and over again – a point already illustrated in 'making the economic habitus' – as well as of comparison (his work in Algeria was followed by 'native ethnography' in the Béarn) and expansion (including more materials than just those collected during fieldwork). Second, he turned to the kind of structuralism then advocated by Lévi-Strauss, in order to find a vantage point which allowed scientific objectivity. In doing this, like Lévi-Strauss, he intended to move from ethnography to ethnology – a search for trans-contextual (or a-contextual) 'driving principles' in the social system observed, by focusing on correlations, contrasts and forms of systemic coherence.

Whereas the first set of measures was maintained throughout his oeuvre, the second set – the turn to structuralism – was abandoned. Fabian, naturally, formulated the same rejection of structuralist abstraction in his work. The main reason, for Fabian and Bourdieu alike, was ethnographic experience. Bourdieu had encountered paradoxes, contradictions and flexible potential in the field, rather than the strict, transparent and mechanistic schemes of structuralism. Furthermore, he had experienced *inter-subjectivity*, so to speak: the fact that the distance advocated in ethnology is, in actual fieldwork conditions, overgrown with sharedness of meaning, joint understandings of 'the logic of the game' and so on. In other words, Bourdieu had ethnographically experienced that the ethnological claim to distance generates another (and a potentially more dangerous) form of ethnocentrism than the intrinsic ethnocentrism of his own observer's role in ethnography. Bourdieu, like Fabian, worries about the specific role of the observer, and this role is not substantially different whether one investigates Algeria or the Béarn. From that point onwards, the notion of 'dispositions' occurs, and Bourdieu theorises how he himself became part of the

WRITING, REMEMBERING AND BEING

object – the objectification of subjectivity. This is also the point where he makes the shift from (Lévi-Straussian) anthropology to sociology: a science in which precisely the objectification of subjectivity is central, and a science which can aspire to eventually develop a mature notion of the subject.

'Subjectivity', thus, is a function of the inevitable positioning of epistemic work. Whenever we know something, we know it from within a particular position, and *what* we know evolves out of the productive confrontation between us and the Other. Crucial in understanding the productive confrontation between Julien and me is the difference in archontic power that characterises our positions. While Julien kept no copies of his three versions, I have full copies of each of them. There are two people in the world who possess Julien's autobiographical archive: Mrs Arens and myself. Julien is not one of them. In addition, I have a corpus of documents that provide useful comparative material for Julien's texts, and I am surrounded by a technology of knowledge – scholarship – which I can apply to this exercise. The consequence of that is that I – and not Julien – can compare the 'facts', can spot coherence and incoherence, similarities, gaps and overlaps, and that I can reconstruct a 'full' or 'complete' account of what he tells us. He himself cannot do that: *he is not in a position to do so*, literally. I am the one who can reduce Julien's three lives to one coherent, unified, 'factual', linearised and 'objective' story (similar observations were made by Barton & Hamilton 1998: 275ff). It is the difference in position that allows me to produce a recognisable voice, a voice that reduces complexity. Julien did not have that privilege and consequently, his voice is one of complexity, hybridity and plurality – of deviations, in sum, from literate European expectations for genres of the Self (Baumann & Briggs 2003).

There are serious ethical implications here. There is a huge risk of my voice becoming stentorian, of my voice silencing that of Julien. In conditions of inequality, such risks are always there, they are systemic and very often define the order of things: some people have voice and others rely on them to be heard. Structural inequalities have a tendency to accentuate individual stances. When no collective, systemic resistance is possible, one is reduced to individual responses, strongly dependent on individual ethical or political principles.

This is more or less the position in which I now find myself. The only way in which I can mitigate that sobering insight is by making my own interpretive procedures explicit (like Fabian); and by showing my own subjectivity in these interpretive procedures (like Bourdieu). The things I can say about Julien reflect my own positioned understanding of how he communicated with me. I can only speak subjectively about his subjectivity, and to some extent this statement should be self-evident. It is, however, an elementary problem that demands perpetual methodological reflection, because it is fundamental to any sensible concept of 'critique'. A critical analysis that claims to use presumed universals as its yardstick cannot stand the test of Fabian's and Bourdieu's epistemological critique. And a critical analysis that thunders from the mountain on behalf of those it claims to represent always risks silencing these others – in other words,

THE LIVES OF JULIEN

becoming an extension of the system of oppression that denied voice to people in the first place.

Julien's self-presentation

Julien did communicate with me, and he has been quite eloquent about himself in these communications. His texts contain quite a bit of material that points towards a clear image that he wishes to project to Mrs Arens. That is the image we can identify, and it is the only one. We cannot speak about Julien's self-image in general and absolute terms, only in relational and contingent ones, on the basis of how he presented himself to his former employer and lifetime benefactor Mrs Arens.

We can again assume that such self-presentations fitted the tradition he developed, of letters to Mrs Arens, and we already know that in this tradition, Julien invoked the relationship he had with Mrs Arens while he was employed by her in 1969–73 by signing as 'your former houseboy'. He invokes this frame explicitly in versions two and three, as an argument for continued support from Mrs Arens:

> A partir de 1969 à 1973 lors de Votre **R**etour
> definitif en Belgique vous m'avez connu comme
> un pauvre boy et jusqu'à maintenant je suis aide
> uniquement que pour ça. (2/15)

Translation:

> From 1969 till 1973 when you returned to
> Belgium for good you have known me
> as a poor boy and until now I have been supported
> just because of that

Apart from that invocation of an older relational frame, what we see is a remarkably constant set of features of his character through the three versions. Three blocks of features can be distinguished:

1 Julien describes himself as a *rational* man, who balances various arguments against each other and takes decisions based on what is best for him and his family in the given situation. Terms such as 'akili' ('wisdom', 'good sense', 'a good idea') and 'wazo' ('thought', 'idea') occur frequently:

> Sasa nikabakia masiku mingi pasipo
> KAZi, NiKApata akili ya kuchoma Makala (2/4)

WRITING, REMEMBERING AND BEING

Translation:

I now stayed many days without
work, and I got the good idea to start burning charcoal

Nikapata wazo yaku**Fanya** fermo (3/7)

Translation:

I got the idea to start a farm

He is a man who makes plans and thinks about his future:

Sasa niko
na furaha na niko na jitengeza namna
yakulima mashamba katika mgini
Katondo (1/9)

Translation:

I now am
happy and I have the possibility
to start a farm in the town
of Katondo

The decision to write letters for support to Mrs Arens is also quite systematically described as a matter of 'akili', of a serious rational process that leads to a decision:

Nikapata aki
li yakumwandia MKOMBOZi wangu bibi
Hèlena ARENs (1/5)

Translation:

I got the wisdom
to write to my saviour, Mrs
Helena Arens

2 While the emphasis on rational and wise decision-making suggests agentivity and some measure of control over one's life, Julien describes himself systematically as a *victim*: of poverty, misunderstanding, jealousy. He does this each time he qualifies Mrs Arens as his 'saviour', directly (as above), or indirectly,

91

THE LIVES OF JULIEN

when he describes his gratitude or the opportunities offered by the support he gets from Belgium. And whenever he describes the negative attitudes of others, they are implicitly contrasted to the normalcy, rationality, integrity and good sense of his own preceding actions. He does not specify the actions that might have triggered the negative feelings of the others:

> Miaka ya 1989 na 1990 nili lima
> nakulimisha <u>mingazi</u> (palmiers) na mashamba
> ya Mihogo. Mingazi ilichomwa kwa moto na watu
> wa chuki

Translation:

> In the years 1989 and 1990 I cultivated
> and let grow palm trees (*palmiers*) and fields
> of manioc. The palm trees were burnt by fire by
> jealous people

> Lakini wa baba na mama walikuwa na ZoeZi
> ya kwa*chance* na mama sababu ya ugoNjwa
> ao ya Matata NYuMBANI, ile njoo ililinetea
> MaiSHA mubaya na KuKOSa kuMaliZA MASOMO (2/1)

Translation:

> But because my father and mother gambled
> and my mother because of illness
> or problems at home, that is what brought me
> a bad life and failure to finish school

He is often a victim, he implicitly signals, because *he is different from the rest*. He is more ambitious, is better than other people and does things better and on a grander scale. This is an effect of the support he gets from Belgium, which allows him to set up his farm, purchase oxen to pull his plough and buy seedlings for his plantation.

> Votre aide pour ma Ferme je suis sûr, d'ici
> deux ans ça n'aura plus de QuiNZE Travailleurs (2/17)

Translation:

> Your support for my farm, I'm sure
> two years from now it will have more than fifteen workers

WRITING, REMEMBERING AND BEING

3 Julien describes himself as a *man of integrity* because he is a *devout Christian*, probably a Jehovah's Witness. We can be more or less sure that he is not Catholic, because, remarkably, he mentions 'Catholic' as an explicit qualification of missions and individuals (as in the opening line of version two: 'I was born in Manono on 10–12–1946 in a family with a Christian father and mother in the Catholic faith'). Given the historically dominant place of Catholicism in the Congo, this explicit qualification appears redundant unless it creates contrasts between Catholics and other Christians, with whom Julien identifies himself. The fact that he calls the God he worships by the name of 'Jehova' (rather than *Dieu*) is further evidence:

> Namtukuza Mungu Jehova aliyeumba MBingu
> Na dunia

Translation:

> I worship the Lord Jehovah who created heaven
> and earth

He often mentions prayer and, as we have seen, he sees the actions of others as inspired by un-Christian feelings. Consequently, while he describes his fellow diamond diggers in Bakwa-Mulumba as addicted to drink and drugs, he himself clearly does not indulge in such excesses. And he clearly anticipates a better world if more people come to follow Christ:

> Si le monde entier devrait croire à l'enseignement de
> Jesus Christ, il n y aurais pas de crises politiques ou
> economiques, on aller vivre tous comme de Frères en
> Christ l'appelation des pays du tiers monde n'aller
> pas voir le jour.

Translation:

> If the whole world would believe in the teaching of
> Jesus Christ, there would be no political or
> economic crises, all would live as brothers in
> Christ, the term third world countries would not see
> the light of day.

If we take these three blocks of features together, we see that Julien presents himself as a man who operates in a rational and moral universe, but with limited control over the course of his life. He never refers to fate or fortune though; when things happen they have a cause in the actions of other people or of God. One of the main actors in his life is, of course, Mrs Arens, and he often takes references to her into a religious frame, mentioning prayer for her and thanking the Lord for her support. Mrs Arens, to him, is a real Christian, better than some other (Catholic) Christians:

> Les aides que vous m'envoyez, pour Jesus-Christ
> Vous surpassez un pasteur qui preche et pecher (
> tromper)

Translation:

> The support you send me, by Jesus Christ
> You surpass a priest who preaches and sins (
> tromper)

As we know, Mrs Arens wasn't overly charmed by the religious allusions in Julien's letters and stories. She also identified his religious zeal as a rather recent phenomenon. It is, in effect, a discontinuity with the older relational framework he invokes and of which he repeatedly signals the continuity across several decades. Yet, and remarkably, his life story does not mention the moment of his conversion to the religious denomination to which he now belongs (and which is different from the Catholic one in which he was born). There is no episode in which he tells, for instance, of his first encounters with members of his Church, nor of a baptism or other form of induction into the congregation. He narrates that part of his life not as an episode, but as a general key in which he conceives of himself and his life: he *is* a Christian, and he looks back on his life *as* a Christian.

And his Christian values largely organise the moral economy in his story: it is a contemporary resource used to reflect on the past. It is, in Bourdieu's terminology, a 'disposition' that structures his subjectivity. It is from within his current religious codes that he distinguishes between good and bad people, good and bad events, good and bad periods in his life, and even good and bad places. Bakwa-Mulumba is a bad place, for instance, where the slavery in the diamond mines leads to excesses and decadence; his farm in Malemba-Nkulu is defined in contrast to Bakwa-Mulumba as a place where one can live a decent life, were it not for the jealousy and hatred of the other people in the town. Note (and perhaps this is another contrast with Catholicism) that Julien never *confesses*. He mentions the fact that his wife suspects him of adultery, but he does not say whether she had reasons for suspicion. He mentions various difficulties he has with people, but he never speaks about his own possible mistakes or transgressions. He becomes the victim of a loan shark but does not mention possible errors of judgment in his business ventures. There is a lot of self-righteousness in his story and very little critical self-reflection.

These features define a kind of 'core', a stable cluster of self-defining characteristics that weave through the complex triple genre exercise he undertakes. It is this character that moves through time and space, with increasing precision

WRITING, REMEMBERING AND BEING

and detail, in three different versions of a life. Central in this life is a stable subject: the particular Julien whom (he believes) is known, loved and understood by Mrs Arens as well as, we can assume, by God.

Textuality and subjectivity

We have reached the end of the story of Julien's lives, and it is time to take a step back and look at what we have gathered so far. We have seen the slow and painful evolving of a particular concept of a life in three texts: life seen and articulated as a rational, factual, chronologically ordered story in which Julien is central. This particular Julien is a stable feature largely defined in terms of a Christian morality and with limited control over the course of events. This rational, factual and chronologically ordered story is, then, a life − a subjectivity that has become the object of a definable genre, 'Récits'.

I think we have surveyed enough evidence to suggest that Julien did *not* have this particular version of his life prior to the process of genring it. At least, he did not have this kind of recognisable subjectivity − recognisable because it is now put in a form that indexes that 'modern' subjectivity. The subjectivity he has acquired is the product of exercise, of effort: an effort to remember and to shape the 'facts', their order and their relative significance. It is not the product of just 'knowledge' of the Self, it is the product of particular textualisations that index that knowledge.

This distinction, between 'pure' knowledge of the Self and practices that shape, enable and articulate such knowledge is central to Foucault's *Hermeneutics of the Subject* (2005). The Greek 'know yourself' was later raised to the cultural paradigm of 'modern' pure knowledge − of 'philosophy' as a formal analysis of Truth. Yet, in ancient Greece it was subordinate to a more general paradigm, 'take care of yourself'. The latter stood for the complex of transforming practices that made the subject ready for the Truth, and so transformed the subject itself. Such practices included meditation, forms of exercise, modes of life that were conducive to a better understanding of the Truth. Any theory of the subject that focuses exclusively on the aspect of 'pure' knowledge misses the point, and we should

> begin with an analytics of the forms of reflexivity inasmuch as it is the forms of reflexivity that constitute the subject as such. We will therefore begin with an analytics of the forms of reflexivity, a history of the practices on which they are based, so as to be able to give the old rational principle of 'know yourself' its meaning − its variable, historical, and never universal meaning.
>
> (Foucault 2005: 462)

As usual, Foucault invokes and invites a vast world of inquiry here, an important part of which ought to be devoted to the 'variable, historical, and never universal' practices that constitute the subject through reflexive knowledge of the Self.

THE LIVES OF JULIEN

I introduce this distinction here because it is an a posteriori motivation for the way in which I have addressed Julien's life: as a form of subjectivity that emerges out of practices of reflexive knowledge formulation – *essais* in the classical sense of the term, exercises in shaping knowledge within particular modes of recognisable representation, within genres. Julien thus necessarily becomes what he has written, and the difficulties we spotted in his writing indexed the practical obstacles that face 'the forms of reflexivity' and 'the practices on which they are based'. They are indeed 'variable, historical, and never universal'. Unless someone else recognises these practices, the forms of reflexivity remain unrecognised too, and the subject does not, practically, exist.

The wider relevance of this is something I have learned from work on asylum application cases. Subjectivity is only recognised when it is recognisably textualised, when the texts allow others to detect the indexicals of subjectivity and convert them into interpretations that (invariably in asylum cases) refer to Truth. Truth and all its peripherals – plausibility, credibility, and persuasiveness – are anchored in the indexical organisation of text; that is, in their shape, structure and organisation, and in the concrete ways in which people gather and deploy textual resources to create such a shape, structure and organisation. And many people just don't have enough of such resources, or they don't have the right ones, not because of choice but because of inequality. An analysis of such patterns of inequality brings us into the realm of ethnographies of power and hegemony, of inquiries into the way in which macroscopic systemic inequalities penetrate the mundane, everyday layers of life through particular norms, expectations and demands that we associate with genred communicative work and start operating there at a microscopic scale.

Julien was definitely a skilled writer. Now that we know the constraints under which he worked, the oeuvre he constructed can only be admired. He surely *could write*. But the conditions under which his writings become meaningful and valuable are *local*: he performed a kind of writing that keeps his texts locked in a particular place in the world, that makes them lose voice as soon as they 'migrate' to a place where different economies of literacy and, consequently, different orders of indexicality prevail. His subjectivity, therefore, is equally *local*, and becomes equally diffuse and complex as soon as his texts enter a different universe. We will see similar things when we turn to Tshibumba, the artist, painter and historian.

Part III

TSHIBUMBA THE HISTORIAN

5

TSHIBUMBA

Artist, painter, historian

Paintings, conversations and texts

In the autumn of 1999 I co-organised a conference called *Belgium's Africa*. Speakers there included Johannes Fabian and Bogumil Jewsiwiecki; both of them spoke on aspects of the work of Tshibumba Kanda Matulu, a popular painter from Lubumbashi.[1] During a conversation with Jewsiwiecki after his lecture, I expressed my interest in grassroots literacy and talked about the lives of Julien. A few weeks later I received a parcel from Jewsiwiecki. It contained a pack of school essays written by pupils in Kinshasa in 1997 (very interesting and rare materials). But it also contained a spectacular document: a copy of a handwritten text by Tshibumba. The text was 73 pages long, written in French in a cheap copybook (a so-called *cahier de brouillon*) and carrying the title:

L histoire du Zaïre
Ecrit par un ZAÏROIS aux années 1980
et cela au ZAÏRE dans la Region du SHABA
à LUBUMBASHI. (TSHIBUMBA-K.M.).

Translation:

The history of Zaire
Written by a Zairean in the year(s) 1980
and this in Zaire in the Shaba region
in Lubumbashi. (Tshibumba-K.M.).

I vaguely remembered having seen this document mentioned. In *History from Below*, Fabian said that apart from the *Vocabulaire*, 'no other document of this kind or comparable scope has so far been made available'. A footnote to this statement reads: 'Bogumil Jewsiwiecki has in his collection a history of Zaire written (in French) by the painter Tshibumba Kanda' (Fabian 1990a: 161). I remembered that Jewsiwiecki had mentioned it in passing during our conversation, but I had made no mental note of it at the time.

A first issue that needed to be addressed was: what exactly was this text? There were clues. Apart from the footnote in *History from Below*, Fabian mentions the text a second time in the superb book he devoted to Tshibumba. In *Remembering the Present*, Fabian (1996) discusses a series of 101 paintings on the History of Zaire, commissioned by Fabian from Tshibumba in 1974 as part of a jointly decided 'history project'. Fabian had previously bought paintings from Tshibumba and the idea of painting a comprehensive history of the Congo emerged out of their conversations. Fabian also presents transcribed conversations with Tshibumba on history, and the analysis in the book thus focuses on the connection between two genres of historiography: paintings and topical conversations. The written document is here described as a '*scenario* for his History of Zaire written in French' (Fabian 1996: 188, emphasis added). A footnote to this says:

> B. Jewsiwiecki has kindly made a copy of the scenario available to me. It consists of seventy-two pages, handwritten in what appears to be an exercise book. It is dated Lubumbashi, September 1, 1980, and signed by Tshibumba with his illegible autograph [. . .] It is impossible to determine exactly how many paintings were planned to go with this account, but the outline as well as much of the detail are essentially the same as the History of Zaire that I recorded with him [. . .].
>
> (1996: 188–9)

This categorisation of the handwritten document as a 'scenario' struck me as strange. As soon as I had read the document I started realising that it might as well be something with a far greater degree of autonomy, a *writing* exercise in its own right – that is, something that creates a different kind of record than the paintings and the conversations: a *typologically* different record. And this different kind of record is constructed *intentionally*, as a separate endeavour and not just as a preparation for a new series of historiographical paintings. I felt at the time that Fabian was trying to detect a single and unified historiographical project in Tshibumba's work. Consequently, the differences between *types* of historiography – each with their own restrictions and affordances – remained underdeveloped, and the handwritten *Histoire* has so far not received the attention it deserved.

We should of course not overestimate the importance of the document. The fact that very few documents of this kind exist in published scholarship does not necessarily mean that such documents do not exist elsewhere and in greater numbers. Absence of evidence is not evidence of absence, and from Julien's writings we have learned that, indeed, other kinds of elaborate writing do exist.[2] The status of *curiosum* of such documents may be due to a failure to search or a failure to take such documents seriously when they appear. But we should also not underestimate its importance. It is and remains a rare, exceptional document; even more so since the author of the *Histoire* also left an oeuvre of historiographical paintings as well as a series of long conversations on history. Tshibumba, in other words, left a historiography that crosses several genres, he left an *oeuvre* (and one of amazing complexity) and this is indeed highly unusual.

Julien's life stories were unusual as well, and the *Histoire* shares an important unusual characteristic with the lives of Julien. Both writings were written *and given away*. They were written for someone else, and the addressee was someone in 'the West'. Tshibumba's text, too, was *written for mobility*, to be transferred to somewhere else and to be read by someone else. In this case, the text was given to Bogumil Jewsiwiecki, a Canadian historian who did extensive fieldwork in Lubumbashi, who evidently shared Tshibumba's preoccupation with history, and whose interest in these matters was, as we shall see shortly, very well known to Tshibumba.

The fact that the *Histoire* was not kept by Tshibumba but was given away to someone whom he knew to be a professional academic historian with a lively interest in popular art, already casts some doubt on Fabian's categorisation of a 'scenario'. Yet there is undoubtedly a close affinity between the *Histoire* and the paintings made by Tshibumba; it is impossible to imagine the absence of such a link. The question is: what exactly is this connection? Here is what Jewsiwiecki wrote to me in 2000 on this topic:

> [Tshibumba] wrote the text for me [Jewsiwiecki], as some kind of companion/explanation to the paintings he sold me. After I left in 1976, he [Tshibumba] brought the paintings to my parents in law who bought them for me. He knew that it was for me and not for them.
>
> (French original, my translation)

And in a conversation with Ellen Schiffer in 2003, Jewsiwiecki mentioned the fact that he had *asked* Tshibumba to write such a text, 'explaining' the paintings he had sold to Jewsiwiecki (E. Schiffer 2005: 12). Whereas Fabian's categorisation of 'scenario' implies that the *Histoire* precedes the act of painting and is (as a preparatory document) subordinate to it, so that the *Histoire* is of relatively minor significance, Jewsiwiecki defines it quite differently. In the latter's account, the *Histoire* is not a scenario or outline for future paintings, but a companion or explanation to paintings already sold to Jewsiwiecki. That means that it *follows* the act of painting, very much in the sense that the recorded conversations in Fabian (1996) followed the painting. In Fabian's case, Tshibumba delivered the commissioned paintings and started talking about them. In Jewsiwiecki's case the paintings are delivered, and later a written text is offered. We see a similar pattern here in which the texts – spoken or written – follow the paintings, and not the other way round.

But there is more. Jewsiwiecki qualifies the relationship in which the paintings and the text were exchanged in very precise terms. He adds the following to the comments earlier quoted:

There thus was some kind of relationship of historian-to-historian, because we knew each other well between 1971 and 1976. He often came to me to sell his paintings, knowing that I was a historian. He had towards Fabian, me and Edouard Vinck a kind of rapport among professionals of knowledge. In that respect he was different from other popular painters.

(French original, my translation)

Three propositions here are of particular interest. (i) Jewsiwiecki speaks of a relationship of *historian-to-historian*, and he highlights the fact that Tshibumba offered his paintings to him *as* a historian, not just a customer. Tshibumba interacted with Jewsiwiecki as a historian, and his paintings as well as his *Histoire* were codes for such interactions. (ii) There is also the phrase '*professionals of knowledge*' (*professionels du savoir*). Tshibumba had frequent contacts, and identified, with some of the expatriate scholars then present in Lubumbashi: Fabian, Jewsiwiecki and Vinck, all of whom were social scientists with strong interests in history, culture and art.[3] And he saw himself as an equal, not as someone who submitted to the authority of their academic voice, but someone who eagerly entered in intellectual discussions (see the conversation reproduced in the opening sections of Fabian 1996: 4–15). Tshibumba was confident in the role of the producer of knowledge, and his favourite domain of knowledge was history. (iii) Jewsiwiecki sees this as something that made Tshibumba '*different from other popular painters*': Tshibumba obviously exudes and articulates something more than just artistic and commercial aspirations. What then? Tshibumba answers the question himself (Fabian 1996: 13): 'Given what I am doing now, I also am a historian'.

He saw himself 'also' as a historian. That much is clear. And he produced historiography in three different genres: paintings, conversations, and a long written text. I suggest we see these three genres as connected but at the same time relatively autonomous, and the analysis in the next chapters will elaborate this thesis. The strongest evidence, I will show, is the effort Tshibumba puts into writing *a specific genre* with rigid, and difficult, genre features. The act of writing the *Histoire* is in itself a highly specific one. It is an act for which he cannot draw on the skills he deploys while painting or while talking about history. But, like Julien, he makes the effort in a *conscious attempt to create a written record of his views on history*. It is the writing that (he hopes) establishes him not just as an artist and painter, but as a historian. In order to be a historian, he must write.

Now, he *had* already written. One striking feature of his paintings is that so many of them have texts written on them. I disregard inscriptions that belong, strictly speaking, to the 'painting' (shop signs, building or factory names, banners belonging to the decor of the painting) and even so, of the 101 paintings that Fabian displays and examines in his book, 92 carry inscriptions that either provide titles, describe events, or comment on the events. I will come back to these inscriptions in later chapters. It is enough at present to establish the point

102

that *painting* history also had a *textual* dimension for Tshibumba. Painting and writing appear to form one composite genre of visualisation, and the writing we see on the paintings is often very much grassroots writing. Thus, painting 17 in Fabian's list (1996: 41) carries as a title 'BODSON FÛT TUER PAR MSIRI' ('Bodson was killed by Msiri'). It contains a spelling phenomenon we have become familiar with through Julien's writings: homophony in spoken vernacular French leading to spelling errors ('tuer' instead of 'tué'). Note that with just a couple of exceptions all the texts on the paintings are in French. Writing in relation to history appears to equal writing in French. The fact that Tshibumba sold his paintings mainly to expatriates naturally explains part of this pattern; but he held his *conversations* with Fabian in Shaba Swahili, while he *wrote* his *Histoire* for Jewsiwiecki in French. This puzzle needs to be solved later.

Tshibumba Kanda Matulu

In contrast to Julien, whom I could only get to know through his life stories and conversations about him with Mr and Mrs Arens, quite a bit more is known about Tshibumba. His association with distinguished academics, of course, contributes to that. The comfort I therefore have now, and did not have when I talked about Julien, is that I can refer the reader to some very good sources for detailed comments on his life and work (Jewsiwiecki, ed. 1992 and 1999; Fabian 1996; E. Schiffer 2005; M. Schiffer 2005). All the same, some points on his life and work need to be briefly made here, especially in order to draw parallels between Tshibumba and Julien.

What a strange and fascinating character we have here. When Tshibumba met Fabian and the other expatriate academics, it was in the context of an emerging post-colonial (or enduring neo-colonial) structure. There was a rather large community of expatriates in the Congolese education system, and many of these people developed an interest in so-called 'genre painting'. Genre paintings belong to the category often identified as 'naïve': simple figurative and descriptive paintings in very bright colours, depicting emblematic cultural or social themes that articulated a certain African 'authenticity'. Such themes included 'mythical' (but often colonial) African items such as the *Mamba Muntu* (a creature half white woman, half fish, painted in front of a river, with a snake and, often, a watch), portraits of Lumumba and other folk heroes, or, after independence, pictures that symbolised the brutality of colonisation or sang the praises of Mobutu (see Szombati-Fabian & Fabian 1976; Fabian & Szombati-Fabian 1980; Fabian 1996, Chapter 1).

Tshibumba was one of these genre painters and his first contacts with the academics were *commercial*: they bought paintings that he sold in the street, and they became his best customers. The intellectual engagements came as a side-effect of what was initially, and mainly, a provider-customer relationship. Material interests generated other interests and more profound forms of engagement. The immense number of paintings he made for Fabian was an effect of their dialogue on history, but it was also a commercial transaction with one of his very best customers.[4] This is similar to Julien's position: Julien, too, was not a disinterested writer when he crafted his life stories, money was a constant concern and topic for him. In addition, we know that the *Histoire* was a document that was written *on request* – another similarity with Julien's texts. The point here is that Tshibumba's oeuvre (in all its genres) is *made for mobility*, made to be 'exported', so to speak, outside of his own community and region.

It is not the only similarity between Tshibumba and Julien. Fabian (1996: ix) mentions that Tshibumba was 'about twenty-seven years old in 1973–4'. He was born in the Kabinda area of East Kasai, close to Mbuji-Mayi, on December 30 1947, and his 'European' first names were Laurent Marcel (see the survey in M Schiffer 2005: 100–6 and E. Schiffer 2005: 13–16). Ethnically, he would be a member of the Luba-Kasai or Lunda. Those elements place him in the same geographical region and in the same generation as Julien, born just after the Second World War and educated in the Belgian colonial education system. Like Julien, who migrated to Lubumbashi in order to find work as a houseboy, Tshibumba's family migrated into Katanga and his father got employment with the railways before starting his own business (a café). Tshibumba spent his youth in the industrial town of Likasi, and (again like Julien) he finished his primary school and a few years of secondary education. At the age of 14 he began to work as a day-labourer, and he began his life as a painter around the age of 17 to 19.

Here is yet another similarity with Julien: Tshibumba's life was characterised by frequent relocations. His family moved from Likasi to Luena and subsequently to Kamina in Katanga. When he began his life as a painter, he travelled around in search of customers to places as far apart as Bukavu (Kivu), Kananga (Kasai) and Lubumbashi (Katanga) – an area covering almost a third of the country. He settled with his wife in Kipushi (south of Lubumbashi) in 1974, around the time when he found a market for his paintings among the expatriates in Lubumbashi. From correspondence received by some of his patrons, we know that he must have moved with his family to the township of Kenia in Lubumbashi. In 1978, however, he disappeared amidst rumours that he had fallen victim to ethnic violence in the wake of the Shaba crisis of that period. Yet, pictures of his continued to appear, and the *Histoire* was sent to Jewsiwiecki in 1980. In 1981, he sent a painting and a letter to Edouard Vinck. The letter is reproduced in M. Schiffer (2005: 105) and contains the following fragment:

> Je ne vous cache pas la verité, dans
> le temps qu'on**t** travaillé avec vous c'etait du travail
> mais aujourd'hui je commence à mandier, c.à.d.
> pas de ~~xxxxx~~ bonnes peintures manque des peinceaux
> etc. . .etc. alors le travail se meurt petit à petit.

Translation:

> I won't hide the truth from you, in
> the times that we worked with you, it was work
> but today I'm becoming a beggar, i.e.
> no good paintings lack of brushes
> etc. etc. so the work dies bit by bit.

Clearly, now that his best customers had left the country, the golden years were over for Tshibumba. The situation in the Congo steadily deteriorated economically as well as politically. From 1982 onwards, all efforts to locate his whereabouts and to re-establish contact with him (by Fabian and Jewsiwiecki among others) have failed and one can only speculate on what has happened to him.

The brief survey I provide here is meant to establish the similarities between Julien and Tshibumba both in terms of life trajectories and in terms of possible sociolinguistic repertoire. Like Julien, Tshibumba is likely to have been born in a Luba (or Lunda) speaking environment. His migrations across Katanga will have provided him with a considerable proficiency in Shaba Swahili varieties.[5] And from his writings, we know that he also used vernacular varieties of French. As we have seen above and shall see in more detail soon, his French literacy skills are very comparable to the ones displayed by Julien. A comparable level of formal education in a comparable educational system and a region close to that of Julien's would account for much of this. But we must also take into account that Tshibumba probably corresponded more with expatriates than most other members of the local population. Like Julien, Tshibumba must have developed a *tradition* of French letter writing to his patrons. The letter to Edouard Vinck cited above illustrates this: Tshibumba did not just write invoices or simple notes on paintings he had sold, he also provided information on his life and situation in such letters. And, like Julien, he knew how to use the material infrastructure of writing: he sent paintings and letters to Belgium, in all likelihood through the good services of the Missions.

As for the *Histoire*, we now know that that document too shares characteristics with Julien's life stories. The *Histoire* was written in response to a request from Bogumil Jewsiwiecki. And while Julien's autobiographies were destined to become documentation for Mrs Arens' own autobiography, Tshibumba's *Histoire* was destined to become part of Jewsiwiecki's historical studies. The same issue of generic recognisability thus arises: to what extent did Julien's historiography match Jewsiwiecki's criteria? The fact that the latter makes only cursory reference to Tshibumba's *Histoire* in his publications, that the document has not yet been published in full, and that no detailed study of it has been undertaken almost three decades after its production, suggests that it was seen as puzzling and problematic, as disappointing in view of its anticipated value, or just as a useless *curiosum*. In any event, the document's reception was as cool as that of

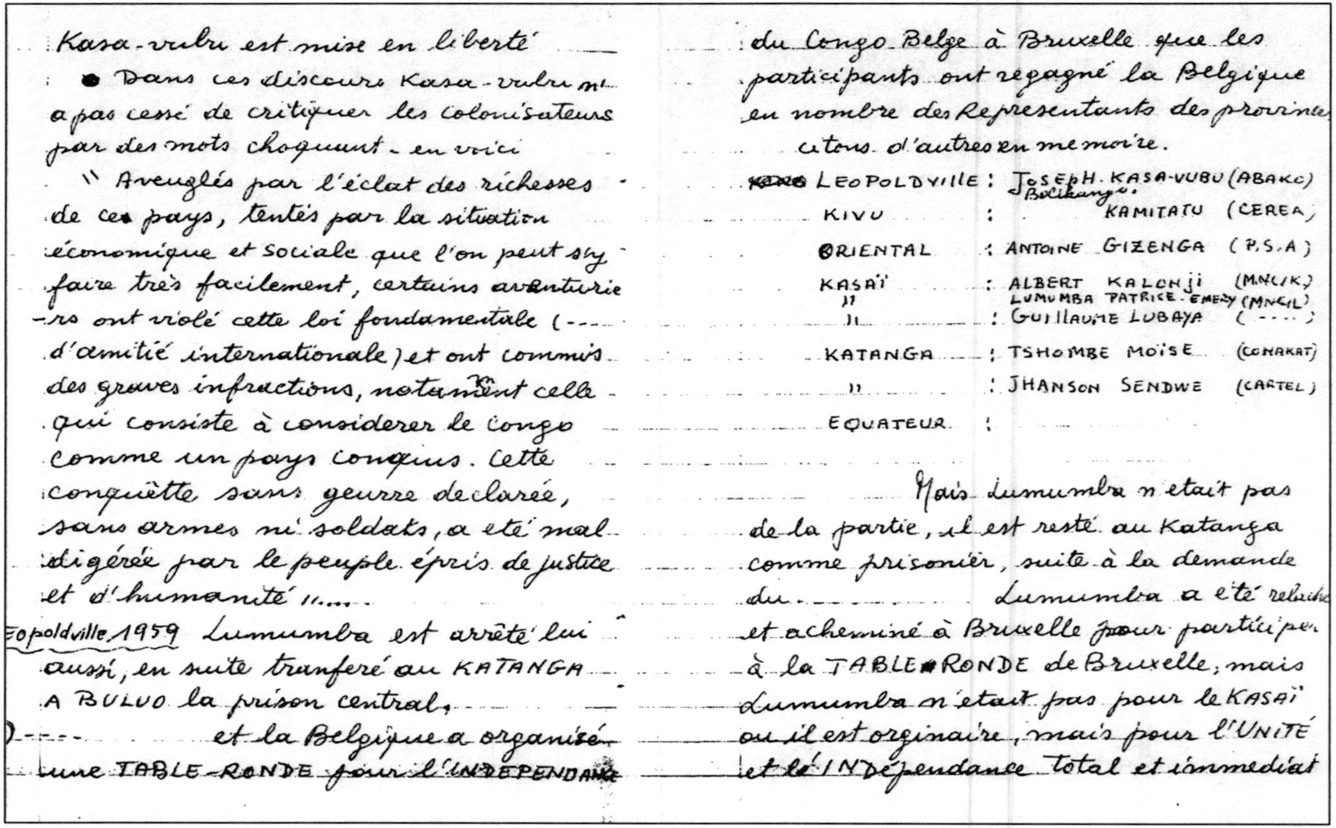

Kasa-vubu est mise en liberté ____

● Dans ces discours Kasa-vubu n'
a pas cessé de critiquer les colonisateurs
par des mots choquant - en voici

"Aveuglés par l'éclat des richesses -
de ces pays, tentés par la situation
économique et sociale que l'on peut s'y -
faire très facilement, certains aventurie
-rs ont violé cette loi fondamentale (---
d'amitié internationale) et ont commis
des graves infractions, notamment cell -
qui consiste à considerer le congo
comme un pays conquis. Cette
conquêtte sans geurre declarée,
sans armes ni soldats, a été mal
digérée par le peuple épris de justice
et d'humanité "......
Leopoldville 1959 Lumumba est arrêté lui
aussi, en suite tranferé au KATANGA
A BULUO la prison central, ____
)---- et la Belgique a organisé
une TABLE-RONDE pour l'INDEPENDANCE

du Congo Belge à Bruxelle que les
participants ont regagné la Belgique
en nombre des Representants des provin-
citons d'autres en memoire.

LEOPOLDVILLE	:	JOSEPH. KASA-VUBU (ABAKO)
		Bolikongo.
KIVU	:	KAMITATU (CEREA)
ORIENTAL	:	ANTOINE GIZENGA (P.S.A)
KASAÏ	:	ALBERT KALONJI (MNC/K)
"		LUMUMBA PATRICE. EMERY (MNC/L)
"	:	GUILLAUME LUBAYA (----)
KATANGA	:	TSHOMBE MOÏSE (CONAKAT)
"	:	JHANSON SENDWE (CARTEL)
EQUATEUR	:	

Mais Lumumba n'était pas
de la partie, il est resté au Katanga
comme prisonier, suite à la demande
du _____ Lumumba a été relaché
et acheminé à Bruxelle pour participer
à la TABLE RONDE de Bruxelle, mais
Lumumba n'était pas pour le KASAÏ
ou il est orginaire, mais pour l'UNITÉ
et la INDependance total et immediat

Figure 5.1 Copy of pages 31–2 of Tshibumba's *Histoire*

Julien's autobiographies, and part of the answer may be found in the grassroots literacy features it displays.

These grassroots literacy features are indeed very similar to the ones we saw in Julien's texts. Visually, Tshibumba's text looks better than those of Julien (see figure 5.1). Julien wrote on cheap airmail paper, Tshibumba wrote in a stapled copybook which had lines on the page and a left margin line. Thus, the curbed and unstable lines we saw in Julien's texts are absent here. Tshibumba writes 'on the lines'; corrections and additions are made above the lines or in the blank margin. He also appears to have the steady hand of a graphic artist: his handwriting is stable and beautifully aligned. And he uses some features of writing that were near-absent from Julien texts: indentation to mark the beginning of new paragraphs, and quotation marks. In spite of these superior features, we see remarkably similar varieties of French being deployed, betraying the same structural constraints as the ones challenging Julien. Consider this fragment (page 16):

[jusqu'à ce]
qu'il a parcourir le KATANGA, arrivé
à **MULUNG**WISHI, LI**V**INGSTONE a \ reïssi
a enseigné la Relligion PROTESTANTE
aux villag**e**ois, ce jusqu'à ce que
LIVINGSTONE est allé trouvé la Mort
parmi les croyants NOIRS à Bagamoyo
et enterré par les Noirs à Bagamoyo

Translation:

[until he]
Travelled across Katanga, arrived
at Mulungwishi, Livingstone was able
to teach protestant religion
to the villagers, this until
Livingstone has gone to die
amidst the faithful blacks in Bagamoyo
and buried by the blacks in Bagamoyo

Note the erratic punctuation, the use of upper case and lower case, the homophony-based error in 'trouvé' (instead of 'trouver'), the writing of 'réussi' as 'reïssi' betraying a local vernacular French accent, and the spelling of 'Relligion'. Despite significant differences, we are facing very similar documents in both cases, and we can start asking similar questions.

TSHIBUMBA THE HISTORIAN

The storyline

I must also use the same problematic procedure as the one I used in Julien's case. In order to clarify what follows, I must provide a purified, coherent and linear storyline of the document. The *Histoire* is a long document, and three main parts can be distinguished in it:

1 preamble or introduction (pages 1–6),
2 the main narrative (pages 7–70) and
3 a postscript (pages 71–3).

The pages are not numbered. In the initial parts of the text, Tshibumba uses chapter titles to mark periods in his historical account; but from page 36 onwards chapter titles disappear (a feature we also encountered in Julien's first two versions). Page 10 contains two chapter titles, 'Royaume de Mongo' and 'Royaume des Bampende', but both chapters are blank. Page 6 is blank, marking the transition from introduction to main narrative. Page 70 is again a blank page marking the transition from main narrative to postscript. Thematically and in terms of episodes, eleven units can be distinguished.

1 An introductory part containing a *preamble* and a set of *methodological reflections* on African history, pages 1–5. Tshibumba discusses the ways in which European historiography has misrepresented African history, giving examples of the Bible, the assassination of Lumumba, and Hitler. Zairian history should be written by Zairians, he claims, and the absence of history from Zairian culture is a problem.

2 A section on the *pre-colonial* period, pages 7–15, initiated by a title 'nos ancêtres' ('Our ancestors'). The whole of this part is structured in separate chapters on pre-colonial kingdoms: the Congo kingdom, the Baluba, Bakuba, Mongo (left blank), Bampende (left blank), Baluba Shankadi, and Lunda.

3 A section on the period of the *explorers*, pages 15–24. This whole period opens with a chapter entitled 'dans le Sud du Katanga' ('In Southern Katanga'). It starts from the important economic role of the Katanga kingdom, something that attracted Livingstone. Livingstone disappears, and this arouses the interest of the Belgian King Leopold I, who calls upon Stanley. Stanley finds Livingstone, and Leopold organises the Berlin Conference. There, a campaign against the Arab slave-trade is launched, and Africa is liberated from slave-traders. Then, Tshibumba returns to the Katanga kingdom led first by King Katanga, then by Msiri (who came to power after having assassinated Katanga's son). Msiri meets Bodson and kills him. Msiri in turn is killed, and something mysterious happens to his head: it is probably taken to Europe. Tshibumba concludes this section with 'Et voilà l'Afrique et complétement libre aux Occidentaux' ('Thus, Africa is completely free to the Westerners').

108

TSHIBUMBA: ARTIST, PAINTER, HISTORIAN

4 The next section treats the *colonisation prior to the independence struggle*, pages 24–31. This section is introduced by the chapter title: 'L'arrivée des Blancs/Colonisateurs' ('The arrival of the whites-colonisers'). After the Berlin Conference, Leopold I acquires the Congo and the establishment of the Congo Free State is proclaimed at Vivi on July 11, 1885 by the King's representative nicknamed Mbula-Matari. Tshibumba provides a sketch of the flag of the Free State (page 25). After the death of Leopold I, the Free State is transformed into the Belgian Congo led by a Governor-General. In 1901 a railway is built connecting the South African railway with that of Katanga: the Compagnie du Chemin de Fer du Katanga. In 1906, groups of white South Africans came to the Congo. In the same year, the Union Minière du Haut-Katanga (UMHK) sets up a major plant in Elisabethville (Lubumbashi), and the Katanga region gradually becomes industrialised. There is migrant labour from other places, and Catholicism becomes firmly established as a religion. The Bishop of Elisabethville is the second most important figure, after the Governor. Tshibumba mentions Kimbangu, the 1941 strike of the UMHK workers[6] (according to Tshibumba, the Governor and Bishop of Elisabethville lured the strikers into the soccer stadium, where they were assassinated), as well as the Batetela revolt in Lodja (Kasai). In Leopoldville (later Kinshasa), the first Congolese political party 'Alliance des Bakongos' (ABAKO) is founded. In 1955, the young Belgian King Baudoin visits the Congo and speaks out against racism, to the dismay of the whites.

5 *The independence struggle*, pages 31–5. On page 30, Tshibumba mentions the first rumours of independence, situated after the local elections of 1957. In 1958, Lumumba attends a pan-African conference in Ghana. In early 1959, there are mutinies in Leopoldville. Kasavubu is arrested, followed by Lumumba. Belgium organises a Round Table conference on the independence of the Congo. Tshibumba provides names of the delegates. Lumumba is released and joins the Round Table. There are different opinions on independence at the Round Table, but on June 30, 1960, King Baudoin declares the Congo independent. Tshibumba provides a sketch of the flag of the new republic. There are no chapter titles in this section.

6 *The first republic and the Congo Crisis*, pages 35–50. With independence, the names of all institutions change. Lumumba is the first Prime Minister, and under the chapter title 'Le Congo et ses fils' ('The Congo and its sons'), the members of the new government are mentioned. Kalonji proclaims the secession of Kasai, and a conflict between Luba and Lulua ensues. Kalonji proclaims himself king, resides in Bakwanga (later Mbuji-Mayi, Kasai) and makes his people dig diamonds. Tshibumba provides a sketch of the flag of Kalonji's kingdom. In Kasai, violent ethnic struggle erupts. In Leopoldville, there are problems between Kasavubu and Lumumba. Lumumba orders all whites out of Katanga within 24 hours, causing an exodus, and Tshombe proclaims the

109

independence of Katanga on July 11, 1961. A sketch of the new Katangese flag is provided. Tshombe meets internal opposition from Baluba and Tshokwe in the north of Katanga. Tshombe organises violent pogroms against people from the north. Lumumba is deposed by Kasavubu and flees to Stanleyville (Kisangani), but is captured and brought to Elisabethville. Tshibumba claims that he is subsequently killed by the French mercenary Bob Denard. A new Congolese government is formed, and UN troops invade Katanga. In the north of the Congo, a new rebellion erupts. UN secretary-general Hammarskjoeld dies in a plane crash. Katanga is defeated in 1962, Tshombe escapes to Europe. The Northern rebellion is crushed by a military intervention by US and Belgian troops in Kisangani. Tshombe is invited to form a government of national unity with Joseph Mobutu as Defence secretary. In 1965, Tshombe is deposed by Kasavubu. Kimba forms a new government and introduces a new national flag.

7 On November 24, 1965, a putsch is organised by Joseph Mobutu, and the *Second Republic* is launched (pages 51–5). Mobutu organises a new government. A new rebellion organised by Mulele erupts, but is crushed by Mobutu. Mercenaries working for Tshombe organise another revolt in Kivu. As Tshombe prepares himself to join his forces, his plane is hijacked. Tshombe dies soon afterwards in Algiers. Other rebellions are crushed as well.

8 The *Third Republic* (pages 55–9) is started by the creation of Mobutu's 'parti-état' MPR (Mouvement Populaire de la Révolution) in 1967. The name of the country changes, the currency changes, *authenticité* causes all people to change their names, there is a new flag, and all place names are Zairianised as well. The structure of government changes profoundly. A conflict erupts between the Church and the State, and the Cardinal has to leave in exile. Industries are nationalised.

9 Next, *the Shaba wars* are discussed at length (pages 60–5). A first Shaba crisis starts in March 1977 with the invasion of former Katangese Gendarmes (members of the army of the independent Katanga republic under Tshombe), supported by the Soviets and Cubans and aimed at ousting Mobutu. Mobutu calls for aid from other countries. The 80-day war ends in victory for Mobutu. In November 1977, Mobutu's first wife dies, and Mobutu is re-elected as president. In May 1978, the mining town of Kolwezi is attacked by Katangese Gendarmes, starting the second Shaba crisis. France and Belgium as well as a number of other countries come to Mobutu's assistance. The local leader Nguz-a-Karl-i-Bond is arrested. Mobutu resides in Shaba for six months, during which the Gecamines workers organise a strike.

10 The final part of the main narrative covers *recent events*, all dating from around 1980 (pages 66–9). A student revolt erupts in Kinshasa and in May 1980, Zaire is visited by Pope John Paul II. In late 1979 the Zairian currency

was changed. Mobutu visits Lubumbashi in the company of his second wife, whom he married in May 1980. The narrative ends with a coda (page 69):

L'histoire n'a pas de fin
ainsi écrit, dit déjà un grand
travail.
Ecrit au Shaba par l'Artiste
Peintre Historien
TSHIBUMBA-KANDA-MATULU
FAIT à Lubumbashi, le 1. Septembre 1980.

Translation:

History has no end
thus written already speaks a great
work
written in Shaba by the artist
painter historian
Tshibumba-Kanda-Matulu
done in Lubumbashi, September 1, 1980

11 After a blank page (page 70), Tshibumba engages in a brief set of *reflections on tribalism* (pages 71–3). Tshibumba sees tribalism at work at various levels in Zaire, causing many problems. Especially in the Shaba Wars, tribalism was rampant. Tshibumba concludes with a MPR slogan:

Sans un Guide comme
MOBUTU, pas le ZAÏRE UNIT et
son ARMEÉ

Translation:

Without a guide such as
Mobutu, no unified Zaire and
its/his army.

As we can see, the scope of the *Histoire* is vast. While the *Vocabulaire de Ville de Elisabethville* was essentially a local and regional history (with some 'national' scope in the description of early colonisation; see Chapter 7 below), Tshibumba's *Histoire* is national in aspiration and spans a historical frame that starts with the 'ancestors' and ends with reflections on the future. And while Julien's texts treated his own life, Tshibumba's text treats the life of his problem-ridden country.

It is an ambitious document, but also a document (as we saw earlier) that does require detailed scrutiny. The ambitions are great, but they are put into practice under severe constraints. These constraints have to do with the material resources Tshibumba can apply, and they have to do with the capacity to have voice by writing a document such as this one. They have to do, thus, with the way in which the writing of the *Histoire* allows him to construct a particular subjectivity – one that can be recognised by, for instance, Jewsiwiecki, Fabian, myself and the other scholars with whom he had contacts and/or who devoted some of their work to him. Let us now have a look at this document in greater detail.

6

THE AESTHETICS OF
GRASSROOTS LITERACY

Writing as drawing

One of the features in which Tshibumba's *Histoire* differs from the lives of Julien is its aesthetic appeal. Whereas in Julien's text forms of embellishment were rare – there would be nicely curved lines under the chapter titles, but apart from that the text was visually austere – Tshibumba has written not just a document but a *beautiful* document. As mentioned earlier, Tshibumba's handwriting is definitely more pleasing to the eye, and he uses visual markers such as indentation to separate paragraphs. The text, thus, looks clearer and more transparent. In addition, his *Histoire* contains some drawings, to which I shall return shortly. Tshibumba has clearly made an effort at making his text not just into an intellectual product, but also into an aesthetic one. He has attended to the aesthetic aspect of the text by elaborating visual text-organising resources.

The use of such visual resources is widespread in grassroots writing. It is widespread in writing *tout court*, even if it doesn't always attract the attention of observers, or even if visual resources are not consciously perceived as a layer of visuality in texts but just as part of the text. Thus, when I perform my writing on a laptop, I use a wide range of visual resources to create the kind of visual structuring that comes with a concept of textuality: I use different fonts and font sizes to mark structural, thematic or textual contrasts such as the beginning of a chapter or a section, or marking emphasis in my text; I use indentation to separate paragraphs; figures and illustrations to illustrate the text, and so on. Writing is the material visualisation of meaning, and aesthetics will therefore always be a dimension of writing. Writing, Kress and van Leeuwen (1996) emphasise, is *design*. The essential role of aesthetics in the production of meaning has, however, not been widely recognised in the study of language. In spite of Jakobson's (1960) widely quoted statements on the topic, the idea that one of the essential functions of language is the 'poetic' production of forms has not made it into the mainstream, and form and content are still firmly seen as separate domains of analysis. It is good to be reminded of the fact that in actual communication, we always produce form-and-meaning at once in one single activity, and that what we say can only be understood by attending to how we say it.[1] Semiotic resources are primarily *formal* resources and their meaningful structuring is

113

TSHIBUMBA THE HISTORIAN

done by formal structuring, by an architecture of forms that can be indexically decoded as meaningful. In the field of writing, the semiotic resources are visual, and the visuality of writing is one of its crucial characteristics.

Every act of writing is, thus, visual; but writing is also an activity dominated by normative conceptions of how to use the visual resources. Just think of spelling rules as a case in point, and Kress (2000) draws a sharp distinction between spelling and writing: spelling is an *institutional* concern, not a *communicative* one. The use of visual resources is, ideally, controlled and fully codified, and this counts for spelling, punctuation, the use of chapter titles, fonts and font sizes, emphasis markers, and so forth. Those of us who are into professional writing can read such dimensions of control from the style sheets or Guidelines for Authors we get from editors and publishers. What we encounter in grassroots literacy, however, very often looks like a visuality which is 'out of control': there is unconventional use of various visual tactics and aids in attempts to embellish the texts. The phenomenon is comparable to graffiti: writers don't seem to 'write' but rather to 'draw' their words, injecting the almost infinite potential and freedom of drawing into the very restricted and rule-governed potential of writing.

Consider the example opposite. It is a copy of a test written by a 16-year old female student in a secondary school in the townships around Cape Town, South Africa. The township is a socio-economically marginalised place, and many of its inhabitants are immigrants from rural areas in South Africa (see Blommaert et al. 2005). The test was on the topic of tourism and the economy. Observe the calligraphic effort: the pupil has circled the test questions with cloud-like shapes, we also see the drawing of a sun in the margin, and the handwriting is remarkably elaborated and stylised. But observe also the grassroots dimensions of the writing. Upper case and lower case are blended in 'INtrests' – one of the words which also contain spelling errors. My corpus of grassroots literacy samples from Africa is replete with such exuberant displays of visual embellishments accompanying highly problematic displays of basic writing skills (see e.g. the documents presented in Blommaert 2004, 2005a, Chapter 5).[2]

The topic fascinates me endlessly, probably because I myself never stopped to consider the essential graphic, visual and material dimensions of my own writing practices until I encountered grassroots literacy documents. This encounter made me realise that the experience of my own writing as non-visual (a purely cognitive/emotive affair for which we have terms such as 'expressing my ideas' or 'feelings') was an ideological effect of considerable complexity. Language ideologies emphasising denotational functions rather than others merged with broader rationalist ideologies about the privilege of 'pure' knowledge in subjectivity. The visuality of my writing has been the object of what Irvine & Gal (2000) called 'erasure': the dominance of a particular ideological model made certain aspects of reality simply invisible (literally, in this case). Undoing that erasure by foregrounding the visual and material aspects of writing thus opens a road to different, and perhaps more precise, kinds of reflections on subjectivity.

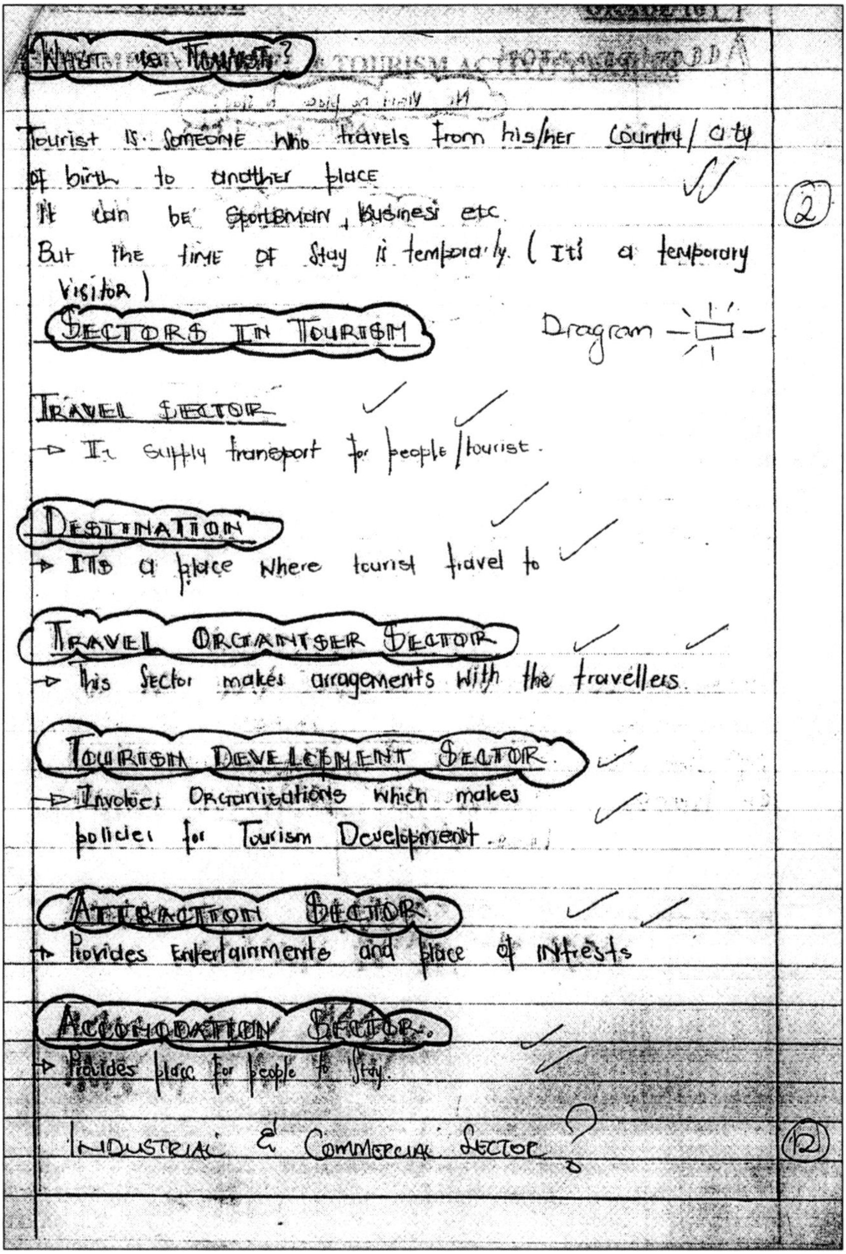

THE AESTHETICS OF GRASSROOTS LITERACY

Figure 6.1 Tourism assignment, Wesbank

TSHIBUMBA THE HISTORIAN

There is an exuberant visuality in grassroots literacy, and the question is, why? I'm not sure that I can answer this question, but I can take a step back and formulate it as a question of available resources versus meaning-making practices. On this issue I let myself be inspired by Gunther Kress' highly insightful *Before Writing* (1997). In this path-breaking study Kress analyses young children's induction into writing. Kress insists that children are not 'tabulae rasae', but that 'in learning to read and write, children come as thoroughly experienced makers of meaning, as experienced makers of signs in any medium that is to hand' (1997: 8). Children use all sorts of objects and techniques of ordering them in constructing a semiosis of, e.g., play (as when a cardboard box can become a 'car'). 'In their world, form and meaning are identical': the box is a form that lends itself to becoming a car. And

> [w]ith that disposition they come to the learning of writing, a system which has all the appearances of a system of signs in which form and meaning have no intrinsic connection: the letters *s h i p*, for instance, do not reveal the meaning that is attached to them in this sequence unless it is pointed out.
>
> (Kress 1997: 9)

Writing, thus, very often appears as a *reduction* and *complication* of the scope of visualisation previously available in the form of drawings or organised objects. The rule is that

> signs are motivated relations of form and meaning, or to use semiotic terminology, of signifiers and signifieds. Makers of signs use those forms for the expression of their meaning which best suggest or carry the meaning, and they do so in any medium in which they make signs.
>
> (12)

Children thus make use of anything that is at hand, but

> [a]s children are drawn into culture, 'what is to hand', becomes more and more that which the culture values and therefore makes readily available. The child's active, transformative practice remains, but it is more and more applied to materials which are already culturally formed. In this way children become the agents of their own cultural and social making.
>
> (13)

There is plenty of evidence in Kress' work to show that the *primary* tendency in sign-making is an aesthetic one. Beauty is fun and the capacity to make a thing of beauty ensures a joy forever, as we know. De-aestheticised products are *disciplined* products: the old German saying *In der Beschränkung zeigt sich der Meister*

THE AESTHETICS OF GRASSROOTS LITERACY

('mastery is shown in moderation') refers to the process of *discipline*, of becoming a master of something, and this process involves the rule-governed reduction of excessive features. The issue now appears as one of ideological regimentation and, consequently, of conventionalisation and normativity. Particular forms – alphabetical writing and (later) spelling, in this case – have acquired a specific cultural load as privileged meaning-makers. This is an ideological process of value-attribution, in which 'good' writing (writing that solidly sticks to the alphabetical code and its rules of organisation) takes hierarchical precedence over the use of other forms such as drawing or 'non-standard' writing. To the extent that writing is seen as a tactic for making sense, for the production of meanings, the whole notion of 'writing' is narrowed to writing in the alphabetical code. This is the erasure I referred to above: it is the effect of a stratification of means of visualisation, in which *ortho-graphy* is ranked higher than all other forms of writing – in short, than *hetero-graphy* – and in which routinised practices of disqualification occur (cf. Blommaert, Creve & Willaert 2006). The induction into this stratified system is largely an institutional matter in which formal schooling plays an important part, and the outcome of which is a 'normal' view of literacy as something that proceeds by means of the regimented, controlled and disciplined deployment of alphabetical signs. Deviations of that normalcy (which is always *normative*) are transgressions into 'abnormalcy'. They can sometimes be perceived as forms of creativity, as deliberate deviations of norms based on a thorough understanding of such norms, but more often than not they are seen as *inferior* or *wrong* forms of 'writing'. If you try to make sense in a hetero-graphical code, you are quickly seen as someone who doesn't make sense at all.

I am cutting a few corners here because the issue of normativity is one of mind-damaging complexity and, hence, there is hardly any statement on this issue that can cover it in its full glory.[3] But clearly, a firmly established and controlled formal education system is a major tool for the reproduction of the regime of literacy described here, as well as (in the well-functioning cases) for the democratic distribution of access to the hierarchically prominent ortho-graphic codes. More generally put: there must be democratic, powerful and effective social institutions to ensure the kind of pretextual conditions in which most people would be able to use ortho-graphic codes and understand them as meaningful, and such pretextualities cannot be generated overnight – it takes a long cycle of reproduction to achieve it. The school in the Cape Town township was not such a case, because there could not be any *re*production of previously established pretextualities. The Apartheid regime was aimed, precisely, at reproducing different (and unequal) forms of cultural capital for the different groups of the population, and the (black and 'coloured') pupils in the township, as well as their teachers, still bore the scars of that long history. The colonial education system in the Belgian Congo was very much of the same order, and post-colonial education systems everywhere in Africa struggle with similar obstacles (see e.g. Williams 2006).

When full access to ortho-graphic codes is absent, people have to draw on the resources at hand, they 'use those forms for the expression of their meaning which best suggest or carry the meaning, and they do so in any medium in which they make signs' (Kress 1997: 12).[4] They shift into *hetero-graphic practices*, or more precisely, they have no choice but to use hetero-graphic media. Thus, we very often see that calligraphic embellishments *complement* the partial control over the ortho-graphic alphabetical writing skills. This was what our student from the township school did: given the problems with ortho-graphic writing, the effort at visual 'upgrading' of her text can be seen as an attempt, on the one hand to make the assignment more fun for herself, on the other hand to be perceived as a 'good pupil', someone who *did well* in the writing assignment – the calligraphic effort is always a *personalisation* of the text. Its features were there as indexicals of a particular identity, part of an indexical architecture in which various formal resources were combined. The visual adornments *complement* but do not *compensate for* the gaps in ortho-graphic skills: teachers in the township school just didn't notice them or, if they did, paid no attention to them – again a case of erasure.

The visuality of texts is part of what they convey in the way of voice. When a professional writer uses illustrations in his or her prose, they are effectively part of 'the text'; that is, of the meaning of the text. One cannot *read* the prose without *looking* at the illustrations. The same goes for grassroots literacy products: their visual embellishment is equally part of the text, very often it is a most eloquent part of it, richly indexical of what the text is supposed to tell us. Such features lead us directly to the author and his/her context and life-world: they are the prime objects for investigating the conditions of production, in a very wide sense.

Tshibumba's writing and drawing

Tshibumba used writing in his paintings and inserted drawings into his written *Histoire*. Both appear as hybridised genres. The hybridisation, however, requires qualification. I shall first look at the inscriptions on the paintings.

Painting history: an emerging genre?

As mentioned earlier, almost all of the paintings Tshibumba sold to Fabian contained inscriptions of some sort. Minimally, there would be his signature on the paintings (and sometimes a date). Maximally, the inscriptions would be several lines long and display features of sub- and superordinate structuring, running over 50 words in a few cases. There would also be inscriptions that quoted direct speech. All of the inscriptions were in French, with a couple of exceptions. Painting 86, for instance, is a painting of Mobutu in uniform rolling up his sleeves (Fabian 1996: 157). Tshibumba called this painting 'Let's roll up our sleeves' – an echo of Mobutu's *Retroussons les Manches* campaign of 1965, which is echoed in a Lingala inscription on the painting ('Salongo alinga mosala', the name of another national MPR campaign of 1969 and the title of a popular song by the Congolese musician Franco).

The inscriptions are not just the titles of the works. Some are, but most are not, and Fabian calls them 'epigraphic, in the classic sense of the word' (1996: 239). Let us look at some examples:

1 *Painting 17* (page 41) depicts the image of Msiri, King of Katanga, who plants his spear into the stomach of a European man. The inscription is

BODSON FÛT TUER PAR MSIRI

Translation:

Bodson is killed by Msiri

2 *Painting 16* (page 40) depicts the image of Msiri holding a sword and standing in front of a kneeling decapitated body; the head of the body is on the ground. The inscription is

LE FILS du CHEF KATANGA
EXECUTER PAR M'SIRI l'AMI de
son père

Translation:

The son of Chief Katanga
executed by M'Siri the friend of
his father

3 *Painting 19* (page 45) depicts four Europeans standing close to what looks like a military barracks, saluting a flag raised on a flagpole next to which Africans are lined up. The inscription is:

DEBUT DE LA – COLONIE BELGE
'SOUS PRÉTEXTE qu'ils étAient venus en AFRIQUE pour nous civiliser, les
    premiers
Blancs "Pionniers de cette civilisation"
commenceront pAR VIDER NOS pAYS RESPECtifs de leur substance
fondAmentAle' (Mobutu)

Translation:

Beginning of the – Belgian colony
'Under the pretext that they had come to Africa to civilise us, the first

TSHIBUMBA THE HISTORIAN

white men
"pioneers of that civilisation"
will start by emptying our respective countries of their fundamental
substances' (Mobutu)

4 *Painting 26* (page 56) looks like a diptych with on the left two shackled people
in a prison cell and on the right the courtyard of the prison with an armed
guard and several people in striped shirts. The inscription on the left reads:

KIMBANGU et JhoN PANDA

Translation:

Kimbangu and John Panda

The inscription on the right is several lines long and reads:

Peu après, kimbangu est transferé a la fameuse prison central
'd'Elisabetville'
a eu l'honneur d'héberger bEAUCOUp d'AFRICAINS aux idées AVANCÉes.
nombreux sont des Africains qui avaient conté de créer des
mouvement politien-relige
MEME CEUX-LA sont tomber SANS l'oubli – Après 30 ANS KIMBANGU a
trouvé LA MORT

Translation:

Shortly afterwards, Kimbangu is transferred to the famous central
prison of 'Elisabethville'
has had the honour of harbouring many Africans with advanced ideas.
Numerous are the Africans who had counted on creating politico-
religious movements
even those have fallen without forgetting – after 30 years Kimbangu
passed away.

Observe, in passing, the grassroots writing skills displayed in these inscriptions:
there is considerable instability in the use of upper and lower case, and the written French variety has some familiar features. We also see that the name of the
king of Katanga is twice written differently – 'Msiri' and 'M'siri' – and 'John' is
written as 'Jhon'.

More interesting is the typological difference we see in inscriptions. Example
(1) is a rather straightforward case of a 'title': the inscription is a descriptive caption to the images in the painting. In example (2) this caption is extended to
include some additional background information: Msiri was Chief Katanga's

THE AESTHETICS OF GRASSROOTS LITERACY

friend. While this is a descriptive statement, it also induces a moral frame: the execution of the late Chief's son now becomes an abominable act perpetrated by a friend. Description here comes with implicit moral condemnation. Example (3) is an explicitly hybrid form: we see a 'title' ('The beginning of the Belgian colony'), but it is followed by a quoted fragment from a speech by Mobutu which retrospectively qualifies colonisation as exploitation. This is political commentary attributed to the post-colonial leader of the country, and the event of the establishment of the Belgian Congo is now politically interpreted as well. Example (4), finally, contains both a caption ('Kimbangu and John Panda') and what looks like a factual as well as evaluative micro-narrative, which we can reformulate in a set of narrative propositions:

(i) Kimbangu was brought to the Central prison of Elisabethville;
(ii) that prison became the place where anti-colonial activists were imprisoned;
(iii) many Africans were involved in such anti-colonial activities;
(iv) they died there and this painting commemorates them;
(v) Kimbangu died after thirty years in prison

The prison became a place of commemoration after independence, because so many freedom fighters were brought there and died there; Simon Kimbangu (the Prophet and founder of the Kimbangist Church) was one of them, and Tshibumba pays his respect to all of them in this painting. The inscription in (4) clearly 'explains' something: it explains the diptych structure of the painting. Kimbangu and Panda were not the only ones, they instantiated a broader category of Africans 'with advanced ideas'. And it explains his intention to commemorate all of them, not just Kimbangu and Panda: the painting is *not* just about them.

The inscriptions, thus, are descriptive, but also interpretive *and narrative*. We see obvious forms of political framing in the examples (3) and (4), and Tshibumba here retrospectively entextualises the depicted historical events in terms of contemporary moral and political categories. The two murders committed by Msiri and depicted in (1) and (2) carry a different type of inscription, and this is suggestive of a different moral framing in both cases. Msiri killing the colonial agent Bodson remains unqualified. From Tshibumba's inscriptions in (3) and (4) we can understand that he had strongly negative perceptions of the colonial period, and so the absence of any moral judgment in the killing of Bodson may be understandable. The killing of Katanga's son, however, is qualified: Tshibumba invokes the close affinity between Chief Katanga and his eventual successor Msiri – a friendship which in a traditional African moral universe would compel Msiri to be the friend and protector of his friend's son.

The bottom line here is that the inscriptions on Tshibumba's paintings are not just *decorative*, they are *writings* meant to be *read* and having a rather important function in the painting. Remove the writings and the paintings would convey very different meanings. While he was painting his history of the Congo, Tshibumba had already started writing one.

TSHIBUMBA THE HISTORIAN

When? Recall that the sequence of historical paintings was *commissioned* by Fabian. Prior to their encounters in 1973 and 1974, Tshibumba had of course painted historical topics, and he manifestly had very developed interests in history. But the idea of a structured, comprehensive and coherent oeuvre of historical paintings evolved out of Fabian's commission. Maya Schiffer (2005: 348–53), in her study of Tshibumba's oeuvre, makes a number of very pertinent observations on the inscriptions. Having compared all the paintings in Fabian's collection in relation to the chronology of their acquisition, she saw a clear development over time in the types and complexity of the inscriptions. Paintings acquired before the start of the 'history project' carried very summary inscriptions, often confined to the artist's signature, dates, a descriptive title and inscriptions on buildings and objects. Longer inscriptions, and especially forms of commentary and quotations such as the one from Mobutu in (3) above begin to appear in late 1974, and develop as the project gains momentum. More complex statements now appear, and many of them have an obvious didactic purpose: Tshibumba wants to teach people about history, and his paintings *together with* the writings on them are the medium he uses for that purpose.

But who is the addressee? Fabian, in comments on the use of French in the inscriptions, writes: '[s]ince he wanted to educate *his fellow countrymen*, French, the language of schoolbooks, would express his didactic intentions' (Fabian 1996: 240, italics added). But the paintings were not sold to 'fellow countrymen' – we know that Tshibumba's main customers were expatriates. The addressees for the words in the paintings were almost certainly middle-class people from overseas, using French as their local lingua franca. And if we accept Schiffer's analysis about the development of the inscriptions in the context of the historical painting project, we can be very precise: the addressee was none other than Fabian, and this explains the way in which the epigrams developed into linguistically and semantically complex propositions *changing* the pictorial representation of events. There was not so much a general and undifferentiated 'didactic' function for the inscriptions, but rather a function also observable in the conversations between Fabian and Tshibumba: a *dialogue among historians*. The paintings with their inscriptions were Tshibumba's first 'historiography' – a writing of history, not just a pictorial representation. The fact that others, like Jewsiwiecki, also benefited from this transition in the work is a side-effect of the fact that Tshibumba now finds his voice as a historian and develops *a changed genre* of paintings, with *more, and more complex inscriptions*, as an effect of the very specific project he has entered into.[5]

The highly specific nature of the exercise on which Tshibumba embarks when he accepts Fabian's commission is also demonstrated in one of their conversations.[6] While talking about the public response to some of his paintings, Tshibumba suddenly remarks:

> 'Now, when you do those other paintings [they say] "Oh, why did you do it that way? It's a bad idea". Because you asked me I went along with

it. I was glad to be able to show that we are intelligent enough to work in this way. But our brothers put a brake on us, especially the authorities'.

When Fabian prompts him to clarify which paintings he is talking about, Tshibumba answers that he is talking about 'this series I did for you [. . .] you are the first to get it'. Not only are these new works of art: Tshibumba knows that they are also *locally controversial* and *only made for Fabian*, as part of the 'history project'.

The historiographical character of the work clearly makes the work a very particular and 'abnormal', even idiosyncratic oeuvre. It is literally born out of the interest of anthropologists and historians and, as in Julien's case, it is best to consider the specific formal features of the work in this light. Tshibumba's painted history is the product of a very specific relationship with a 'globalised' audience. It is an emerging genre, and the remarkable features it has – its volume, themes, and increasingly 'hybrid' character – are features of genre development.

Writing history: a further development?

Let us now return to the written *Histoire* and remind ourselves of two things. First, the *Histoire* was produced after the production of a painted history of the Congo. It was produced significantly later: Fabian and Tshibumba embarked on their history project in 1973–4, and the *Histoire* was written in 1980, at a time when Tshibumba probably did not have any realistic prospect of producing another large-scale sequence of historical paintings. This we can infer from his letter to Vinck in 1981, in which he complains about the difficulties in his career as a painter. The letter came with paintings for Vinck, so we can see that Tshibumba was still productive. But no other coherent history-painting project was undertaken after the episode with Fabian. The *Histoire* thus came several years after the completion of the history painting project and, as I suggested earlier, it is best seen as a relatively autonomous writing exercise.

The second point we need to recall is that the text looks good. The regularity and style of the handwriting and the careful construction of chapters and paragraphs create a smooth and transparent 'look'. Whenever lists are given (e.g. page 33), the lists are very neatly aligned and graphically separated from the text by the uniform use of upper case. It is a calligraphic text, exuding great care for *how* things are written. In addition to these graphic features, the text also contains six small drawings, illustrations to particular parts of the text. Let us take a look at them (see figure 6.2 overleaf).

A first observation is that the number of illustrations is modest. Tshibumba, a fine painter, definitely had the skills to include far more and more elaborate illustrations (portraits of some of his protagonists, for instance). Not only is the number of illustrations modest, their theme is modest too. All the illustrations are drawings of new *flags* introduced at particular moments in the Congo, and we get, consecutively:

TSHIBUMBA THE HISTORIAN

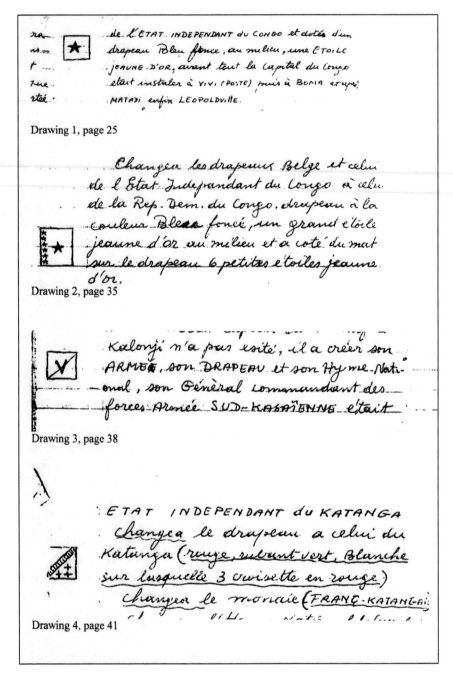

Figure 6.2 The six drawings in Tshibumba's *Histoire* (above and next page)

THE AESTHETICS OF GRASSROOTS LITERACY

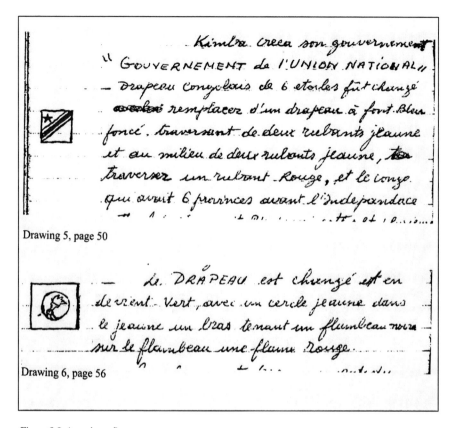

Figure 6.2 (continued)

The flag of the Congo Free State;
That of the (first) democratic Republic of Congo;
That of the secessionist independent republic of Kasai, founded by Kalonji;
That of the secessionist Katanga Republic;
The new flag of the Congolese Republic under Kimba;
And the flag of Mobutu's 'parti-état' Zaire.

The drawings are undistinguished. They are simple line-drawings, accurate of course, but without colours or much detail. Such attributes are, however, provided in the texts that accompany them. Thus we read next to the flag of Mobutu's Zaire:

> Le drapeau est changé et en
> devient Vert, avec un cercle jeaune dans
> le jeaune un bras tenant un flambeau noire
> sur le flambeau une flame rouge.

Translation:

The flag is changed and
becomes green, with a yellow circle in
the yellow an arm holding a black torch
on the torch a red flame

That's it: six very modest and simple drawings, minimally illustrating what is maximally explained in words. For an outstanding graphic artist like Tshibumba, this is a remarkably wordy text. There has not been an attempt at creating a hybrid genre in which drawings and text are blended; the effort has been to perform an *orthodox written* genre, a genre in which words are organised in relation to each other and not in relation to figurative illustrations. *In die Beschränkung zeigt sich der Meister* and the mastery that Tshibumba attempts to demonstrate here is in writing, in the construction of a 'normal' text.

This is remarkable because we saw how his paintings gradually contained more and more elaborate texts, how writing became part of his painting, resulting in a highly intricate hybrid image. Fabian partly explained this co-ordination between painting and writing as a genre influence: according to him, Tshibumba was 'an avid reader of comic strips' and elements of the cartoon genre may thus have entered his paintings (1996: 236). This explanation, however, is not conclusive because too many techniques of incorporating words in images remained unused (e.g. text balloons or the separation of text and image in a text box).[7] A more sustainable hypothesis, according to Fabian, is to see the writings as 'epigrams' on (what Tshibumba himself calls) 'monuments' – his pictures commemorate history in very much the same way as statues and other monuments do (236–9). The epigrams 'give these pictures a voice', and they are in French because that choice of code offers the 'prospect of making his voice heard among the largest number of those he wanted to educate [. . .]' (240–1).

We have already seen that this hypothesis invites revision as well, for the writings on the paintings appear far more complex and diverse than the label 'epigraphic' would suggest, and their development and differentiation occurred in a highly specific communicative context. It was a genre that emerged from the history project with Fabian. I suggest we look at the *Histoire* for answers. Tshibumba's multi-generic oeuvre offers us the possibility to speculate about his repertoire, and the *Histoire* can clarify the role of writing in his repertoire.

Let us first establish one point. The *Histoire* is obviously another entextualisation of the historical 'stuff' that Tshibumba elaborated in his paintings and discussed in his conversations. Some parts of the conversations display very strong textual similarities with the versions afterwards written in the *Histoire*. The *Histoire* is, however, also a *different* entextualisation, one in which the 'stuff' is reordered and reorganised according to a particular (distant) genre model. We will return to this specific issue in the next chapter; for now I should point out that in his written *Histoire*, there is a conscious attempt at *chronology* – a feature

THE AESTHETICS OF GRASSROOTS LITERACY

that appears far more loosely organised in the sequence of paintings and in the conversations. Chronology becomes the basic formal resource for constructing the story. This is by now a familiar phenomenon; we saw it in the genre development in Julien's writings as well. And here, too, we can take our clues from the way in which the division of chapters in the text is done. The chapters are the main text-structuring tool applied in the *Histoire*, and we will see presently that their use is not unproblematic. But by means of chapters and chapter titles, *episodes* are created and *chronologised*. Let us take the storyline I reconstructed in the previous chapter and map the chapters onto it. I will mark some noteworthy features in italics and bold (see table overleaf).

There are 29 chapters in the text, and the way in which such chapters are graphically marked by Tshibumba differs quite a bit throughout the text. Upper case and curved lines underscoring the words are frequently used markers. Sometimes such markers are accompanied by blank lines above and under the title, clearly separating it from the remainder of the text. But we see that none of these graphic tools is used systematically and consistently. The clearest examples can be found in the first part of the text: they combine upper case, underlining and blank spaces (see the titles 1, 2, 8 and 9 in the table). From that point onwards, two features remain: the use of upper case (as in the examples 10–15) and, increasingly and sometimes underlined, *dates*. Especially from the middle of the text onwards, as soon as Tshibumba starts telling the story of the independence struggle, dates become key parts of chapter titles. Of the 16 chapter titles occurring from page 31 down, no fewer than 11 contain dates, either just a year (e.g. '1970'), or (in 8 of the 11 instances) a full day-month-year string. *Chronology becomes the formal principle on the basis of which chapters are organised*: the *Histoire* becomes a chronicle. And as we saw in Julien's texts as well, a chronologically organised narrative is about accuracy. Note how in the list of chapter titles, four of them begin with a phrase that indexes chronological consistency: *revenons* ('let's return to') or *reculons* ('let's go back'). In each of these instances, the chronological flow had been interrupted by a digression, and Tshibumba restores the flow of the narrative by returning to an earlier episode. Chapters 16 and 17 show another feature of accuracy: the bold fragments are clearly added afterwards. In (16), Tshibumba adds '4' to complete the date he gives. In (17), he adds 'Leopoldville' to the date he had provided. None of this is random; all of this is the product of a conscious genre effort.

Tshibumba wrote dates on his paintings too. In fact, he wrote quite a few of them. 27 of the 101 paintings discussed by Fabian contain dates as part of the inscriptions. The occurrence and frequency of these dates follows the pattern of development of the inscriptions discussed above: they do not occur frequently in the earlier works but become a steady feature when the 'history project' is well underway. The first date appears in painting 20 (Fabian 1996: 46), which depicts the foundation of the Congo Free State in 1885. And from that point onwards until painting 56 (on the Katangese independence), one out of three paintings has a date in its inscription. In terms of historical periodisation, paintings that

TSHIBUMBA THE HISTORIAN

1. The pre-colonial period, 7–15	1) NOS ANCETRES ('Our ancestors'), 7 2) 1° LE LONG du fleuve CONGO (NZADI)/ou le Royaume du Congo ('1st along the River Congo (Nzadi), or the Kingdom of Congo'), 7 3) Royaume des Balubas ('Kingdom of the Baluba), 8 4) le Royaume de BAKUBA/Le Roi de BAKUBA ('The Bakuba Kingdom, the Bakuba King'), 9 5) Royaume de MONGO ('Mongo Kingdom'), 10 6) Royaume des BAMPENDE ('Kingdom of the Bampende'), 10 7) Royaume de Baluba SHANKADI ('Baluba Shankadi Kingdom'), 11 8) EMPIRE LUNDA ('Lunda Empire'), 13
2. The explorers, 15–24	9) Dans le SUD du KATANGA ('In the South of Katanga'), 15 10) STANLEY HENRI MORTON, 16 11) LA CONFERENCE DE BERLIN ('The Berlin Conference'), 19 12) Les ARABES en AFRIQUE ('The Arabs in Africa'), 20 13) Revenons un peu à KATANGA le Chef ('Let us return to Chief Katanga'), 21
3. Colonisation prior to the independence struggle, 24–30	14) L'ARRIVÉE des BLANCS/COLONISATEURS ('The arrival of the white colonisers', 24 15) 'Ni POLTICIEN NI RelligIEUX' ('Neither politician nor religious [leader]'), 28
4. The independence struggle, 31–35	16) **4** Janv.-En 1959 ('January 4, 1959'), 31 17) **Leopoldville** 1959, 32
5. The First Republic and the Congo Crisis, 35–50	18) LE 30-JUIN-1960 ('June 30, 1960'), 35 19) Le Congo et SES FILS ('The Congo and its sons'), 37 20) ETAT INDEPENDENT du KATANGA ('The Independent State of Katanga'), 41 21) Revenons au conflît KASA-VUBU et LUMUMBA ('Let's return to the conflict between Kasavubu and Lumumba'), 42
6. The Second Republic, 51–55	22) 24 NOVEMBRE 1965 ('November 24, 1965'), 51
7. The Third Republic, 55–59	23) 1970, 55
8. The Shaba wars, 60–65	24) le 8-Mars 1977 ('March 8, 1977'), 60 25) Le 22.11.1977, 61 26) le 12-MAI 1978, ('May 12, 1978'), 62 27) Revenons à l'Agression du 22-MAI 78 ('Let's come back to the aggression of May 22, 1978'), 64
9. Recent events and Coda, 66–69	28) 1980, 66 29) (Reculons) Le 24 Déc. 1979 ('(Let's go back) December 24, 1979'), 67

128

THE AESTHETICS OF GRASSROOTS LITERACY

treat events between 1957 and 1961 most often contain dates; dates are less frequent when the paintings depict other periods in the history of the Congo. But the appearance of dates as part of the inscriptions goes hand in hand with the solidification of the 'history project'; when Tshibumba consciously starts painting his history of the Congo, accurate chronology becomes part of the organisation of that project. The conversion from a painting to a writing project, then, offers the opportunity to *make chronology into the central structuring feature* of this version of history, and that is what he does. The events, previously moulded in figurative and evocative images, are now structured around the actual points in time of their occurrence. It is a conventional textual way of structuring a historical narrative, and if historiography is Tshibumba's general ambition, this conventional textual way becomes a compelling format: a more rational, factual, 'objective' and thus truthful way of telling the story of his country.

Seen from that perspective, it is the completion of his historiographical project that forces Tshibumba into this genre shift. In order to tell the history of the Congo accurately and correctly, it needs to be written. The writings on the paintings, given their specific genealogy, can be seen as the beginning of this genre shift. The more precise the concepts of history and historiography become, the more text appears. We see the birth of the genre in Fabian's collection of paintings; we see the mature genre in the *Histoire*. So after all, there may have been a unified historiographic project in Tshibumba's mind; not one of *painting* however (and here I differ with Fabian) but one of *writing*. In that sense, the paintings were (or at least *became*) a 'scenario' for the writing, and not the other way around. The minimal use of graphic illustrations in this text is an effect of conscious genre choice. This choice, as we can expect, is severely constrained and constraining.

Tshibumba's voice

The choice is constrained and constraining, because Tshibumba seems to surrender his best and most powerful communicative resources. As a painter, he can draw on his own talent and on a vast range of technical and material instruments: perspective, colour, the architecture of images on a canvas – the things that made him into an artist of international significance. His paintings are extraordinarily eloquent and they have become emblematic of a period and style in Congolese art. They have been displayed in some of the world's most prominent museums and galleries, and (as we know) they have become the object of an art-historical, anthropological and historical cottage industry of sorts, the book products of which sometimes carry reproductions of his work on their covers. He is one of those few African artists who actually has a *name*.

When he opts for writing, then, he clips his own wings and he becomes considerably less eloquent and evocative. He is thrown back onto a very restricted range of semiotic resources: a linguistic and literacy code, and some graphic, stylistic and organisational writing conventions such as chapter, paragraph and

129

emphasis marking. While his painting skills raised him to the level of international exposure, commentary and circulation, his writing brings him back to the level of someone like Julien: grassroots literacy. While his voice was loudly and widely heard when he painted, he produces a muffled and less than clear voice when he writes. He chooses a genre and finds himself with the range of resources that fit that genre. None of these resources is unproblematic. I have already commented on his use of chapter titles; let me now turn to the use of a code – French – and of some stylistic and narrative techniques he uses in his *Histoire*.

The monoglossic code

Tshibumba uses monoglossic French in his *Histoire*: a code of which we know that it was not his native language, and that, in the sociolinguistic ecology in which he lived, it was a resource of restricted use and function. It was used *orally* and in *a vernacular variety*, most often blended with Swahili in the different forms of Shaba Swahili employed there. And when written, it probably only served the purpose of correspondence with his expatriate customers. Like Mrs Arens, these people were extraordinarily tolerant of spelling and other errors and even if his 'accent in writing' is quite outspoken, it was left uncorrected. If we return to the examples I gave earlier, where we saw that he drew images of flags and described them, we see the following features.

Homophony in speaking leading to errors in spelling:
–   'le Capital du Congo était installer' (= 'la capitale du Congo était installée', 'the capital of Congo was installed'), page 25
–   'Kalonji n'a pas esité' (= 'Kalonji n'a pas hésité', 'Kalonji didn't hesitate'), page 38
–   'rubant vert' (= 'ruban vert', 'green ribbon'), page 41
–   '3 croisette' (= 'trois croisettes', 'three little crosses'), page 41
–   'union national' (= 'union nationale', 'national union'), page 50
–   'fût changé remplacez' (= 'fut change [et] remplacé', 'was changed and replaced by'), page 50
Orthographic traces of vernacular pronunciations:
–   'Independant' (= 'indépendant', independent), page 35
–   'indepandace' (= 'indépendance', independence), page 50
Incomplete mastery of French orthographic peculiarities:
–   'jeaune' (= 'jaune', 'yellow'), page 35, 50, 56

As for the latter, Tshibumba gets the infamously complex French graphemic compound 'eau' right in 'drapeau' ('flag'), and this pattern is probably carried over into 'jeaune'. In other examples, we saw how he also wrote 'peinceaux', a complex graphemic structure which he gets right as well.[8] So there are traces of awareness of the 'correct' forms, alternated with evidence of confusion and of absence of such a fully developed awareness. Similar phenomena occur in his

THE AESTHETICS OF GRASSROOTS LITERACY

choice of grammatical forms. On several occasions, he opts for the *passé simple* tense, an emblematic marker of 'high', elite code use and a notoriously arcane aspect of French verbal inflection. Thus we saw in our examples how he used 'changea' (from 'changer', 'to change', page 41) as well as 'fût' (from 'être', 'to be', page 50). Note, however, how in the latter form he uses the *accent circonflexe*. This turns the word into a noun, meaning 'barrel'; the correct form would be 'fut', without *circonflexe*. The grammatical complexity is here stretched into an ortho-graphic complexification of the form. The use of French ortho-graphic accents on vowels is, in general, highly problematic, as several examples have already shown.

Standard French is thus 'there', it transpires in the correct spelling of ortho-graphically complex words and in his choice of 'high' French grammatical forms. It is there, but at a distance: none of these selections of 'high' code use is systematically and completely realised, and the *Histoire* is packed with the kinds of vernacular, 'sub-standard' forms we also encountered in the lives of Julien. Standard French, thus, may be *available* in Tshibumba's (and Julien's) sociolinguistic environment, but not necessarily *accessible* for people with his social and economic background.

I do not intend to redo the analysis I did earlier on Julien's repertoire. But the conclusion is identical: this monoglossic French, of course, is a highly *special* code, a register which is part of the Shaba Swahili repertoire used by Tshibumba. His oral vernacular code is densely 'mixed', as we can see from the transcripts published in the *Archives of Popular Swahili*. Consider just these examples from APS 3b; I put French items in bold:

- '**ou bien** nitaweza kufansia **cinq**: **cinq**' ('or else I could do five − five')
- 'sichangule **territoire** ya Kambove hapana / kwa sababu ma**tableaux** mingi' ('I did not choose the *territoire* of Machambove / because [there are] many paintings')
- '**et puis** asubui' ('and then in the morning')
- 'sawa vile unaone **policier** na **numéro matricule**' ('like you see a policeman with his badge number')
- 'sawa vile **chef de l'état** na anakala ku: Kinshasa' ('like a head of state and he lived in Kinshasa')

And so forth, the point should be sufficiently clear: writing a monoglossic French code, for Tshibumba and for Julien, is a matter of eradicating 'mixed forms' and 'purifying' vernacular language use, distilling the 'pure' French they want to use in writing. In Tshibumba's case more than in Julien's, we also see an indexical arrow pointing upward: he distinctly attempts to write 'high' French. In this attempt he has to build the required register from the materials he has at his disposal. As I hope to have demonstrated, these materials are few and many are missing; these are clumsy and recalcitrant tools for the complex genre exercise he embarks on.

TSHIBUMBA THE HISTORIAN

Creating a factual narrative

The conversations between Fabian and Tshibumba reveal the latter as a competent storyteller. He picks up on anecdotes or points from his paintings and develops them into a 'plot' with lively characters whose speech he often quotes. So, too, at some points in his *Histoire*. The following fragment illustrates his capacity to create lively micro-narratives in his text. The fragment is inserted in a chronicle-like episode about King Baudoin and Mr Pétillon. Baudoin succeeded his father in 1955, and he made an appeal against racism. This appeal, however, is seen by Tshibumba as a tactic to delay independence. Baudoin sends Pétillon as his emissary to convey that message to the Belgians in the Congo. Then follows this paragraph (page 30):

> Fou de rage les Blancs du
> Congo on jetté des fruits des Tomates
> pourrit en signe de protestation
> contre le répresentant du Roi ✖✖✖
> poursuivant leur plan d'intimida-
> tion démocratic, réfusant le cadeau
> offert par le Roi

Translation:

> Enraged, the whites of
> Congo have thrown fruits rotten
> tomatoes as as sign of protest
> at the representative of the King
> following their plan of democratic
> intimidation, refusing the present
> from the King

Tshibumba attaches importance to this episode. Two paintings are devoted to it as well: painting 33 in Fabian's collection depicts Baudoin giving a speech, and the inscription reads: '"Eat, drink, and dance together with the blacks of the Congo" (Baudoin) to hinder independence' (Fabian 1996: 67); painting 35 depicts Pétillon in front of microphones, with white people throwing objects at him. The inscription here reads 'Mr Pétillon at the residence of the Mayor of the town of Jadotville in 1957' (pages 70–1). The fragment of the conversation between Fabian and Tshibumba about this painting is an example of Tshibumba's capacity for narrative performance. He quotes Pétillon and his opponents and the story turns into a small piece of role-play:

> 'Then in 1957 came Mr Pétillon. He travelled all over the Congo, as the country was called then. So he got to Likasi. He was at the lord mayor's residence in Jadotville, which was the name of Likasi at the

132

THE AESTHETICS OF GRASSROOTS LITERACY

time. He called together the whites, and many came. He explained to them: "Brothers, I am just an emissary, sent to settle the matter that King Baudoin left unfinished. What do you say? What have you agreed on?" They picked up tomatoes, threw them at him, and chased him away, saying, "You can inform him that we reject what he said".'

(Fabian 1996: 70)

In his written *Histoire* version as well we see how Tshibumba enters into the description of an emotional crowd (*'fou de rage'*, 'enraged'), although he represents the verbal interaction in reported speech ('refusing the present of the King'). This was an event from Likasi in 1957; Tshibumba could have been there as a witness or may have heard lively stories from witnesses at the time. Yet we should not immediately walk into the trap of suggesting that Tshibumba's style here mirrors his position of an eye witness: it is a stylistic and rhetorical matter. The capacity to produce an eye witness-like account also transpires from the next fragment, set in a period of which Tshibumba could not possibly have been a witness. Here, Henry Morton Stanley reports back to King Leopold (page 18):

> Et il a raconté a S.M.
> LEopold Ier, tous ce qu'il a vu
> lors de son éxploration jusqu à
> MALADI-KANANGA
> **Stanley** 'J'ai vu de LOBITO des hommes
> s'emblable à nous, ils parlent
> et marcherent, mais avec une couleur
> NOIRE et un peu plus loin dans
> la forêt, j'ai vu de loin des gends
> aussi NOIRS mais avec des queus
> s'enfuillant dans la forêt, laissant
> des huttes et des ~~maisons~~ cases)'
> Fort interesser le Roi a
> confié à STANLEY une mission

Translation:

> And he told H.M.
> Leopold I, all he had seen
> during his exploration to
> Maladi-Kananga
> **Stanley** 'I saw in Lobito people
> similar to us, they talked
> and walked, but with a black
> colour and a bit further in

133

the forest, I saw from afar people
also black but with tails
hiding into the forest, leaving
huts and ~~houses~~ mud-houses'
    Strongly interested the King
gave Stanley a mission

This is a genuine micro-story in which two real characters appear: Henry Morton Stanley and King Leopold I. I will return later to this remarkable *lapsus* in which Tshibumba confuses Leopold I with Leopold II. In this little episode, we see how Stanley reports directly, in quoted speech, to the King, who was 'strongly interested'. Stanley's words describe the people of the Congo: these people are like us, but they are black and some of them (only observed from a distance) have tails.[9] He puts in Stanley's mouth the stereotypes of Europeans about Africans, and the conscious effort at making these words sound authentic can be measured from the correction he makes in Stanley's final phrase. There, '*maisons*' – the normal 'modern' dwelling – is struck out and replaced by '*cases*', a term that belongs to the vocabulary of exotic differentiation in which African 'houses' are described as 'huts' and 'mud houses'. Note also that Tshibumba afterwards added 'Stanley' to the beginning of the quote. The author is emphatically identified: the stereotypes are his, and Tshibumba here describes the Africans as seen through the eyes of a white explorer.

This lively episodic style, however, gradually disappears as the *Histoire* progresses. We have seen how Pétillon's contact with the Belgian settlers in the Congo was rendered in reported speech. On page 32, there is a quote from a speech by Kasavubu, but beyond that point a factual, indirect reporting style becomes a constant feature. Thus, no speeches from Lumumba are quoted. This is remarkable given the prominence of Lumumba in Tshibumba's work, and the fact that fragments from Lumumba's Independence Day speech were widely known by Congolese of Tshibumba's generation. This speech, however, is represented as follows (page 36):

Lumumba a fait un long discour
dans lesquelle il a injirier la colonie
et ses chefs, après passé a tous ce que
les Belges ont fait comme mal a nos
ancêtres et a notre pays ~~en remer~~ il a
fini par remercié, les Congolais **en les**
felicitant d' acceurir leur Indepandance par le
Sueur de leurs fronts.

Translation:

> Lumumba gave a long speech
> in which he insulted the colony
> and its leaders, after having reviewed all that
> the Belgians have done wrong to our
> ancestors and to our country he
> ended by thanking the Congolese while
> congratulating them on acquiring independence
> by the sweat on their faces.

While there was direct involvement between the author and his characters in the encounter between Stanley and Leopold, the tone here is distant and factually reporting. This tone is maintained throughout the remainder of the story. Tshibumba quotes from documents (e.g. from an ultimatum by Kalonji to the Congolese government, page 54) but not from speeches, and we do not encounter any other lively rendered conversations in the *Histoire*. From an engaging and sometimes almost cinematographic style, the *Histoire* develops into a factual account, dominated by the chronological organisation of neutrally reported events. This stylistic shift, of course, raises questions about the sources that Tshibumba used and, consequently, about the range of genre models he could employ. To these we will devote the next chapter.

A disciplined voice

Tshibumba's *Histoire* is strangely 'un-aesthetic'. This is of course a relative statement: the document has an aesthetics of its own. It is relative when measured against the enormous range of semiotic resources that someone like Tshibumba had at his disposal. As an accomplished painter, he could have brought a thoroughly, even spectacularly visual architecture to his story. The fact that he didn't is a matter of choice: a choice for writing, and writing in an orthodox fashion. This results in a monoglossic text, devoid of any exuberant visuality. Images are replaced by chronology as a formal-structuring tool, and by a clear and controlled handwriting and some visual-textual instruments such as chapters and paragraph markers. This still makes the text 'look good', but it is a very serious reduction of what was available.

This reduction of the aesthetic resources for constructing the text is an effect of *Beschränkung* – of disciplined moderation. It is a disciplined reduction of the possible means for constructing a story. Disciplined means that there is a discipline, history, and the *Beschränkung* is an attempt at displaying mastery in history writing. The fact that his handwriting is stable, regular and 'on the lines', as well as other features such as the increase in dates as chapter titles, the attempt at producing monoglossic 'high' French, and the decrease of performance-like stylistic features as the story moves on, all add substance to this. Writing 'on the lines' is writing in an orthodox, disciplined way – a way that emphasises uniformity, transparency, clarity. The uniform shape, size and format of the six little flags he drew also suggests regimentation. There, too, we saw the conscious avoidance of exuberance. The aesthetics of the *Histoire* is a regimented *textual* aesthetics, one that deploys a very narrow range of visual features in an orthodox – and ortho-graphic – way.

The voice Tshibumba attempts to construct in the *Histoire* is a rational and disciplined voice, a voice of which he hopes that it matches the expectations of and carries resonance with his addressee, a professional historian. In order to achieve that goal, he must use the resources at hand, and the choice of genre here involves a serious reduction of these resources. More resources apart from the formal and visual ones examined here are needed to create a 'history'. While Julien's texts were *Récits*, Tshibumba claims to write an *Histoire*. Julien's genre allows an articulated 'subjective' narrative; Tshibumba's genre imposes 'objectivity' and comprehensiveness on the text. Recollections are not enough, and Tshibumba is facing a more momentous task of collecting and ordering available materials.

7

SOURCES AS RESOURCES

The archive again

One of the most difficult tasks of the historian is that of assembling those documents which he considers necessary. He could hardly succeed without the help of various guides: archival or library catalogues, museum indexes, and bibliographies of every kind. There are people who express contemptuous amazement at the time sacrificed by some scholars in composing such works and by all the rest in familiarizing themselves with their existence and use.

(Bloch 1953: 69)

This is what the great historian Marc Bloch writes in *The Historian's Craft*. Historical research proceeds, first, by delineating the terrain on which the inquiry will take place; next, the sources need to be identified. If we intend to examine the evolution of wheat prices in a 17th century Italian village, we will need to identify and select documents that provide information on that – for instance, town accounts and correspondence between traders and farmers, preferably from that area. Throughout the process of identifying and selecting the sources, we should keep an open mind, for '[i]t would be sheer fantasy to imagine that for each historical problem there is a unique type of document with a specific sort of use' (1953: 67). We will have to locate these sources, find out whether they are accessible, try to get into contact with them, and study them. In addition, we should collect relevant literature on that or related topics, so as to check and develop a preferred methodology for that piece of research. The contact with the documents, and their study, is in itself a seriously complex affair. Among historians it has given prominence to the sub-discipline of historical criticism, the careful and methodical scrutiny of documents in an attempt to separate facts from gossip, true and correct accounts from errors, and original (that is, truthful) versions from copies and forgeries. Bloch spends a long chapter on historical criticism, because historical *analysis* can only proceed on the basis of sources that have withstood the test of such criticism. The sources must first be there, they must be thoroughly verified, and only then can the historian embark on more ambitious and adventurous enterprises.

TSHIBUMBA THE HISTORIAN

Naturally, historical work, thus conceived, can only proceed where there is an adequate technology for creating repositories of collective memory. The archives, libraries and bibliographies that Bloch mentions are core elements of such a technology. In this respect, Bloch remarks that 'our civilization has always been extremely attentive to the past' (1953: 4). He refers of course to European societies in which, indeed, there has been a clear archival tendency for many centuries. Even so, the abundance of archives and other repositories of collective memory does not necessarily create a historian's heaven. Not *everything* is archived, and Bloch mutters that sometimes a calamity such as the eruption of Vesuvius is the best method for guaranteeing a complete and comprehensive record. 'A good cataclysm suits our business better', he writes, and the historian will always be plagued by the incompleteness of the archives:

> until society begins to organize a rational self-knowledge by controlling its records, instead of depending on calamities for its information. To do so, it must come to grips with the two principles responsible for forgetfulness and ignorance: that negligence which loses documents; and, even more dangerous, that passion for secrecy – diplomatic secrecy, business secrecy, family secrecy – which hides or destroys them.
>
> (Bloch 1953: 75)

An ideal historian's world is one in which everything is archived, ready to be examined and used in later accounts of events. The quest for adequate sources as well as the methods of historical criticism both attempt to fill the gap between ideal and reality.

We have seen in our discussion of Julien's three versions that the gap between ideal and reality is much bigger for someone living in a village in Northern Katanga. And while Julien could still be allowed a measure of 'subjectivity' in the construction of his auto-histories, we now see what a colossal burden Tshibumba has placed on his own shoulders by calling himself a 'historian' and calling his text an *Histoire*. In Julien's case, the act of remembering was something that proceeded slowly and assumed the shape of more and more accurate chronological situating of events from his own past, with minimal references to wider events. Tshibumba's ambitions are different, and he takes upon himself the task of writing a serious, rationally organised history of a national space, the Congo, or Zaire as it was known at that time.

I have already mentioned that the definition of this national scope sets Tshibumba's document apart from the *Vocabulaire de la Ville de Elisabethville* by André Yav. The latter was primarily a local account, with some wider regional angles but still essentially confined to Katanga, and it aspired to be nothing more than that. Thus, even when events are mentioned that happened elsewhere, they are quickly repatriated to Katanga and Katangese interests. I quote from Fabian's translated version of Yav's text (Fabian 1990a: 65):

SOURCES AS RESOURCES

At that time, the King watched this in his home 'Bruxelles' and studied the news that came from Africa. Many groups informed him that food and equipment did not arrive fast enough from Europe. And the King studied with his eyes on the map of the country. He told himself: Where can I find a road to transport equipment, one that is short, so that I could construct a railroad quickly to expedite shipment of material to Africa, and [get] a train that will get material there quickly? That way one would not have to use porters. [. . .] In order to organize all this the King gave orders, on March 11, 1902, to set up the 'Compagnie du Chemin de Fer du Katanga'.

We see how an event that happened in Brussels – King Leopold pondering over logistical problems in the exploitation of his Free State – is immediately converted into regional history. Far more than just the construction of the Katanga Railroad happened, to be sure, but Yav selects the item which is of immediate concern for his regional history. And interventions in Katanga quickly convert into interventions in the Congo as a whole; when Yav arrives at the foundation of the Union Minière du Haut Katanga, he qualifies it as 'this "big society" which was needed for the progress of the Congo' (ibid.). We can note here in passing that in Yav's account King Leopold is depicted as equally interested and active in the affairs of the Congo as in a fragment from Tshibumba's text I quoted in the previous chapter. I'll return to this below.

Tshibumba did not have the comfort of a restricted scope. He wants to write a national history and in doing so he adopts a spatial and temporal framework that compels him to be comprehensive for that national scope. He also had this national scope in his paintings. Fabian affirms (when discussing the use of French in the inscriptions on the paintings) that: 'his conception of the history of Zaire, indeed his political position, was decidedly national, not regional' (Fabian 1996: 240). Tshibumba believes that Zaire has what Foucault called a 'positivity'; it is a 'historical a priori' (Foucault 2002: 143). 'Every country has a story', he claims (Fabian 1996: 270n). The Congo has, thus, a firm discursive existence, as can be seen from the following fragment of a conversation with Fabian:

'Thus, without following the teaching [. . .] of religion, such as the Catholic, Protestant, or Kimbanguist [denominations], our Zaire existed, it existed from the days of old. And [there were] our ancestors, they were as you can see them here [he refers to paintings 1–3 – JB], those [were] our ancestors. And they knew how to dress; they had raffia clothes [. . .]. They knew how to work. They were the ones who worked on the water, fishing, and, in Katanga, they began to make copper ingots at that time . . . They knew how to govern themselves (*kujigouverner*)'

(270)

TSHIBUMBA THE HISTORIAN

Zaire was not created by the missionaries; there was a pre-colonial 'Zaire' in Tshibumba's mind, and the history of that country can thus be described from 'the ancestors' onwards. But note how, as in Yav's case, the national and the regional appear intertwined: Zaire is immediately followed by Katanga, and his statement on what ancestors did in Katanga is more specific than the general statement that precedes it. There is regional bias in his description of the Congo, and I will elaborate this thesis in the remainder of this chapter.

This regional bias does not deny national aspirations. Fabian points out that Tshibumba manifestly and conspicuously avoids an *ethnic* perspective in his paintings and conversations, and that the idea of national unity is a prominent trope in his work (1996: 271–3). Thus, Fabian is 'fairly certain that Tshibumba would have agreed had I proposed to him that the subject of his [painted and narrated – JB] History was *le peuple congolais* [. . .]' (272–3), and I can join him in that certainty. The issue is rather more complex though. It revolves around the fact that Tshibumba writes his national history *from Katanga*, and from *within a sub-elite stratum of Katangese society*. That is, he writes from within an economy of literacy and knowledge which is strongly local and which *determines* what and how he can write. The only sources he can use are local sources, and they are local *re*sources too. He can only see the national space from the place where he looks from: a sub-elite social space in Katanga. His *Histoire* shows the kind of positioning which Eric Hobsbawm once defined as 'the Fabrice Syndrome':

> There are perfectly sound reasons why participants at the bottom do not usually see historic events they live through as top people or historians do. One might call this (after the hero of Stendhal's *Chartreuse de Parme*) the 'Fabrice Syndrome'.
>
> (Hobsbawm 1983: 13n)

This particular kind of positioning is again a matter of resources. Transcending it is the capacity that Marc Bloch locates in historical analysis and interpretation. But as we have seen, one can only get to that stage when the necessary sources are available, have been collected and criticised. Tshibumba did not get to that stage.

A national history with local resources

The King and I

Let us begin with a very remarkable *lapsus* occurring in the *Histoire*. Here is a fragment immediately following an account of Livingstone's travels and achievements (page 16):

> Plusieurs jours ont passé sans
> les nouvelles, mais il y avait une
> personne qui s'est xxxx s'interesse de

l'Afrique central à la personne
du ROI des Belges LEOPOLD Ier
qui à organiser **des** éxpèditions
sous la direction des **p**lusieurs éxplo-
rateurs, pour la tentative de trouvé
la trace de LIVINGSTONE qui reste
sans (succès) nouvelle.

Translation:

Several days passed without
news, but there was one
person who was interested in
Central Africa in the person of
the King of the Belgians Leopold I
who organised expeditions
directed by several explorers
in an attempt to find
traces of Livingstone which remained
without (success) news.

Leopold II, the infamous founder of the Congo Free State, is here wrongly named
the first. It is not a one-off. On page 18, we read:[1]

le Roi LEOPOLD Ier qui avait tout
ces désires d'Etudier l'exploration
de l'Afrique central, a fait appel
a STANLEY l'anglais, qui celui-ci
a repondu favorablement.

Translation:

King Leopold I who had all
these desires to study the exploration
of Central Africa, made an appeal to
Stanley the Englishman, who in turn
responded favourably.

This fragment is immediately followed by one we have already seen (page 18):

Et il a raconté à S.M.
LEOPOLD Ier, tous ce qu'il a vu
lors de son éxploration jusqu'à
MALADI-KANAGA.

TSHIBUMBA THE HISTORIAN

Translation:

And he told H.M.
Leopold I all that he had seen
during his exploration to
Maladi-Kananga

And on page 24 we find:

et les Belges choisissez le Congo (ZAIre)
le Burundi et le Rwanda
comme colonie Belge et le Roi
LEOPOLD Ier a fait le Congo s**on**
proprietér privé

Translation:

and the Belgians chose the Congo (Zaire)
Burundi and Rwanda
as Belgian colony and the King
Leopold I made the Congo his
private property

And finally, on page 25:

Après la mort du xxx Roi LEOPOLD Ier
de belgique, la Belgique a changé cette
système d'appelation de l' E.I.C. à celui
du CONGO-BELGE.

Translation:

After the death of King Leopold I
of Belgium, Belgium changed this
system of naming from E.I.C. to that
of Belgian Congo.

In the *Histoire*, Tshibumba *systematically* confuses the two first Belgian kings. Leopold I (1790–1865) was the first King of Belgium and was evidently not in any way involved in the colonisation of the Congo; his son Leopold II (1835–1909) was the architect of Belgium's imperial plans, and he acquired the Congo as his private 'Free State', a corporate enterprise quite ruthlessly governed by a mercenary army and a nucleus of a colonial administration (1885–1908). Leopold II, the monarch who should have been mentioned in all the episodes described here, is *never* mentioned in Tshibumba's written text.[2]

142

SOURCES AS RESOURCES

This is a quite astonishing error, for several reasons. First, Leopold II was an iconic figure in the colonial Congo. His role in acquiring the Congo was very well known, and there must have been plenty of portraits of Leopold II as well as hagiographic stories about him, spread by colonial authorities and notably by the colonial education system. The presence of visual images of Leopold II is manifest in Tshibumba's paintings. The King is twice portrayed in Fabian's collection: painting 20 ('The Congo Free State', Fabian 1996: 46) and painting 27 ('The monument to Leopold II', page 57). In both instances, the face of the King bears strong resemblance to his official portraits, with short hair and the characteristic square beard. Especially in painting 20, where we see the king wearing his uniform and decorations, the echo of official portraits is outspoken. As the founder of the Belgian colonial empire, Leopold II must have been very much part of the collective memory in the Congo.

This brings us to a second reason: Tshibumba was clearly aware of the Belgian Monarchy. Apart from the two paintings of Leopold II, there is a painting of Prince Charles, brother of King Leopold III and Regent of Belgium in the years following the Second World War. The painting is entitled 'Prince Charles visits the Congo' – a royal visit happening in Tshibumba's birth year, 1947. In the narrative given next to the painting, Tshibumba expresses a rather detailed awareness of the Belgian royal genealogy and, especially, of the royal visits:

> That was in 1947. Before that there had been the tour made by Prince Leopold, the future king. Leopold became the ruler after Albert died, and he had travelled here in 1925. In 1928 King Albert and Queen Elisabeth travelled in the Congo.
>
> (Fabian 1996: 64)

The Royal visit of King Baudoin in 1955 is the object of two paintings: painting 32 ('King Baudoin visits the Congo', page 66) and 33 ('King Baudoin gives a speech', page 67). Baudoin appears another two times: in painting 48 ('Lumumba signs the Golden Book', page 91) and in painting 49 ('Lumumba makes his famous speech', page 92). Both paintings describe moments from the Independence Day ceremonies, and in both paintings the King is presented as a smiling bystander in events dominated by Lumumba.

Royal visits were, of course, events of some magnitude in a colony situated many thousands of kilometres from the motherland, and one can imagine the avalanche of propaganda messages and images that preceded and followed them. No wonder that they appear in Tshibumba's paintings as moments that punctuate history. To this he adds, as we have seen, ideas about the agentive role of the Belgian king in governing the colony. We saw how he imagined Stanley reporting his encounters with Africans to a king who was 'strongly interested' and decided to send Stanley on further explorative missions, and we also saw how he imagined Baudoin sending Mr Pétillon to tell the Belgian settlers in the Congo that they should revise the institutional racism in the colony if they wished to avoid

143

decolonisation. In Yav's *Vocabulaire*, too, we encountered a king who thought, worried and took decisions that brought 'progress' to the Congo. The Belgian Monarchy was clearly an important element in local imaginings of power.

A third reason why this error is so remarkable is that, elsewhere, Tshibumba got it right. The painting of the monument to Leopold II in Kinshasa (painting 27) carries a plaque on which we can read 'Monument Roi Leopold II'. The error in the *Histoire* shows that Tshibumba did not use his paintings as a source that could be 'quoted'. Here is a fragment of the transcribed conversations between Fabian and Tshibumba in which they comment on the painting (APS 1b):

> F: All right. Now this the Leopold
> T: It's the monument
> [. . .]
> F: Did Leopold have a name?
> T: Leopold?
> F: Did he have a nickname among the people?
> T: No, we know him only as *Leopold Deux*
> F: Leopold Deux?
> T: Yes. Before that he was Prince Leopold
> F: Prince Leopold?
> T: And then his father – or was it his grandfather – died, *Albert Premier* (Albert I). He replaced him as *Leo Deux*.

There is no confusion here between Leopold I and Leopold II. The king is Leopold *Deux*, not *Premier*. But there is confusion here about royal genealogy. Compare the fragment we gave earlier (from Fabian 1996: 64), where Tshibumba correctly said that Leopold III was the son of Albert I. In the conversation with Fabian, however, Albert I (1875–1934) becomes the father or grandfather of Leopold II. In the *Histoire*, Tshibumba also gets the transition from Leopold III to Baudoin factually right, but note the many hesitations surrounding the name 'Leopold III':

> 1955 la Belgique a un nouveau
> ROI à le personne de S.M. BAUDOIN Ier
> remplaçant son Pere ~~ALBE~~ LEOPOLD III
> ~~LEOPOLD III~~ demissionaire

Translation:

> In 1955 Belgium has a new
> King in the person of H.M. Baudoin I
> replacing his father ~~ALBE~~ LEOPOLD III
> ~~LEOPOLD III~~ who was resigning

We see traces here of a particular knowledge economy. Tshibumba has obviously been exposed to knowledge of the Belgian monarchy, and members of that monarchy, through their royal visits, had certainly acquired considerable notoriety among the Congolese. Factual accounts as well as mythologised ones circulated about them. Part of the myth was that image of the king as omnipotent and omniscient that we encountered in Yav's *Vocabulaire* as well as here.[3] The factual accounts must have included the genealogies connecting the different monarchs, some of which were clear, others more complex. The linear succession from Leopold I to Leopold II was followed by an indirect succession – Albert I was the nephew of Leopold II. Albert's son Leopold III was replaced as Regent by his brother Charles after the Second World War, and Leopold's son Baudoin became King in 1951. In Belgian school history, the brief Regency of Charles is often treated as a footnote; in Tshibumba's case it becomes an event worthy of inclusion in his painted history because of direct autobiographical reasons (see below). But note that Prince Charles is not mentioned in the written *Histoire*.

The relationship between Albert I and Leopold II, in contrast, is a detail that can fade in memory: a point of little significance. Remembering such insignificant details is a function of complex state apparatuses that sustain the reproduction of such details. Absence of such apparatuses – an efficient and democratic education system with a clear curriculum, but also mass media and other state propaganda instruments – allows historical 'facts' to shrink to their essence. In writing the *Histoire* years after having made his historical paintings, we see that Tshibumba remembers the name 'Leopold', but not whether it was Leopold *Premier* or *Deux*. It is a case of genuine historical confusion fixed in several repeated errors, produced over a period of time. It teaches us that while the same economy of knowledge informed all the genres covered by Tshibumba, the actual way in which the resources provided by that economy were converted into semiotic products can differ. Processes of cultural reproduction are not linear.

We see the connection between remembering and an apparatus that sustains the reproduction of memory when Tshibumba talks about Mobutu. The last page of the historical narrative in the *Histoire*, page 68, contains an almost formulaic statement about Mobutu's wedding:

> Le chef de l'Etat
> etait a compagné de son épouse
> MAMA-BOBI-LADAWA, son séconde
> épouse après la Mort de son première
> épouse MAMA-MOBUTU.
>   Son 2eme mariage a ete
> anoncé officiellement, le 1 MAI 1980
> a la suite, de la fête du TRAVAIL.

TSHIBUMBA THE HISTORIAN

Translation:

the Head of State
was accompanied by his spouse
Mama Bobi Ladawa, his second
spouse after the death of his first
spouse Mama Mobutu.
His second marriage was
officially announced on May 1, 1980
after the May Day celebrations.

This could have been directly copied from a formal communiqué by that new king of Zaire, Mobutu. Sometimes the sources are clear because such sources are abundantly present and compelling; in other instances the sources of knowledge have faded into the past and only exist as distant memories. More about this will be said below, because we have reached the issue of sources as resources here.

Sources

Recall how Marc Bloch emphasised that the collection and ordering of sources is crucial in the work of the historian. This requirement, I stressed, can only be satisfied where such sources are available and accessible, and it is clear that Tshibumba did not have much in the way of archives and libraries at his disposal. His *Histoire* needed to be constructed out of the materials at hand, and some of his sources are clearly identifiable, others not. The ambition of comprehensiveness implied in his project of national historiography faces a massive obstacle of sources, betraying the particular economy of knowledge in which he must be situated: one in which information circulates in a variety of shapes and formats, rumours and stories being among the most important channels for such information, and in which formal repositories of knowledge and information are not generally democratically distributed instruments. Let us begin by having a look at the recognisable sources. Since (with the *caveats* I expressed earlier) we can assume that the sources that informed his paintings and conversations also informed his writing, we can broaden the spectrum of our inquiry a bit and include sources we spot in all the genres performed by Tshibumba.

1 There is some influence of *official Belgian colonial history*, notably in the way in which Tshibumba discusses the Bakongo Kingdom, the early period of exploration, the campaign against Arab slave-traders, the Berlin Conference and so on. The whole sequence of description of the period until the 1950s is structured very much along the pattern of official Belgian colonial history. Tshibumba went to school in the heyday of the Belgian colonisation, the 1950s, and the impact of official Belgian schoolbook history is unmistakable.[4] Tshibumba not

SOURCES AS RESOURCES

only displays considerable enthusiasm in describing the adventures of Livingstone, Stanley and King Leopold – as we have seen earlier – but he also adopts the geopolitical perspective of the colonial rulers. Thus, King Leopold's campaign against the 'Arab slave-traders' ends in the liberation of Africa (page 21):

> et voilà l'Afrique noire est libre
> malgré leur lutte de chassé les Arabes
> un peu partout en Afrique-central.

Translation:

> and so black Africa is free
> in spite of their struggles the Arabs were chased
> a bit everywhere from Central Africa

In a conversation with Fabian (1996: 310), Tshibumba explicitly makes the connection between school history and his views on particular episodes in the history of his country:

> 'So we would sit by the fire in the evening with our parents [and he would say] "You see, in the old days [. . .], this is how our country used to be [. . .]". And then we entered school, and school also taught us how it used to be in the past [. . .], [our] ancestors, we had the Arabs, and how they treated us. And some told lies and some spoke the truth.'

The school histories were not always correct – Tshibumba knows that. The way in which the colonial Congo was organised is consequently described factually and in a detached way. Note the official voice in the next fragment, expressed in a long complex syntax (page 25):

> Gouverner directement par la Belgique
> à Bruxelle, d'un gouvernement réprèsenter
> par UN GOUVERNEUR-GENERAL à LEOPOLdville
> avec ces Réprèsentants dans 5 provinces du
> Congo Belge, puisque durant la colonie
> au Congo Belge, LEOPOLDville etait considerer
> comme 9^{em} provinc**es** de la Belgique.

Translation:

> Governed directly by Belgium
> from Brussels by a government represented
> by a Governor-General in Leopoldville
> with his representatives in 5 provinces

of Belgian Congo, because during the colonial
era in Belgian Congo, Leopoldville was considered
the 9th province of Belgium

Tshibumba here mentions the direct system of colonial rule (as opposed to 'indirect rule' in the British Empire) as well as the structure of governance in the Congo, and he does it in an accurate but hardly involved way. It is just a factual description of the colonial state infrastructure, as learned by colonial subjects in their primary education. This is how the colonisers described themselves to the colonised.

2 The colonised kicked back, however, and the *Histoire* contains many fragments where we hear an outspoken anti-colonial voice, distinctly critical of the colonial enterprise and probably derived from a range of *post-colonial political and historical sources*. They blend in with the colonial sources. The chronography of the colonial era is, as we saw, derived from Belgian colonial history. But the events get anti-colonial footnotes, as in the next example (page 19):

Le Roi des Belges satisfait
du Travail d'HENRI-Norton-STANLEY
a fait convoquer une conference INTE-
RNATIONAL à Berlin appelé
LA CONFERENCE de BERLIN
et cette conférènce avait une but
significatif, nom pour etudier l'Afrique
Central, mais pour eliminer nos pouvoir
Africains et leurs chefs

Translation:

The King of the Belgians, satisfied
of the work of Henry Morton Stanley
called for an international
conference in Berlin called
THE BERLIN CONFERENCE
and this conference had a significant
aim, not to study Central
Africa, but to eliminate our African
powers and their chiefs.

We see how Tshibumba starts from empathic images of the King, who is 'satisfied of the work of Henry Morton Stanley' and who organises the Berlin Conference of 1885. When he describes the purpose of that conference, however, Tshibumba slips into an anti-colonial perspective. The conference was not, as Leopold claimed, a merely scientific enterprise. It was in actual fact an instrument for colonial expropriation and oppression.

Remarkably given the devastating impact of that period on the African population, there are no such anti-colonial statements in the discussion of the Congo Free State. Leopold's private enterprise was, even by contemporaries, known as the most ruthlessly brutal example of colonial exploitation and in the anti-colonial struggle, the images of Africans being whipped by supervisors or having their hands cut off for not having produced enough rubber were powerful mobilising tools. Tshibumba's 'Colonie Belge' (painting 34, Fabian 1996: 68) does refer directly to this period: it is a genre piece in which we see an African stretched out on the ground with a soldier brandishing a whip towering over him, and a European official overlooking the punishment.

The anti-colonial perspective enters more clearly as soon as early anti-colonial rebellions emerge. Thus, Tshibumba describes Simon Kimbangu's predicament – thrown in prison until his death – and has it followed immediately by an episode in which protesting workers of the UMHK are brought into the company's football stadium and executed by the colonial army. He also describes the Batetela revolt, and the description of this event leads directly into the creation of the first anti-colonial political organisation, ABAKO (led by Kasavubu). The history of the anti-colonial political mobilisation is always described from the perspective of the Africans. The Belgian colonial authorities are systematically seen as opponents.

3 There is an influence of *Congolese mass media and popular culture*: a rather diffuse set of images, tropes and accounts derived from an apparently widespread body of messages and information disseminated in the Congo during the early years of independence. This source would inform most of the stories on the Congo Crisis, including the political events involving leading figures such as Kasavubu, Lumumba, Tshombe, Ileo, Kimba, Kalonji, Adula and others, as well as the rebellions of the mid-1960s. Some of the anti-colonial voices in his narrative must also have been borrowed from mass media in which the views of leading post-colonial politicians could be found. Such mass media appear as *national* sources, sources that often articulate an ideal of unity and condemn ethnic strife and separatism. Stories that bear the traces of such sources are clearly structured and precise. In an episode in which he describes the secession of Southern Kasai under 'Emperor' Albert Kalonji, we read the following account (pages 39–40):

> TSHINYAMA et NGALULA qui étaient
> du HAUT-KASAÏ ont renversé l'Empereur
> KALONJI par un coup d'Etat militaire
> et suprima le pouvoir Imperial au
> Sud-KASAÏ, et Ngalula devenait Gouve-
> rneur de la province du Sud-KASAÏ

sous l'autorité du governement du
central.

Translation:

Tshinyama and Ngalula who were
from Upper Kasai ousted Emperor
Kalonji with a military coup d'état
and terminated the imperial power in
Southern Kasai, and Ngalula became
governor of the province of Southern Kasai
under the authority of the central
government.

Tshinyama and Ngalula were both high officials in the government of Emperor Kalonji; the fact that they are mentioned here reflects Tshibumba's desire for precise detail as well as the availability of sources in which such details can be found. The absence of a moral condemnation here — the coup could also have been seen as an act of betrayal, for which at least one perpetrator was later generously rewarded — has to do with the fact that national unity is restored. The idea of unity runs through the story of the post-colonial troubles as a constant beat. Even a notorious separatist such as Moïse Tshombe is at times qualified as someone fighting for the unity of the country (page 41):

[. . .] et c'est
ainsi que TSHOMBE lutta a deux fronts
politique, pour LEOPOLDVillE l'UNITE
du CONGO et pour le CARTEL au KATA-
NGA toujour l'UNITE du Congo [. . .]

Translation:

[. . .] and it is
thus that Tshombe fought on two
political fronts, for Leopoldville the unity
of the Congo and for the Cartel in Katanga
still the unity of the Congo [. . .]

Such traces from national mass media are indirect; sometimes however, traces from media and popular culture are direct. Earlier, we also saw how the inscription on painting 86 ('Mobutu rolling up his sleeves', Fabian 1996: 157) bore the Lingala inscription 'Salongo Alinga Mosala', which was the title of a song by the immensely popular (and very strongly pro-Mobutu) musician Franco. We also know that Tshibumba used pictures he found in newspapers, magazines,

SOURCES AS RESOURCES

billboards and other places, and some of his paintings have a 'snapshot' quality (Fabian 1996: 263–5) – think of the 'photographic' qualities of his paintings of King Leopold II. The following fragment from APS 1b testifies to this use of photos as direct sources for his work. Fabian and Tshibumba are discussing painting 25 ('Simon Kimbangu in Court', Fabian 1996: 54):

> T. Mh mh. That's it. This is not [something I did] with all these [paintings]. Those I did by myself with the exception of the one about Kimbangu.
>
> [. . .]
> T: [The painting of] Kimbangu I took from this paper *Mwana Shaba*, right?
> F: Yes
> T: And there I wrote at the bottom that it was [a picture taken from a play] by Elebe Lisembe

The direct inspiration for the painting was a picture in a newspaper, of a scene in a theatre play on Kimbangu. Tshibumba read newspapers and comic strips, and he heard reports on the radio. He was integrated in the (very modest and fragmentary) media culture of the post-colonial Congo.

Related to this type of sources are *books*. In a conversation on painting 17, 'Bodson was killed by Msiri' (APS 1b), Tshibumba turns to the *History of Rwanda* by Abbé Alexis Kagame:

> T: Everything I am bringing to you was worked out while painting. I take a while to think, then I make a sketch, and there it is. In this particular painting, however, his particular pose I tried to reproduce from a book on the history of Rwanda. If you look at one particular place in that book you see two chiefs killing each other, right?
> F: we have it, we have that book here
> T: mh mh. That's where I took it from.
> F: I see
> T: Yes I copied that pose, but . . .
> F: Msiri's pose?
> T: Yes only Msiri's. Yes I think that is correct
> F: I see
>
> [. . .]
> F: Mh mh. Ah yes, [so] this is the History of Rwanda. You read it? You read it?
>
> [. . .]
> T: I read it, I read the whole book.

TSHIBUMBA THE HISTORIAN

The connection between the book and the historiographic work, however, is marked as exceptional. Normally, his own mind is the main source for his history – that is, his memory.

4 An easily identifiable source is *official Mobutist propaganda*, probably performed by MPR sections in Tshibumba's environment and, of course, broadcast by the media. It is illustrative of the hegemony organised by MPR over many years that this kind of vision of Zaire penetrated Tshibumba's discourse on history. Note that Tshibumba was aware of the fact that some of what he did in the way of historiography was locally contestable. He made particular historical statements *specifically* because his customers were non-Congolese. And the *Histoire* was written and then sent to Jewsiwiecki, it was not a document for local circulation. He could have deviated from official state propaganda if such discourses were around and would fit his perspective. The fact that he didn't suggests a very powerful hegemony of MPR propaganda.

There is a shift in general footing and framing as soon as Tshibumba embarks on the Mobutu period in his history – a phenomenon noticeable both in the written *Histoire* and in the sequence of paintings presented to Fabian. In some paintings, Tshibumba only represents symbols of Mobutism and '*authenticité*': slogans, emblems, political principles. Similarly, when writing on the Mobutist period, a striking degree of distance and reverence can be distinguished. I have already mentioned the way in which he wrote about Mobutu's second marriage – a copy, it seemed, of officially broadcast announcements – and there is quite a bit more. Tshibumba begins his account of the Mobutu era with another statement that sounds as though it has been copied from official accounts (page 51):

> Le GÈNÈRAL MOBUTU alors lieutenant-
> GEneral, commandant en chef de l'A.N.C.[5]
> **assisté du colonel MULAMBA-LEONARD**
>   **ont a** pris le pouvoir sous le haut patronage
> du Haut commandement Militaire.

> *Translation:*

> General Mobutu then Lieutenant-
> General, commander-in-chief of the ANC
> **assisted by Colonel Mulamba-Leonard**
>   **have** has taken power under the high authority
> of the Military High Command.

Mobutu's brutal coup of 1965 is here formulated as a legitimate intervention on behalf of the Military High Command (of which General – later Field Marshal – Mobutu was of course the chairman). A chronicle is given of many of

152

SOURCES AS RESOURCES

Mobutu's decisions and interventions in social and political life. All of them are reported in a quasi-official voice and with care for detail and accuracy. In the fragment above, we saw how Tshibumba added 'assisted by Colonel Mulumba-Leonard' to the sentence, changing the verb from singular to plural. In the following fragment, we see how he adds the precise date of the event in another account of Mobutu's antics (which is, by the way, evidence of the fact that Tshibumba reread, edited and corrected his text afterwards):

à <u>Kinkole</u> à quelques Kilometrès de
LEOPOLDVILLE le President Mobutu annonça
le 20 MAI 67 la creation du nouveau Parti cette fois çi
politique, le M.P.R. parti unique

Translation:

In Kinkole, a few kilometers from
Leopoldville, President Mobutu announced
on MAY 20, 67 the creation of a new party this time
political, the MPR, single party

The 'Zairianisation' campaign of 1971 is described in detail. Tshibumba lists the different symbolic name changes, again attending to detail and comprehensiveness. Lists and accurate dates are recurrent stylistic features of the description of Mobutu's reign, and all of this is done in the most factual and detached style. Significantly, all the chapter titles of the period after 1965 are dates: Mobutu's era is structured as a chronicle, and official voices dominate in its contents. Tshibumba adopts even the official emotions that surround events (page 61):

Le <u>22.11.1977</u>
en plein election Presidentiel et
legislative et des ZONES-URBAINES la
Radio a anoncé la mort du regrettée
MAMA-MOBUTU epouse du Chef de l'Etat
décédé en europe

Translation:

On 22.11.1977
in the middle of the presidential and
parliamentary elections and of the Urban Zones
the radio announced the death of the deplored
MAMA-MOBUTU, spouse of the Head of State
passed away in Europe

153

TSHIBUMBA THE HISTORIAN

Mobutu's 'spouse' is 'deplored' because she 'passed away' in Europe. The whole tone and style of this fragment is that of official state discourse – of the radio. Not only Mobutu's emotional state but his political interpretations as well are echoed. We have already seen that Tshibumba inscribed a fragment from one of Mobutu's speeches on painting 19, 'Beginning of the Belgian Colony' (Fabian 1996: 45). When he arrives at the Shaba crises of the late 1970s, the defensive geopolitical frame invoked by the Zairian dictator is copied as well (page 60):

> L'Agression dit coalision RUSSO-CUBAINES
> a eté declare, soulevement Général
> et le President Mobutu a fait appel aux
> pays d'Ami du ZAÏRE.

Translation:

> The aggression of the Russian-Cuban coalition
> has been declared, general mobilisation
> and President Mobutu has made an appeal to
> the countries that are friends of Zaire.

And Tshibumba ends his *Histoire* with a Mobutist slogan (page 73):

> Sans un Guide comme
> MOBUTU, pas de ZAIRE UNIT et
> son ARMEE.

Translation:

> Without a guide like
> Mobutu, no united Zaire and
> its/his army

There is an interesting similarity between this distancing, factual and conspicuously neutral reporting style in the *Histoire*, and the paintings of Mobutist symbols and emblems. In both genres, Tshibumba detaches himself from his topic. The involvement and identification we have seen in other parts of the *Histoire* (and other parts of the painted history) is all but absent when Mobutu's reign is reached, and Tshibumba prudently copies the dominant state rhetoric and symbolic currency. He does this factually and accurately, emphasising chronology and the official – that is, uncontroversial – version of events. There is little in the way of explicit reflection in these parts of the *Histoire*. There may be irony, of course, but it is hard to find overt traces of it. The bedrock of irony, detachment, is there, and it dominates the narrative.

SOURCES AS RESOURCES

5 Indisputably the most important source is *Tshibumba's own historical experience.* We will see below that this experience is strongly 'placed': it is tied to Katanga and Kasai, and these places function as an epistemic and affective filter on history (see also the essays in Jewsiwiecki, ed. 1999). More generally, one can say that Tshibumba's own life is the organising principle for the way in which he gets informed. He often emphasises in the conversations with Fabian that he himself had 'thoughts' and that his historical paintings reflected things he himself had constructed in his mind.

Let us first consider the immediate effects of a life trajectory on historical perspective. We see direct traces of autobiography when he discusses the paintings. A first trace, already mentioned, is the painting of the royal visit of Prince Charles in 1947. As we know, 1947 is Tshibumba's birth year, and the visit of Prince Charles is accompanied by a weird apocryphal story that was summarised in an inscription on the painting: 'All the children born in 1947 should have an eye ripped out' (Fabian 1996: 64). The story told by Tshibumba (and presented by Fabian next to the painting) is as follows. Prince Charles had 'a deformity in one of his eyes'. When he arrived in the Congo, he announced (and Tshibumba again uses direct speech here): 'To mark my trip to the Congo, the order should be given that every child born in 1947 [. . .] should be picked up and should have one eye removed'. The Regent also decreed that, while he took a nap, all African men should have their hair cut. Fortunately, the Belgian parliament intervened on behalf of the men and boys, recalled the orders given by the Prince, and nothing came of it. We see here, apart from another instance of the image of the king as omnipotent (and of Prince Charles as somewhat eccentric, which he surely was), the influence of rumour and gossip as a mass medium in Tshibumba's world. It is easy to imagine that such stories of a weird royal visitor who threatens the well-being of the Congolese newborns could spread like brushfire, and be transformed years later into a story told to a child about the circumstances of his birth. It becomes a story of Tshibumba's origins with distinct Biblical undertones.

A second trace of autobiography can be found in the story accompanying painting 32, 'King Baudoin visits the Congo' (page 66). This very spectacular and widely mediatised visit took place in 1955. Tshibumba was 'a first-grader in elementary school', and Baudoin visited Jadotville (Likasi), the town where Tshibumba lived. Tshibumba recalls:

> And they put a flag in my hand and I kept cheering him. I saw him coming in a black car, and when he arrived he got out in front of the church.

We get a glimpse here of the propaganda techniques surrounding big events such as the royal visits: school children were given small flags and served as a cheering audience for the king. The connection between these events and his own life creates strong memories in Tshibumba, and his paintings and (even more so) the conversations with Fabian contain several direct links between life experience and visions of history. Note, however, that one will look in vain for such clear autobiographical traces in the *Histoire*. They are there, but at a more general level and more tacit, as assumptions that create particular stances and orientations towards historical events.

The *Histoire*, however, is replete with traces of Tshibumba's own experience in a wider sense. Tshibumba is the mediator for the information he gets from all of these sources. This explains the ways in which information is represented together with a particular moral or epistemic stance: sometimes he writes in a very detached style, sometimes in a very involved one. He clearly finds particular people (Lumumba, for instance) more sympathetic than others (Kalonji, for instance), and manifestly wants to stay away from judgmental comments on certain people or events (on Mobutu, for instance). He is also a living subject in an environment where rumours, stories and gossip circulate. I already pointed to this in relation to the painting on Prince Charles' visit. The story about Charles' order to cut out an eye from every child born in 1947 is a myth that reflects images of the colonial system and of the unrestricted powers of the King.

I also already mentioned (in footnote 3 to this chapter) the curious moment in a conversation with Fabian (APS 1b), where Tshibumba says about Leopold II that 'up to this day there is the suspicion that he was also Hemptinne'. The story of the King being an illegitimate child (or father, see footnote 6 below) of the Bishop is again a myth that reflects images of power – the power of the Bishop this time. De Hemptinne was born in 1876, more than thirty years later than Leopold, and died in 1958. In Tshibumba's lifetime, de Hemptinne must have existed mainly in the stories of older people. The man arrived in Katanga in 1910 as a Benedictine missionary and became one of the most ardent defenders of the necessity of religious work in the colonial system.[6] His views of religion, missionary work and colonisation were, mildly put, conservative; those he held of Africans were, equally mildly put, racist. He was ordained Bishop of Katanga in 1932 and was, as such, one of the most influential and powerful people in the region and a reliable ally of the colonial authorities and the industrial powers there. He had a long white beard, and photographs of the Bishop show a *prima facie* similarity with those of King Leopold. Images of power merged with visual similarities here, and in the eyes of local people, de Hemptinne was a synonym for oppressive colonial power. Thus, when Tshibumba narrates an incident dated 1941 in which protesting UMHK workers are shot in the football stadium in Elisabethville, we read (page 28):

le gouverneur d'Alors: Mr MARRONS
en présènce de MONSEIGNEUR-DEHPTINE
on les a fait venir au stade de
FOOTBAL de l'U.M.H.K. a ELISABETville

SOURCES AS RESOURCES

Translation:

the governor of that time, Mr Marrons
in the presence of Monseigneur de Hemptinne
they made them come into the
football stadium of the UMHK in Elisabethville

The 'Holy Trinity' of the Belgian Colonial system is united in this fragment: the State (the governor), the Church (Mgr de Hemptinne) and business (the UMHK).

Stories of Mgr de Hemptinne may have flourished more widely in Katanga than, for instance, in Kinshasa. The proximity of events prompts intense circulation of rumours and gossip, often grounded in the authority of (presumed) eye witnesses. This also goes for events such as the speech of Governor-General Léon Pétillon in Likasi (Jadotville). Pétillon was Governor-General of the Congo from 1952 until 1958, and the incident occurred in 1955, when Tshibumba was of a very tender age. Even if the thing happened in his home town, it is very unlikely that Tshibumba had first-hand knowledge of the revolt of the colonial settlers and of the tomatoes thrown at Pétillon's head. It was a local event, but one in which the public facade of colonialism was changed – whites were fighting among each other. This was a typical 'hidden transcript' (Scott 1990), something that probably caused quite a bit of hushed-up tension in the settler community, and was picked up by Africans but could only circulate as whispered rumours: a medium the power and credibility of which are well known.

Tshibumba is fully integrated in his environment; he is a subject among subjects placed in a specific sub-elite position in a social and political system. It is from that point that he looks at events, listens to stories, perceives the reports in the media, and transforms them into his own 'thoughts' and, later, into versions of his history. The different sources identified here offer us a glimpse of this economy of information, which seems to dominate the environment in which Tshibumba works. It is an economy dominated by specific voices at specific times: the colonial school authorities in one period of his life, Congolese official history and the media later, Mobutist propaganda still later. The sources are thus anchored autobiographically, with particular sources dominating stages of his life and – consequently – of his version of history. Interwoven through all this is Tshibumba's own experience as a Katangese subject with a keen interest in all these matters.

The locus of history: Katanga

Bourdieu never failed to remind us of the fact that there is no knowledge which is not inflected by someone's position in the world. Sometimes, this position needs to be understood literally, as a place from where one constructs knowledge. The knowledge constructed in the *Histoire* will display traces of its locus of production, because Tshibumba does not 'move around' in his history: he

157

writes it from Katanga, from the place where he lives. He expresses an interest in what happens in his home region and in the predicament of his ethnic group, the Luba, a group living largely in the Katanga and Kasai regions.

The storyline and survey of chapters given earlier already indicate this. Tshibumba writes more and more detailed stories on events in Katanga and the neighbouring province of Kasai (his birthplace). In his survey of the pre-colonial period, he provides some information on the Kongo Kingdom (Lower Congo), the Baluba (Kasai and Katanga) and Bakuba kingdoms (Kasai). Then two chapters on kingdoms from other parts of the country are initiated but left blank: one on the Mongo (Equatorial region) and on the Bampende (Bandundu region). Finally, he addresses two more Katanga–Kasai kingdoms, that of the Baluba-Shankadi and that of the Lunda.

The presence of two empty chapters is telling (see figure 7.1). The two kingdoms he mentions (of the Bampende and the Mongo) were both situated in areas thousands of kilometres away. Tshibumba knows that these kingdoms have existed, and that their existence is important enough to deserve being mentioned in his survey of the pre-colonial Congo. But he clearly cannot remember anything about these kingdoms: no historic leaders or events, no dates or periods, no specific places. The contrast with his detailed descriptions of kingdoms in the Katanga–Kasai area is huge. We probably see various forces at work here. There is the awareness that the genre compels him to be comprehensive, which prompts him to mention both kingdoms. The kingdoms were probably known to him from school history: things he heard many years before and did not, perhaps, find overly informative at the time. Given the distance between his home region and the location of these two historic kingdoms, stories about them may not have existed beyond the walls of the school, and this may be a contrast with the kingdoms of Katanga and Shaba about which he appears to know (or have remembered) quite a bit more than just school history.

This becomes clear when Tshibumba describes the reign of Msiri, the king of Katanga. Observe the amount of detail and historical relocation going on in the following passage on Msiri (page 21):

> celui-ci n'est pas originaire du KATANGA
> aujourd'hui (SHABA) mais c'est un BURUNDAIS
> chassé du Burundi après être conquit
> et considerait comme criminel est
> revenu demandé réfuge chez: KATANGA
> , on l'a confié une partie de la terre
> aujourd'hui BUNKEYA

Translation:

> this one was not originally from Katanga
> now (Shaba) but he's a Burundese

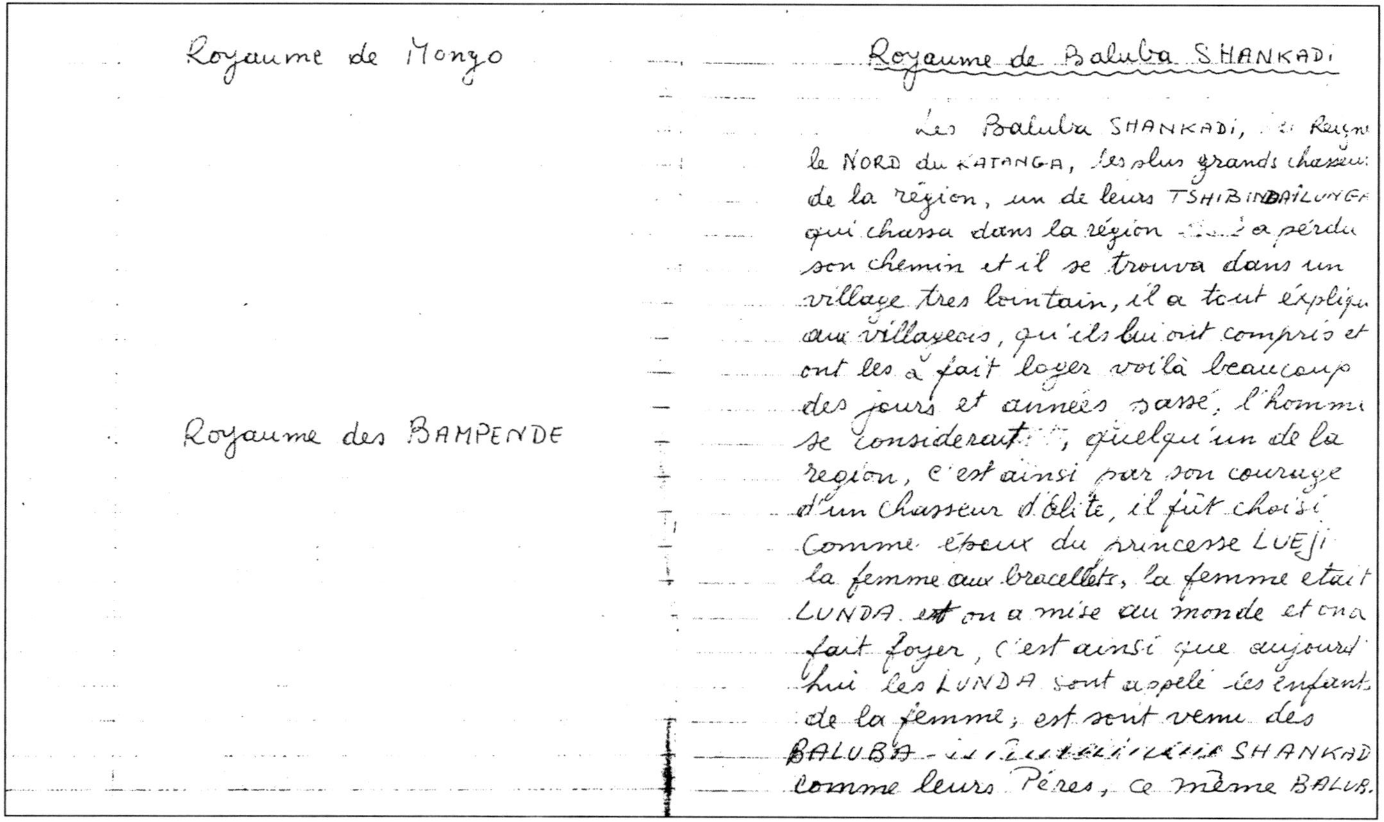

Royaume de Mongo   <u>Royaume de Baluba SHANKADI</u>

    Les Baluba SHANKADI, qui Regne
le NORD du KATANGA, les plus grands chasseurs
de la région, un de leurs TSHIBINDAILUNGA
qui chassa dans la région s'a perdu
son chemin et il se trouva dans un
village très lointain, il a tout expliqué
aux villageois, qu'ils lui ont compris et
ont les à fait loger voilà beaucoup
des jours et années passé, l'homme
se considerant, quelqu'un de la
region, c'est ainsi par son couruge
d'un chasseur d'élite, il fût choisi
comme époux du princesse LUEJI
la femme aux bracellets, la femme était
LUNDA. est on a mise au monde et on a
fait foyer, c'est ainsi que aujourd'
hui les LUNDA sont apelé les enfants
de la femme, est sont venu des
BALUBA ... SHANKADI
comme leurs Pères, ce même BALUB.

Royaume des BAMPENDE

Figure 7.1 The empty chapters, pages 10–11 of the *Histoire*

TSHIBUMBA THE HISTORIAN

chased from Burundi after having been caught
and considered a criminal, he
returned to ask asylum with Katanga
they gave him a part of the land
now Bunkeya

Tshibumba relocates Msiri's itinerary in the contemporary topography of his region. The description of the episode of Msiri is lively and engaged. Tshibumba quotes from the words spoken by Chief Katanga to Msiri on his death bed (page 22):

[. . .] je te confie mon pouvoir
provisoirement en attendant que
mon fils soit une personne mûr
après quoi tu vas lui restituer
son pouvoir, etant donné que
je n'ai pas des enfants d'autre.

Translation:

[. . .] I hand you my power
provisionally until my
son has become a mature person
after which you will return his
power to him, given that I
don't have other children.

We are familiar with the remainder of the story: after Chief Katanga's death, 'M'siri devient malin' ('Msiri becomes shrewd', page 22); he kills the son he was supposed to guard and becomes king. That makes him, in Tshibumba's eyes, 'le chef le plus criminel' ('the most criminal chief', page 22). Needless to say, there is no record of Chief Katanga's final words; they existed as local stories about pre-colonial Katanga and, in this particular form, they are the product of Tshibumba's imaginative powers.

The Katangese bias is also manifest when the early colonisation period is treated. Tshibumba moves quickly from the proclamation of the Free State to immigration by white South Africans in Katanga, the creation of the UMHK and industrialisation in Katanga and the role of the Bishop of Elisabethville, the formidable Mgr de Hemptinne. He mentions the workers' strike at the UMHK in 1941 and the way in which this strike was crushed by the Bishop and the Governor of Katanga. In the section on the First Republic and the Congo Crisis, Tshibumba pays a lot of attention to Kalonji's Baluba Empire in the Southern Kasai (and provides a sketch of the flag in the margins of the text) and to ethnic struggles caused by this secession. Evidently, the Katangese seces-

SOURCES AS RESOURCES

sion under Tshombe is also discussed and a sketch of the new Katangese flag is given. The Shaba Wars of the late 1970s are discussed at great length, and the story ends with a visit to Katanga by Mobutu and his second wife. Finally, in the postscript, Tshibumba (speculatively, see above) discusses 'tribalism', focusing strongly on the situation in Katanga. So Katanga prevails, it is the window through which Tshibumba perceives his country. He narrates the history of the Congo as it occurred to a man in Katanga. The country is his unit of narration, but the material entering the narrative is geographically and experientially 'placed'.

Remarkably, this local footing abruptly changes as soon as Mobutu enters the story. Tshibumba still comments extensively on events in Katanga, but the discussions of the Second and Third Republics are not so much written 'from Katanga' as presented from a 'national' point of view. The point from which history is now written is Kinshasa, not Lubumbashi. We have seen earlier, however, that Tshibumba's treatment of the Mobutu era is intriguingly detached. None of the empathy he has when he talks about the local kingdoms of the Luba, about Stanley or Leopold, or about Chief Katanga, Msiri and later Lumumba can be found. The Mobutu period is caught in a 'national' perspective, but this perspective reflects a hegemony, a view from above. It is a hand-me-down from the official MPR discourses in which Mobutu's main claim to power rested on the fact that he brought 'unity' and 'peace' to the country. It is, in other words, a borrowed or imposed viewpoint.

Let us now briefly return to what Fabian (1996: 240) said about Tshibumba, that 'his conception of the history of Zaire, indeed his political position, was decidedly national, not regional'. Looking at the collection of paintings discussed by Fabian, this interpretation is plausible: although a lot of attention goes to Katangese or Kasai topics (Msiri, Kalonji, air raids on Lubumbashi, ethnic struggles, Tshombe, massacres in Katanga), there is more that speaks to 'Zaire' as a unit of reflection and imagination. Note, however, the figures: of the 101 paintings in the collections, 40 are either situated in Katanga (the meeting of Stanley and Livingstone, for example, is set in Katanga, and emphasis is given to the fact that Lumumba's assassination took place in Katanga) or treat 'Katangese' topics such as Tshombe. And of the remaining 61 paintings, 12 treat Mobutu, the MPR or Mobutist political principles. Most of these Mobutist paintings are not anecdotal but abstract: they show a monument, Mobutist emblems, or general developments such as the Zairianisation of the economy.

So whereas Tshibumba's personal ambitions may have been situated at a 'national' level – speaking to the people of Zaire – the way in which he actually performs this bespeaks deep situatedness as a Katangese subject. Katanga is an epistemic and affective filter on what he finds in the variety of sources we reviewed here.

Tshibumba's voices

I concluded the previous chapter by describing Tshibumba's voice as a disciplined voice. His choice of a monoglossic French code and of an austere, orthodox aesthetics of writing betrayed an attempt to write *as a historian*. The writing itself needed to be done in such a way that all the indexicals were in place: indexicals of *gravitas*, factuality and precision. He had imposed upon himself a particular regime of textuality which, given the potentially vast range of other resources of visualisation he could mobilise, was seriously constraining. But he saw it as an indispensable tool for writing history.

The constraints are even more outspoken when we look back on the way in which he handles that other crucial element of writing history: access to sources and a method of sifting and critically reviewing sources of historical information. The knowledge economy of which he shows traces in his *Histoire* is that of a sub-elite man from Katanga. He is integrated in the modest media and culture economy of his time and place, as well as in circuits of stories, rumours and gossip. He has also been exposed to the kind of information contained in colonial schoolbooks as well as some post-colonial sources on politics and history, and, since 1965, he has been bombarded with official messages from Mobutu and his MPR. All of this proceeded in Katanga, and the lens through which he looks at the Congo is that of a man living his community life in Katanga.

There is no single body of sources that dominates the account: Tshibumba did not have a complete and finished master plan on the history of the Congo, a skeleton around which he could put the tissue of information he culled from this variety of sources. He could, for instance, have used one history book as a skeleton structure for the *Histoire*, adding detail and elaboration to the structure he adopted from it. We know that he read books such as the *History of Rwanda* by Kagame, and such books could have become models to be copied. There is no evidence whatsoever of such a master text, or of a single dominant source from which he could draw his historical narratives. There is no evidence of a clear and rigorously followed 'book plan' either – we have seen enough features that testify to that. In that sense, he is not an 'autodidact' who could apply fully developed existing models to his own enterprise. Such a self-teaching process requires resources and skills he did not possess and could not acquire.

The result is a thoroughly polyphonic complex in which everything is used that he can possibly use, from relatively reliable factual sources (such as the colonial schoolbooks on the governance structure of the colony) to very doubtful local lore such as that on de Hemptinne. Tshibumba uses his disciplined genre writing to produce dense mixtures of various sources. They sometimes occur in one statement – recall the example in which he comments on the Berlin Conference:

> et cette conférènce avait une but
> significatif, nom pour etudier l'Afrique
> Central, <u>mais pour eliminer nos pouvoir</u>
> <u>Africains et leurs chefs</u>

SOURCES AS RESOURCES

Translation:

and this conference had a significant
aim, not to study Central
Africa, <u>but to eliminate our African
powers and their chiefs.</u>

Consider also the following one. Tshibumba again refers to King Baudoin's decision to send Pétillon with the message that the settlers should abandon their racism against the Africans (page 30):

[. . .] afin que les NOIRS
soit permis, dans des HOTELS, BARS
et RESTAURANTS dans leurs pays le Congo
et qu'on puisse se marier noirs et
Blancs, <u>afin de masqué aux noirs</u>
<u>l'idée de l'Independance</u>

Translation:

[. . .] so that blacks
would be allowed in hotels, bars
and restaurants in their country Congo
and that blacks and whites
could marry each other, <u>in order to mask</u>
<u>the idea of independence to the blacks</u>

The text slips from positive to negative, from a summary of Baudoin's words – the colonial voice – to an imputation of his intentions – the anti-colonial voice. The slippage is marked by underlining in the fragment, and the *Histoire* contains numerous examples in which we see such slippage from one voice into another, concentrated in the period of the colonial state and the early post-colonial troubles. Clarity comes with power. The text is only monovocal when it deals with Mobutu – a ruler not remembered as a lover of dissidence. There, Tshibumba submits to the absolute and totalising clarity of the official version of events, even if such events – the Shaba wars of the late 1970s, for instance – are likely to have had a deep impact on his personal life. Even if Tshibumba had other sources available – stories, rumours, pamphlets from the rebels, perhaps even local radio broadcasts – that could cast a different light on these events, he plays it safe and sticks to what comes from Kinshasa.

We should not reduce Tshibumba to a passive user or consumer of available information. We have seen plenty of evidence of the way in which the information he gives is shot through with moral and political commentary, and how he shows sympathy and antipathy for figures and incidents. He *voices* his sources,

163

he adds his own emotive and epistemic stances to them. And he knows that some of his sources are more reliable than others. Recall his comment on colonial schoolbooks: '[a]nd some told lies and some spoke the truth' (Fabian 1996: 310). He is aware that sources need to be treated critically, and we will see in the next chapter that he spends time reflecting on issues of methodology. The trouble is, however, the availability and accessibility of sufficient, and sufficiently reliable sources. In a knowledge economy such as the one that characterises his position in society, access to such sources is severely restricted. Tshibumba does not live in a place – physically, socially and culturally – where he can get to such sources, and he consequently needs to manufacture his *Histoire* out of grassroots materials: the things almost anyone in his position could get access to. He did not live in a society which, in Marc Bloch's words quoted at the outset, had begun 'to organise a rational self-knowledge by controlling its records'. His writing was, in fact, a rare moment in which such a record was created.

8

THE GRASSROOTS
HISTORIAN'S CRAFT

Tshibumba's historiographic methodology

I believe we have collected evidence in the two previous chapters of the particular situatedness of Tshibumba's writing. Both in terms of writing skills, genre awareness, and access to sources, the *Histoire* is a deeply situated document, placed, so to speak, in a sub-elite social space in Katanga. The code he uses, his ortho-graphic effort, and the way in which he organises and reviews the information that enters into his *Histoire*: all these things must be seen as determined by the particular position that Tshibumba occupies as a subject. They are defined by that position, and what we have learned so far all points towards one conclusion: he was not in a position to write a history of his country, at least not one that satisfied the criteria of what historians would understand by 'history'.

Then why did he *write* one? Why did he make this tremendous effort of carefully and thoughtfully writing a 73-page document? Why, in sum, did someone who had so brilliantly painted historical stories turn to an unwilling medium such as formal writing? The answer, I believe, must be sought in the remarkable preamble that fills the first pages of the *Histoire* (pages 1–5) and in the brief postscript with which he concludes his text (pages 71–3). We have so far mainly concentrated our effort on the main body of his text, the historical narrative. But that narrative was sandwiched between two more peripheral parts, a preamble and a postscript. There is a lot to be found there. In these peripheral texts, Tshibumba makes important methodological remarks. Both parts are pieces of meta-historiography, a set of comments on how to conceive of and write history. They deserve close examination.

The preamble opens with a title and an identification of the author, place and time of the production of the *Histoire* (page 1):

> L histoire du Zaïre
> Ecrit par un ZAÏROIS aux années 1980
> et cela au ZAÏRE dans la Region du SHABA
> à LUbUMBASHI. (TSHIBUMBA. K.M.)

TSHIBUMBA THE HISTORIAN

Translation:

The history of Zaire
Written by a ZAIRIAN in the years 1980
And this in ZAIRE in the region of SHABA
In LUbUMBASHI (TSHIBUMBA K.M.)

Immediately following this formal opening, he produces what is in my view the conclusive argument in favour of *writing*: Zairian history should be written by Zairians. As an authority, he (anachronistically) quotes his political favourite Lumumba (page 1):

Tous pays a son histoire, je
crois que chaque chose a son histoire aussi,
Lumumba, Emery Patrice l'a dit:
"L'histoire du ZAÏRE sera écrite par un
ZAÏROIS".

Translation:

Every country has its history, I
believe that every thing has its history as well,
Lumumba, Emery Patrice has said it:
'The history of ZAIRE will be written by a
ZAIRIAN'

He will elaborate this argument at length, beginning by identifying an obstacle: Africans did not know how to write. Consequently, the history of the Congo 'est mal écrite' ('is poorly written', page 1) by Europeans and later by Africans with specific interests in mind. This, to Tshibumba, is a problem and a threat (page 3):

Mais cela est une erreur très
grave pour l'avenir de ce grand pays,
un poison pour nos futurs historiens
pourquoi pas, pour nos enfants.

Translation:

But this is a very serious
mistake for the future of this great country,
a poison for our future historians
why not, for our children

THE GRASSROOTS HISTORIAN'S CRAFT

Tshibumba then embarks on a discussion of 'errors' in history, starting with examples from the Bible: the fact that Adam and Eve are presented as whites, not as blacks, and the story of Noah's son Cham in which the origin of the black races is located. Tshibumba sees these biblical stories as historical frauds with a massive influence on Africa (page 4):

> Voilà ce qui prouve déjà que
> l'histoire en Afrique était fort falcifiée
> **pe**nsée et même truquée.

Translation:

> See what already proves that
> The history in Africa was strongly falsified
> Thought and even forged

These problems persisted after the Africans had acquired literacy. Even then, history was dominated by 'ASSISTANTS des MERCENAIRES même des MISSIONAIRES' ('assistants mercenaries even missionaries', page 4) who had 'too much complicated' the history of Zaire. Examples of this are the multiple existing versions of the assassination of Lumumba. As an aside, he remarks that the situation is not better in Europe, where there are different opinions on Adolf Hitler's death. We see here a kind of historical–critical awareness, one that affirms the existence of different versions of events and tries to find a balanced appraisal of them (pages 4–5):

> Cas LUMUMBA par Exemple
> celà devient aujourd'hui un secret de l'Etat
> plus personne ne vous dira la verité
> de sa mort
> – d'autre: Lumumba est mort au SHABA
> (KATANGA) tué par un français BOB-DENARD
> – d'autre: Lumumba est mort trempé
> dans l'acide SULFURIQUE de U.M.H.K.
> aujourd'hui GECAMINES
> – d'autre: Lumumba est mort au KATANGA
> tué par MUNONGO-Godefroid alors MINISTRE
> KATANGAIS de l'Interieur de ses propres mains

Translation:

> The case of Lumumba for example
> it becomes these days a state secret
> no one will tell you the truth

anmyore of his death
– others: Lumumba died in Shaba
(Katanga) killed by a Frenchman Bob Denard
– others: Lumumba died soaked
in sulphuric acid from the UMHK
nowadays Gecamines
– others: Lumumba died in Katanga
killed by Munongo Godefroid then Katangese
Minister of the Interior with his own hands.

The issue of sources is obvious here: given the absence of a publicly available historical 'truth' – those who know, won't tell – all sorts of contradictory stories circulate on the assassination of Lumumba.[1] Some are manifestly wrong (the involvement of the legendary mercenary and *putain de l'impérialisme* Bob Denard, for instance), while one can only be astonished by the level of accuracy of others: Lumumba's corpse was indeed put in a bath of acid, and Munongo was indeed involved in the assassination.[2] The big question is, however: how to differentiate between truth and fiction, between reliable stories and unreliable ones.

Tshibumba does not answer the question, but he describes and metapragmatically situates his own effort (page 5):

Moi aussi qui ai écrit cette
histoire du **Congolais** j'aimerais tracer
mes lignes historiques sans préciser
les date et des mois xx xxx xxxxxx par fautes
des mémoires pour n'est pas semer
des confusions et pour prouver que nos
ancêtre dans leur existence ne savaient
pas lire ni écrire, mais sauf chez les
Bampende et les Bakuba qui nous ont
laissé quelques objets d'Arts, tel que
des MASQUES, des STATUES et CANES.
Et divers, mais qui ne parles a au**cu**n
point l'histoire du Zaïre.

Translation:

Me too who has written this
history of the Congolese I'd like to trace
my historical patterns without specifying
the dates and the months xx xxx xxxxx because of failures
of memory not to create
confusions and to demonstrate that our
ancestors in their existence didn't know

168

THE GRASSROOTS HISTORIAN'S CRAFT

how to read and write, but except for the
Bampende and the Bakuba who left us
some objects of Art, such as
MASKS STATUES and STICKS.
And others, but who do not talk
anywhere [about] the history of Zaire

So Tshibumba intends to *clarify*, he wants to help in avoiding more *confusion* on the history of Zaire. The existence of various different and contradictory stories is what causes confusion; there must be a clear and authoritative version. He also wants to fill a blank: hitherto, Africans have left no documents on history, with the exception of some groups whose sculptures can be seen as informing history. And as he mentioned before: it is essential that a Congolese writes the history of the Congo. It is a matter of bias and perspective: the right bias produces the truthful and authoritative version of history, the wrong bias is what made history into a problem. Tshibumba underscores the importance of *writing* in the larger problem: Africans have been voiceless when it came to articulating their own history. Consequently, their history was within the realm of the whites; the main reason for this is illiteracy, and the main result is confusion. The remedy is a *written historiography*.

We now know why Tshibumba wants to write a history: *he attributes something special to writing*, something that transcends the level of popularly circulating stories and that creates an authoritative record. If it is done by a Congolese, and if it is done well, such a record will be created and it would solve a major problem for the Congolese people. The carved objects of the ancestors, even though they represent cultural achievement of the highest order, are not sufficient. History needs to be written.

How? He is helpful in this respect too. The main requirement for historiography is *an orientation to the past*. History, as a neutral, unbiased and literate discourse, needs to be a story of past events; one cannot speak as a historian on the present or on the future. We can see this from the brief postscript (pages 71–3) where Tshibumba explicitly opposes 'history' versus the future and the present (page 73):

Ce que l'Historien ne parler
pas cette fois-ci de l'Histoire mais
de l'Avenir et de ce qui existe actuellem
ent

Translation:

What the historian does not
speak this time of History but of
the Future and of that which exists
nowadays

The historian is Tshibumba, of course, and the fact that he does not speak now on the past but on the future and the present is explicitly mentioned: readers must know that these words are of a different order. The postscript, in general, is produced on a very different footing: 'l'Historien, peu nous proposer quelques lignes de:' ('The Historian can propose to us some lines on:', page 71). This is no longer the factual declarative and confident mode of narration which dominates the *Histoire*, but a more speculative, putative set of reflections on what will or may happen in the Congo. The past can be told objectively, the future is a conjecture by the historian – an interesting set of generic aspirations mapped onto epistemic modes and semantic domains. He clearly marks his postscript as a different text, produced now by someone who has stepped out of the disciplined pose of a historian. It is literally a different text as well. He puts his signature under the historical narrative on page 68; the postscript is signed again on page 73. There is a momentous genre break reminiscent of Julien's shift from historical narrative to 'letter', in which more general issues could be addressed. We will come back to this later.

In the postscript, we also come to understand the *purpose* of Tshibumba's written *Histoire*. As we have seen, he writes it in order to eradicate the confusion that now dominates the history of his country. The postscript is completely devoted to what he now perceives to be the most pressing problem in his country: 'tribalism'. He briefly reviews the ethnic dimensions of some of the conflicts previously treated in his *Histoire* – the secessions of Katanga and Kasai, the Shaba wars. This form of 'confusion' should cease and be replaced by 'un seul chef, une seul partie et une seul NATION' (page 71). And he concludes his postscript with the Mobutist slogan we already saw: 'Sans un guide comme Mobutu, pas de Zaire unit et son armée' (page 73). Whether this alignment with Mobutu is genuine or not should not concern us here. We can see the statement as an expression of belief in the virtue of national unity – Lumumba comes to mind again – and his *Histoire* is an instrument for forging such a united country. It is henceforth a country that has a 'native' historical record *as a country*: recall his line 'tous pays a son histoire'.

We are perhaps a long way now from the moralising, factual and restricted 'didactic' aims identified by others in Tshibumba's work. I think we now have sufficient scope and depth of evidence to see the *Histoire* as an exercise in historiography with a significant degree of autonomy. Tshibumba has thought deeply about its specific structure, architecture and purpose, and he has identified it as an opportunity to do more and different things than in his other historiographical genres. The purpose of his written history is also *political*. He intends to instruct – undoubtedly this is the case – but he also makes a statement on the political troubles of his country, and on the possible role (and responsibility) of historians in addressing them. The fact that this statement was buried in the archive of a professional historian living half a world away is bitter irony. The fact that this text *became an archive* is itself a token of structural misrecognition. I can't abstain from wondering how the years in which he spent time with dis-

THE GRASSROOTS HISTORIAN'S CRAFT

tinguished historians did not result in a transfer of 'professional' method and technique. When his expatriate friends left, Tshibumba remained as 'grassroots' as before they had arrived. This brings us to the next topic.

Grassroots historiography and popular consciousness

Tshibumba's history is a grassroots effort. If there has been any influence on his historiographic practice from his expatriate comrades, it is perhaps in the privilege he now gives to the act of writing. He must have known that people such as Fabian and Jewsiwiecki wrote texts, and he must have seen that their houses were stacked with books and papers, typewriters and file cards. We have seen in Chapter 7 how in a conversation on a painting, Fabian drew Kagame's *History of Rwanda* from his shelves. The bottom line is that Tshibumba must have witnessed the way in which the practices of professional scholars were organised around literacy processes and products; he must have had a rather precise idea of the materiality of being a *professionel du savoir*.

His own writing, however, does not show traces of a learning process in which he gradually adapted his own practices to those of his fellow intellectuals. We can speculate, of course, on the ways in which this documents not just the absence of a learning process but also of a *teaching* process, in which Tshibumba's friends explained and demonstrated their ways of producing an intellectual product in a kind of give-and-take fieldwork relationship with someone who was, to be sure, a fascinating and hugely interesting 'informant'. The *Histoire* could then be seen as a document that expressed a unilateral pattern of knowledge transfer, in which Tshibumba gave and his expatriate friends received. This, I am sure, would not reflect the intentions of his friends, and I wish to abstain from any further comments on this topic. I suggest that, instead, we try to establish the way in which Tshibumba's writing carries the features we previously encountered in other sources – Julien's life stories and the *Vocabulaire* – and then see what particular form of knowledge it could have represented for his friends.

The grassroots technique

In Chapter 4 I commented on the difference in archontic power between Julien and myself. This archontic power – the fact that I had been able to construct an 'archive' of his texts – allowed me to compare and analyse across texts and make observations that Julien could never make. Here, too, my position is privileged. I can not only compare Tshibumba's *Histoire* to his paintings and the conversations he left, but also to Julien's texts and to that other piece of grassroots historiography from Katanga, the *Vocabulaire de Ville de Elisabethville* by André Yav. I will draw attention to some striking resemblances between these three documents.

171

TSHIBUMBA THE HISTORIAN

1 The three documents use *accurate chronology* as a major structuring device in the construction of a historical narrative. We have seen this in detail in Julien's three versions, where the development of a more definitive story could be witnessed from the rather spectacular increase in precise dates mentioned in the text. We have also seen this in Tshibumba's *Histoire*. The text gradually became a chronicle in which chronology became the most important text-structuring characteristic. Especially in the period documenting Mobutu's reign, we saw how dates became the keystone in the textual architecture. Let us now turn to the *Vocabulaire*.

Fabian, in his analysis of the use of dates in the *Vocabulaire*, argues that the use of 'standard chronology' 'is far from simple and straightforward' (1990a: 193). There is no chronological *development* of the historical narrative, because the text moves *topically*, on the basis of topics and places rather than of periods and moments. Thus, 'the succession of dates plays, if at all, only a minor role in ordering the succession of topics' (197). Fabian therefore chooses to 'turn from chronology to "topology", i.e. to those principles, manifest and inferred, which served to assign each of the significant topics its "place" in the text' (ibid.). There is much to be said for this interpretation, but there is a different way of looking at chronology in the *Vocabulaire*: one that understands its occurrence as a significant genre feature in its own right, as something that adds *diachrony* to the structure of the text and so indexes *history*. The occurrence of dates in a text then becomes indexical of the historiographic genre ambition of the author, something that textually suggests the accurate location in time of events which is the hallmark of historical narrative.

Seen from this angle, the *Vocabulaire* is indeed quite strongly organised – generically – around chronology. The booklet carries the date of its release on the cover: 'LE 5/ SEPTEMBRE 1965'. It is in itself a document which is clearly set in time and space. In addition to that, I counted no less than 79 dates in the text, which is 33 pages long. Each page would thus on average contain more than two dates – an average roughly comparable to that of Julien's third version. And if we look at *how* chronology is used, we also start noticing quite interesting things. The *Vocabulaire* alternates between sections in which precise chronology is absolutely central, and lists and enumerations from which chronology is absent. As for the former, let me quote the following fragment from Fabian's translation (1990a: 69):

> Truly, they got together with complete mutual understanding to set up the different projects: 1. To found the 'Union Minière du Haut Katanga' on October 28, 1906; 2. to found the 'Compagnie du Chemin de Fer du Bas-Congo au Katanga', which was first SFK, BTK, and, in the end, BCK, until this day; this was in the year 1906, October 31; 3. To found the 'Société Internationale Forestière na Minière du Congo' on November 6, 1906. This was the year the 'big societies' originated.

THE GRASSROOTS HISTORIAN'S CRAFT

Fragments such as this one testify to a desire to produce accuracy in the chronological location of historic events; they also testify to the existence of some kind of record in which such accurate dates could be remembered. The events described here occurred almost sixty years prior to the moment of writing of the *Vocabulaire*; it is highly unlikely that Yav himself was a contemporary of these events. He must have learned them (and memorised or noted them) in school, from mass media, or from other published records on the foundation of these industrial complexes in Katanga. Further in the document we find several similar examples in which dates are given for events that happened long before. Thus Yav writes things like: 'until the railroad arrived in Elisabethville on September 27, 1910' (Fabian 1990a: 71) and 'Finally came the year 1927. This is when Bwana Hollémas constructed the water tanks' (95). Chronology here, too, structures events and their connections to other events.

The importance of chronology can also be seen from points in the *Vocabulaire* where Yav wants to restore the temporal sequence of events. Thus, he tells the story of a priest called 'Père Dédec'(85–7). This priest 'had this Bwana François hanged'. The man François was an African who had caught a Belgian *in flagrante delicto* with his wife and had during that incident killed another white man who kept the lookout outside François' house. Dédec made sure François was hanged for that murder, and 'Bwana François died in the year 1922'. Yav then closes the chapter and opens a new one on the arrival of Simon Kimbangu in Elisabethville, also in 1922. He speaks about Kimbangu's miraculous powers and then of his arrest and lifelong imprisonment. After he died, 'his relatives came to carry away his body in the year 1959' (89). Then the Swahili text reads (page 14 of the facsimile; Fabian 1990a: 22):

> tunakumbusha tena ya yule bwana François yule balitundi
> kaka 1922

Translation:

> we recall again [the story] about this Bwana François, the one
> they hanged in 1922

We are reminded here by Yav of the temporal frame which was broken by the story about Kimbangu. That story took the year 1922 as its point of departure and then carried Yav to 1959; but he needs to go back to 1922 in order to resume the storyline he was developing prior to his expatiation on Kimbangu. This is a concern for chronological sequencing that reminds us clearly of Tshibumba's repeated use of *revenons* ('let's return to') and *reculons* ('let's come back'). Both authors handle chronological sequencing in a rather inconsistent, even clumsy way, and both have difficulties sustaining the rigour of chronological sequencing throughout – a phenomenon we also encountered in Julien's texts. But this problematic use of chronological sequencing does not mean that

173

chronology is not important or neglected by the authors. It is *very* important, and the considerable efforts at remembering chronological details as well as the occurrence of corrections in which the temporal sequence is restored testify to that. Chronology of this kind is a resource that these authors must painfully conquer. It isn't just there to be used; its use requires a special effort, just as the use of a monoglossic code requires a special effort too. The effort is generic: *history requires accurate chronology.*

2 The use of *chapters and chapter titles* is another striking similarity between the three bodies of text. In Julien's case, we saw how the increase in the use of chapters and chapter titles, and their more measured distribution throughout the text, were features of increased structural and stylistic tightness in the versions. The more and longer he worked on the story of his life, the more this story became organised in distinct units – chapters – that got a title and a particular layout. Tshibumba used chapters as well, and he used quite a few of them: the *Histoire* contained 29 chapters that form the largely (and increasingly) chronologically dominated organisation of the text. We saw how Tshibumba used different formats to mark these chapters, and while some of them are very clearly marked others are much less clear. This mirrored Julien's struggle with finding a 'system' in the use of chapters, and I pointed towards several unexpected places and formulations of chapter titles in the latter's texts.

Yav's *Vocabulaire* is even more characterised by the use of chapters. The document (again, just 33 pages long) is divided into an amazing 43 chapters. Each of these chapters is transparently marked by a title, always written in a distinct typography: upper case is used throughout, the title is indented, and a blank space above and under the title clearly separates the chapters. There is great rigour in the typography of chapters in the *Vocabulaire*. There is much less rigour, though, in their actual style and construction. Yav appears to have particular difficulties with punctuation throughout his document, and chapter titles contain lots of punctuation symbols. They sometimes also contain questions or appeals to consider a particular topic, and sometimes they seem to be part of the story itself. Thus, for example, we read (page 17 of the facsimile; Fabian 1990a: 23):

" " NYUMBA YA MUNGU MUKUBWA YATIWA KAMA
CATEDRAL " "
ST PAUL DE PAUL YILIYENGWA MWAKA GANI? 1922,

Translation:

The main church called the Cathedral
of St Paul of Paul was built in which year? 1922,

The next example shows how the title is actually part of the story, which spills over into the first line of the chapter itself (page 15 of the facsimile, 1990a: 22):

THE GRASSROOTS HISTORIAN'S CRAFT

KUFIKA KWA BWANA STRONG NI MWAKA WA 1928
FASI YAKE NI WAPI?NI/PALE PEKO MAGASIN
MUKUBWA YA B.C.K.,BUREAU (BUREAU)MUKUBWA
YA NJU ETANGE.

kutoka pale amehamia wapi Hotel Léo II [. . .]

Translation:

THE ARRIVAL OF BWANA STRONG WAS IN THE YEAR 1928
HIS PLACE WAS WHERE? IT IS WHERE THE B.C.K.
SUPERMARKET WAS, THE BIG BUREAU (BUREAU)
WITH MANY FLOORS

Where did he move from there [?] to the Hotel Léo II [. . .]

Yav's use of titles is at once the most systematic and the least systematic of the different texts we examine here. It is the most systematic in its graphic layout and organisation; the least systematic in the function of chapter titles in the narrative flow of the text. We encounter highly peculiar titles in the *Vocabulaire*. Like chronology and (as we have been able to notice from the examples) ortho-graphic conventions, the well-oiled use of textual structuring devices such as chapters is a resource which appears to be just beyond the reach of the author. The fact that we encounter them, however, points to an awareness of their significance and usefulness *in terms of a genre*. Writing this particular type of text demands such stylistic features, even if realising them proves hard and troublesome.

3 Julien, Tshibumba and Yav all write in *generically modified vernacular language varieties*. All three of them use particular registers from their Shaba Swahili repertoire, and in each instance we see that this variety, when written, is far from unproblematic. Schicho (1990: 33) notes that '[t]he Vocabulaire was written without clear reference to a prescriptive, normative system', because such a system is not in place for Shaba Swahili. In the case of Julien and Tshibumba, there were manifest attempts at producing *monoglossic* documents. Shaba Swahili was 'purified' in such a way that 'unmixed' Swahili and French varieties could be deployed – the code for writing is a 'pure' code. In Tshibumba's case, we also saw traces of attempts to write a 'high' variety of French.

Yav's text contains far more code-switching than those of Julien and Tshibumba, but all the same, Schicho points towards its 'somewhat formal character' (35), a formal level of language usage commonly identified as 'Swahili Bora'. The three authors all used materials from their language repertoires – Shaba Swahili – and adapted them to the particular genre they tried to write. In all these texts, we encountered accent in writing: clear and abundant traces of a lack of comfort in deploying these modified language varieties in the task at hand. The texts all struggle with stability in ortho-graphic writing conventions, spelling and grammar. In all of these texts, names prove to be particularly challenging, even when such names are frequently used and (one can imagine) very familiar – think of the various versions of 'Helena Arens' in Julien's texts.

4 We could see many traces of *an awareness of genre conventions* in the documents. The previous points all fit into this image of a genre: the authors all appeared to believe that the genre needed to be chronologically organised, structured into clearly defined units (chapters), and written in a 'high', monoglossic code. The genre is rational, serious and formal: the *gravitas* of the texts is quite overwhelming, and none of the texts we have examined here contains jokes, word-play or other forms of humour. In Julien's and Tshibumba's texts, we also saw *transitions* from one genre to another. In Julien's texts, this transition was signalled by a shift from monoglossic Swahili to monoglossic French, by a reordering of the participant framework in which Mrs Arens changed from a character in the story to the direct addressee of a letter, and by a change in tone and footing from detailed factual storytelling to general reflections on politics and society.

In Tshibumba's *Histoire*, we saw how the postscript was separated from the rest of the text by means of graphic features (it was signed separately) and a change in footing and contents. Tshibumba announced that he would now not address past events but current and future ones, and he qualified his remarks as conjectural. Such shifts identify the presence of images of particular genres, even if such images are distant and hardly precise when it comes to details of realisation. But Julien and Tshibumba clearly excluded certain parts of their writing from the 'historiographic' genre, to be included in a different genre, differently written and presented. It is through such shifts that we see how genre becomes a directing framework for organising texts, something that compels the author to write specific things in specific ways.

5 The three authors clearly belong to a *particular type of knowledge economy*, one in which access to the resources required for the genre they try to perform is restricted. All three *write an elite genre with non-elite resources*. The 'incomplete' realisation of that genre, then, shows the structural constraints of their position as writers of history. Julien did not possess an archive of his life, not even copies of his own texts, and he had to remember his story again while writing new versions of his autobiography. Tshibumba had to draw on a very diverse range of sources, ranging from relatively reliable ones to locally circulating stories of limited credibility. In the texts of both, the locality of their perspective was a striking feature. Both wrote from a particular place in the world.

The pattern is very similar, even more outspoken, in Yav's *Vocabulaire*. There are traces of formal sources in the accuracy of dates for past events, and the way in which he describes the Belgian colonial development suggests an influence from Belgian schoolbooks. But there are even more traces of locally circulating rumours and folklore. Thus, Bishop de Hemptinne is described as the (illegiti-

THE GRASSROOTS HISTORIAN'S CRAFT

mate) son of Leopold II, and the arrival of Simon Kimbangu in Elisabethville is the start of a number of miracles he performs. Yav, too, sees the Belgian King as an omnipotent and omniscient figure who decides over the fate of the Africans. Yav's sources are, like the ones Tshibumba could draw on, a very diffuse set of formal and informal channels of information. Consequently, Yav's text is equally polyphonic, and we see similar forms of discursive slippage in the *Vocabulaire* to the ones we encountered earlier in Tshibumba's *Histoire*. Consider the following fragment from Fabian's translation (1990a: 61). Yav treats the very beginning of colonial exploration:

> These agents knew how to look for ores and [knew] what the ore-bearing soils were in the Congo. <u>These agents knew how to find clothes</u> [? to distribute] and to bring peace to the country of Africa, especially in the Congo, everywhere in the Congo and the territories of the Congo.

The fact that the colonial agents knew how to 'find clothes' is a proposition that reflects a very different perspective than the fact that they could find ores and bring peace. These are statements of a different order: the 'bringing clothes' reflects the perspective of the African recipients of such clothes; the work of finding ores as well as the peace-making effect of colonisation belong to official Belgian historical discourses and reflect the perspective of the colonial powers. Two voices, and two very different positions, inform this intensely polyphonic sentence.

The three authors share much of each other's background. All three of them are from Katanga–Kasai and native speakers of Luba (or, in Yav's case, Lunda) languages from that region; they all use Shaba Swahili varieties (including 'pure' Swahili and French) in their everyday lives in that region. All three of them are what we could call (while stretching the term a bit) lower middle-class people who had an elementary education in the Belgian colonial system. All three of them had also worked with expatriates: Tshibumba maintained very productive contacts with expatriate academics, and Julien and Yav were former houseboys. All three wrote elaborate, complex and formal texts in which history was a central concern, and all three struggled manifestly with the successful completion of that task. It shows us how narrow the elite is in their society: in spite of their lower middle-class background, basic education and contacts with highly educated expatriates, none of them possessed the resources required for the task they undertook.

These are pretextual conditions, structural constraints on what and how they could write; such constraints are rarely negotiable. They are relatively stable and enduring conditions, too. We have seen them re-occur in three separate bodies of text, the oldest one of which was produced in 1965 (Yav's *Vocabulaire*), the most recent one in 1997 (Julien's third version). Three decades separate the different documents; even bearing in mind that our body of evidence is small and eccentric, we can suggest that the literacy regime for people like Yav, Tshibumba and Julien did not fundamentally change. The same cluster of constraints could be detected in clear features in each of their texts: we have bumped into something systemic.

Popular consciousness and authenticity

In the eyes of professional Western scholars, the result of the writing exercise was, in all of these cases, a *curiosum*. We know of the reception of Julien's life histories and of that of Tshibumba's written *Histoire*. As for the *Vocabulaire*, Fabian (1990a: 169) concludes that 'the very least that can be said is that this document did not leave traces even remotely comparable to those of popular painting (or popular music and theatre)'. The *Vocabulaire* may have had a local readership (it was written for and on behalf of a local association of former houseboys), but it surely didn't hit the market. The inconsequential character of these writings is baffling; their very modest impact does not reflect the massive effort invested in them – an effort to be read, to have voice *as a writer of history*. The meanings that were so carefully and painstakingly composed clearly fell into a pretextual gap, the gap between what is expected and what is achieved.

Documents of this kind can become 'data', though: data for other researchers who can then decide how to represent them. To be sure, they are 'data' in the present book. Their failure to have voice as 'serious' historiographies did not preclude other functions – functions, however, that depended not on the author but on the receiver who could attribute value to them in terms of his/her own preoccupations. This means, of course, that the documents are consecutively de-voiced and re-voiced by someone else, and that they become *new* texts, texts that are framed in universes of meaning and orders of indexicality that may be far from the ones that informed their creation.

Fabian gives us some clues in this direction in relation to the reception of the *Vocabulaire* (1990a: 165–9). A first observation he makes clarifies the professional habitus from which he encountered the *Vocabulaire*. Initially, very little happened to the text, because

> we conducted our research in a frame of mind which, although we felt immediately that there was something remarkable about this text, directed our inquiries among Africans above all to oral information. Occasional written statements by Africans were welcome as supplements to that primary source.
>
> (1990a: 165)

Studies on African societies started from the (still quite powerful) image of Africa as non-literate, and written 'data' did not fit the picture. Interest in the text grew, however, and Fabian sees an influence from the particular academic climate in Lubumbashi in the early 1970s. In the History Department (where Jewsiwiecki

THE GRASSROOTS HISTORIAN'S CRAFT

worked), people had begun collecting 'history from below' in attempts to document the way in which historical change (colonisation and the transition to independence, in particular) was perceived and experienced by 'ordinary people'. The *Vocabulaire* acquired some notoriety in that movement: '[i]t was now recognised as pioneer work, possibly the first in the line of a decolonised, genuinely Zairian historiography' (166). More precisely,

> 'Domination and Resistance' replaced social change as a dominant theme in the 1970s. Responses and resistance to colonial rule were looked at in much greater historical depth than before and various expressions of 'popular culture' were seen as intellectual, esthetic, and emotional resistance to new forms of domination.
>
> (167–8)

And, later still, there came an interest in 'the creative aspects of "*savoir populaire*" or "popular modes of action"' (168). Documents such as the *Vocabulaire* could now be seen not just as (negative) acts of resistance but also as (positive) acts of re-creation and re-building.

Fabian's account is helpful, because it points us towards several structural issues. One: written documents are 'unusual' in a society defined as primarily 'oral', and 'unusual' quickly becomes 'a-typical' or 'not authentic'. Written texts will rarely be seen as 'the best data' when research is premised on the primacy of oral data. They trigger uncomfortable reactions among scholars, because it is hard to find a clear category in which such 'data' can be placed. Two: conversely, their 'deviant' character can be absorbed to the extent that documents such as these articulate a kind of 'authenticity' which is inscribed in their formal characteristics. They become creative aspects of *savoir populaire* when they appear as *populaire*, of the people, that is: grassroots. The peculiarities of these documents then become reasons for scholarly interest: their orthographic instability and vernacular code allows a categorisation of 'authentic', unfiltered expression. In contrast to Africans who write polished scholarly prose, the authors of such 'authentic' documents become 'popular', and their work can become 'data' in research on popular consciousness. That is all very nice, but there is a catch. The texts of the fully professional African scholars, naturally, are not 'data'. Their authenticity is not an issue, because they write 'like us' and we can engage in a mature academic dialogue with their works. We quote them as authorities on a particular topic. Texts such as the *Histoire*, however, will not be recognised as authoritative historiographical texts; their very authenticity prejudges such a dialogue, and the best they can become is 'data' in a study on popular consciousness.

The misrecognition is institutional: given what history means *as a discipline*, a text such as Tshibumba's *Histoire* could never get in there. His voice as a historian is, at best, that of a grassroots historian, and this is not a matter of choice but of structural inequality. This voice is particularised: Tshibumba is made to

179

speak not as a scholar but as an interesting anthropological subject – the ordinary man. While a professional historian's voice is collective, articulating the common discipline and addressed to a worldwide congregation of fellow professional historians, Tshibumba's voice is idiosyncratic, and he can only speak to someone very different: a professional scholar who finds interest in his texts.

This is what Tshibumba's writing effort achieved: it created an interest among a handful of professional scholars, who, perhaps, 'felt immediately that there was something remarkable about this text' but also felt uncomfortable about it. He was a painter who had done magnificent work in painting history (an equally 'special' project, recall, evolving out of his contacts with Fabian). He had also written such a history, but the text fell far short of the power and creativity that emanated from his paintings. Thus, the focus remained where it was: on Tshibumba's outstanding paintings, not on his text. The *Histoire* remained an inconsequential text.

Artist, painter, grassroots historian

It was in many ways destined to remain inconsequential. The structural conditions under which it was produced made Tshibumba's identity claims – artist, painter, *historian* – a *curiosum* as well, something that people should not wish to take too seriously, because it takes a whole lot more to call yourself a historian. It takes a massive instrumentarium of skills, as well as a developed technology and infrastructure in which this instrumentarium can be used. These conditions would allow one to become an autodidact. In order to become a professional historian even more is needed: one must go through an institutional filter and submit to the rigours of disciplinary training and practice. None of these things were available and accessible for Tshibumba: he could not even become an autodidact, because the conditions for becoming one could not be satisfied by someone like him. He could not transform his interests in history into a controlled, disciplined form of mastery, because none of the actual resources needed for that process of auto-didactics was within his reach.

In the end, the only resource he could use was *the very act of writing*: his 'can write' was the thing he could apply to a practice onto which he projected a kind of definitiveness that his paintings did not have. Of all the resources required for writing history, only the grassroots writing skills could be used; other resources did not offer themselves, and he performed this elite genre with distinctly non-elite instruments. He stretched his writing skills to their limits and beyond in ways one can only admire, but they remained grassroots skills. As a consequence of all this, the very brief *précis* of the history of the Congo I wrote in Chapter 1 can be read as a *prima facie* reliable account of 'history', while Tshibumba's text can be dismissed as such. As we know, discourses of truth – Foucault's *épistèmes* – are well guarded behind institutional and professional–practical walls.

His self-qualification as a historian is therefore aspirational, it reflects an ambition which he probably grounded in the congenial contacts he had with professional Western academics who expressed strong interests in his historical views. They had this interest because of the authenticity of his views, because of the fact that his views reflected a *savoir populaire* which, rather than a partner in a dialogue, was an object of reflection and study. While he believed that he spoke as a historian, he was, in fact, listened to as an informant. What was denied in the process was that Tshibumba's views of history reflected his position *in* history: he writes *on* history *from* history, from within a particular structural position that enables him to articulate particular views and not others (cf. Blommaert 2005a, Chapter 6). And rather than as an idiosyncratic, deviant character, he could have been seen as a *structural* voice, as someone whose voice articulated things bigger than himself. This area of inquiry awaits attention; little has been done on it so far, and in the meantime, the best people such as Tshibumba can aspire to is to become 'informants' who generate 'data'.

To be sure, he was not alone. We can identify in his work, but also in the texts written by Julien, a powerful set of beliefs in which writing in and of itself is perceived as something that propels meanings to higher levels and vast spaces, and in which the act of writing itself is believed to produce new, more prestigious, identities. Writing is seen as the technique for de-localising meanings, for making meanings mobile. The features of their writings, however, make them very local, they tie them to a particular literacy and knowledge regime in a restricted space. Writing itself (regardless of the capacity to produce generically adequate texts) is often seen as synonymous with 'publication'. I have received letters from African friends of mine with requests to 'tell everyone' about what is written there; Liisa Malkki (1995) reports similar experiences with her Hutu friends in Tanzania during the 1994 genocide in Rwanda.

This idea, that writing directly involves a universal readability of texts, testifies to a very undifferentiated notion of 'writing' which is definitional of grassroots literacy. Writing is writing, and the hugely complex aspects of generic differentiation in writing as well as the stylistic minutiae required of particular text types, are either unknown or exist as a latent form of knowledge. One is aware that very different kinds of texts exist, but there is a limited capacity to differentiate one's own writing across different text types. We have seen this in Julien's texts as well as in Tshibumba's *Histoire*: both made conscious efforts at writing a historiographic genre, and both separated this historiographic genre from another one – a letter in Julien's case and a more conjectural postscript in the case of Tshibumba. The efforts at constructing a particular genre, however, were severely handicapped by the structural constraints that characterise the literacy and knowledge economy in which they wrote their texts, and these texts therefore do not communicate easily to us.

Tshibumba, like Julien, definitely 'could write': he wrote a book. This act of writing articulates a particular subjectivity: we see someone present himself as a committed and dedicated intellectual, someone in possession of knowledge and ideas of relevance to someone else. He presents himself as someone who rises to the intellectual call to arms that he attributed to Lumumba: for Congolese to write the history of the Congo, as part of the effort of building a unified country. He does not write as an artist but as a *professionel du savoir* and as a citizen – but then he didn't paint as just an artist in the works he made for Fabian either. He was a complex man, undoubtedly brilliant and deeply fascinating, and, given his place in the world, perpetually in danger of being reduced to a quite interesting 'authentic' artist and painter from Katanga.

Part IV

JULIEN, TSHIBUMBA, AND BEYOND

9

REFLECTIONS

It is time now to pull together the different threads that ran through the analysis of the documents by Julien and Tshibumba. These documents raise several rather fundamental issues. In part, these issues have to do with what they represent – what did we read in them? – and in part they have to do with how they represented it – with our own gaze and approach to such documents. Let me first recapitulate and summarise some of the main points of my analysis.

1 The documents I examined here were clearly *oriented towards particular genres*. The genre that dominated Julien's accounts as well as Tshibumba's *Histoire* was a serious, rational and formal genre in which events were organised chronologically. I called this genre 'historiography': Julien and Tshibumba wrote 'history', and this act of writing history assumes a particular generic shape. The texts were monoglossic and organised into textual units – chapters – but they were also 'serious', factual and detailed. The perception of genres piloted the writing process towards a particular formal–textual structure.

2 We could see in both cases how this work of genring a text was *conscious and deliberate*, and what a considerable effort it represented. Julien wrote three versions of his life story, each time moving closer to the model of genre he had in mind. The work of writing this particular story was spread over many years and involved complicated journeys to places where he could write such documents. In Tshibumba's case, we saw how he abandoned much more effective semiotic resources – the graphic art he was so good at – in favour of a medium in which he was far less accomplished. Tshibumba explicitly argued that *writing* history created a superior record, a record of political relevance.

3 We could also see how writing this genre was a *productive* act in which Julien and Tshibumba attempted to articulate particular forms of subjectivity. They produced themselves *as* someone specific by writing a 'special' genre. In Julien's case, he wrote 'his life', that is, he started organising his memories of events in a pattern that betokened comprehensiveness, precision, and location in time. Julien constructed an 'autobiographical' Self while writing the different versions of his story. Tshibumba systematically emphasised

185

that he wrote his *Histoire* as a historian, not as an artist and a painter. The written genre he tried to realise was the vehicle that could produce such a Self: the act of writing (and not that of painting or talking) was the practice in which the historian Tshibumba could come into being.

4 The genre, however, needed to be realised with *locally available resources that inhibited a translocally adequate realisation*. This had to do with the fact that the documents were *requested* by someone else and that the genre, consequently, was quite unfamiliar for Julien and Tshibumba alike. For both, written historiography was a *distant* genre, something that existed primarily as an image of how things ought to be written. Full access to that genre, however, demanded access to and control over resources that were beyond their reach, and both, consequently, produced an elite genre with non-elite resources. This makes the texts examined here exceptional, even eccentric: they do not represent 'normal' writing practices but rather *special* writing practices in which images of what is valid elsewhere in the world begin to dominate the writing. The particular genre is imagined as something the addressees – both 'Westerners' – will understand and appreciate. This is 'writing for export'.

5 In so doing, the documents lay bare the 'maximum' resources that Julien and Tshibumba have at their disposal for this exercise. Julien and Tshibumba both have to stretch their writing skills to the limit, and they have to construct some new skills in the process. We thus get a glimpse of the *structure of their repertoires and of the wider conditions under which texts such as these are made*. This is the point where we can start seeing grassroots literacy as something *systemic* rather than accidental, and as something which is *locally organised* in relation to economies of signs and meanings: in short, as a particular literacy regime that governs particular non-elite strata in society. It is because the texts cross such regimes – they cross from Katanga into Europe and North America – that we can begin to see the patterns of such regimes, of the processes of transfer and of the mobility potential of the resources deployed by Julien and Tshibumba. The texts become 'grassroots' because they have been lifted out of their local ('grassroots') environment and transferred to a different ('non-grassroots') environment. We can see a particular system when items produced there leave that system and enter another system.

While I have focused on these particular documents here, the analysis was informed by work on other grassroots texts, mostly from Africa and produced in educational and administrative contexts typical of globalisation: education in which hopes are articulated to become part of a globalised and cosmopolitan middle class on the one hand, asylum applications and immigrant-related legal issues on the other hand. I opened this book with an example of such documents: a written police statement by a Congolese woman arrested in Belgium. The advantage offered by Julien's and Tshibumba's texts is that they provided the largest and most coherent body of grassroots writings, features of which can be found to recur across almost all the documents I have come across elsewhere. The complexity and scope of the remarkable historiographies written by Julien and Tshibumba provide a macroscopic image of what occurs elsewhere in a more fragmentary form.

But the recurrence is there, it is systematic and widespread, and that is why I strongly believe that highly exceptional and peculiar documents such as these have a wider and more immediate relevance. They direct our gaze towards structural inequalities in the field of literacy, and such inequalities are still insufficiently understood. We see this on a daily basis in all sorts of globalised communication events, many of them with a dramatic outcome of which the same kinds of people become victims. Let me now specify some of these points of wider and more immediate relevance.

Lives, literacy, subjectivity

Several years ago, I overheard a philosopher greet another philosopher with the words: 'Hello Etienne, you look so Heideggerian today!' Being less than thoroughly acquainted with Heidegger's oeuvre at the time, I spent a while pondering about what exactly a Heideggerian look would be, scanning Etienne's face for traces of such a look and asking myself what I should do to acquire a Marxian look. The anecdote of course proves a well-known point: that we are what others ascribe to us, and that such ascriptions proceed on the basis of categories and criteria specific to the ones who do the ascription work. If these categories and criteria are unknown to us, or if we do not immediately perceive their relevance and applicability, the ascribed qualities become incomprehensible and puzzling.

Describing and interpreting someone else's life, work and personality, therefore, can say more about the one who described than about the one who is described, and I know that my own descriptions and interpretations of Julien and Tshibumba cannot be exempt from that. There is always an autobiographical bias, one that is inflected by questions we want to answer for ourselves. We can run but we cannot hide from such a bias, and the best way for me to handle this issue is by specifying the questions and sources of inspiration that guided me in my descriptions and interpretations.

Autobiography is an uncomfortable genre for me, but a little story needs to be told here. I did not grow up in the centre of the world, I spent my childhood in a rural village in Flanders in what one could call strict localism. The village was the world, and we recognised foreigners from the fact that they spoke with an accent we could hardly understand. The idea of eccentricity was very much part of that localism. There were a good number of people who were seen as weird, fools and strange by others (some of these fools were veterans of the First World War) and often I found these people extraordinarily interesting. Some were great storytellers, others were taciturn to the point where communication seemed like a punishment to them. The Congo was there as well: an uncle was a missionary in the Congo and would tell glorifying stories of colonisation and heroic missionary work during his visits to the homeland. At school, I was instructed in the official versions of colonial history, and my geography book still had a chapter on that province of Belgium called the Congo.

My life changed when my family moved to Brussels, a place where my native language was a minority language and where my Dutch accent in French would betray me as a country bumpkin from Flanders. It was there that I acquired an acute sense of what linguistic and communicative resources could mean in someone's life, how limited they often were, and how tricky communication often was when limited resources needed to be turned to complex and demanding tasks. I later became a fully globalised person, if you wish, someone propelled into a worldwide community of academics because of communicative resources I started assembling late in life: academic written registers in English. I now write texts that I would not have been able to read at the age of eighteen, and these texts define me in the eyes of others. I produce myself in highly specific, sometimes hermetic genres of writing, the acquisition of which was a slow and often frustrating process. As for my village dialect: it was frozen when I left the village, and when I return there now I catch myself speaking the language of a 1960s adolescent. In that village, I am now weird, I have no voice there.

I do not expect readers to find this little auto-narrative profoundly thrilling, but perhaps it clarifies a thing or two about the direction from which I approached the texts by Julien and Tshibumba, why to me they raised certain questions, why I chose to address these questions in this particular way, and why I felt this was necessary. To start with, I was clearly dissatisfied with the way in which lives are described in mainstream anthropological work (as well as, I should add, by the conspicuous avoidance of this topic in mainstream sociolinguistics). Authors often are less than successful in transcending the anecdotal and exceptional and identifying the larger systemic and structural lessons that can be learned from working on small and strongly contingent cases. (I find this a problem, for instance, in Caplan's 1997 book on Mohammed, the man from the Swahili coast). What is often lacking is a solid theory in which individual things can be used to understand bigger, structural things. Two sources, in particular, seemed to me to elaborate Marx's crucial statement about social being and social consciousness: Bourdieu's (e.g. 1990) concept of habitus as enduring, structural 'dispositions' that influence the smallest bits of everyday practice and thought (which I found a very useful implementation of Marx's point) and Foucault's (1975, 2003a, 2003b) views of the individual as the product of regimes of power. Individual lives are 'determined': they evolve under conditions that are changeable but constraining at each moment in the evolution of lives. We can only understand ourselves if we see our Selves as set in the collective and enduring frames we often label with terms such as 'culture' and 'society'.[1]

The concept of a 'life' – something that defines an individual – becomes a problematic object from this perspective. Yet, lives are often seen as self-evident givens, things everyone possesses. Communicating them is then an epiphenomenal, almost coincidental practice and what matters is whether you can discursively disclose 'your life' adequately or not. If you do it well, you have an identity, if you don't your identity is in doubt. Giddens (1991: 53, cited in Castells 1997: 10), for instance, insists that 'self-identity is not a distinctive trait possessed by the individual. It is the self as reflexively understood by the person in terms of her/his biography'. This biography, apparently, is just there, and the task of identity-formation is to find an adequate mapping of practices onto that biography: the 'reflexive understanding' in Giddens' terminology.

Biographies are themselves a highly specialised, complex and demanding type of practice, and in our late-modern lives, we perform such practices with the invaluable assistance of many professional biographers drawing on an elaborate technology of administrative and commodified biography. We exist as individuals because individuals also have a *systemic* existence. The 'individual' is, in the classic sense of the term, a 'social formation' whose life trajectory is a matter of structural organisation and control, something which is literally 'produced' and 'reproduced'. I make no effort at dissimulating the influence of Foucault's (2003b) arguments about biopower here: people's concept of a life is to a large extent an effect of a regime of power in which each aspect of such lives is subject to scrutiny and 'management'. My work on asylum applications greatly helped me grasp the specific ways in which such regimes operate. Foucault's arguments are compelling, and they force me to de-naturalise the concept of a 'life' and to look for the actual regimes, technologies and practices that allow (or inhibit) the 'production' of lives. Such regimes – this is evident – are specific, contingent and situated. They are not universal and in spite of what the rhetoric of globalisation makes us believe, they are not even uniformly 'globalised'. Globalisation describes the transport from one place to another, and these places are not empty: they are 'localities', fully formed social and cultural spaces that have their own patterns and systems. If we want to understand 'lives', we need to look at the actual practices that produce them, and these practices are local and systemic.

I see writing as a technology for the production of Selves operating within locally systemic conditions. Writing is productive: it offers a rich indexical terrain for others to judge, and others rarely refrain from such judgments. It is locally conditioned as well: the particular forms of writing, the way writing is organised culturally and socially as a technology for producing Selves, the way in which writing enters people's repertoires and acquires particular functions there – none of that can be taken for granted but needs to be examined. In that light, I was of course deeply uncomfortable with the rapid a priori categorisations of communication cultures one finds in much literature. Africa, for instance, was caught in totalising dichotomies of oral versus literate, pre-modern versus modern, authentic versus 'acculturated'. Such a priori dichotomies are forms of 'the denial of coevalness' (Fabian 1983): a refusal to situate African

JULIEN, TSHIBUMBA, AND BEYOND

societies in the same space and time as late-modern 'Western' societies (which are, of course, equally totalised in such dichotomies), and an idea that prejudges any attempt to think about globalisation in ways that transcend stereotypes. Writing was quite consistently seen (and dismissed) as something 'new', something that actually did not belong there and distorts the (pre-modern) authentic sociocultural African fabric. The essays in Jack Goody's collection on *Literacy in Traditional Societies* (1968) illustrate this, but one should not be led to believe that such views died in the more sophisticated 1980s or 1990s. There is still a lot of literature in which 'exotic' societies are defined as 'pre-literate' and 'traditional', and in which these pre-literate traditions affect whatever there is in the way of literacy. Thus, according to such literature, African writings should bear the traces of an 'oral culture', and this unilateral influence from a strong and resilient oral tradition to a new and vulnerable complex of literacy practices makes African writings so 'authentic'.[2]

In my view, societies are literate as soon as people write. It does not matter whether *many* or *few* people write: as soon as there are literate people, the sociolinguistic patterns and hierarchies of that society have quite drastically been transformed, and people with restricted literacy skills can often participate in highly intricate literacy practices, be it only under certain conditions and in a restricted set of roles. Writing becomes part of the world of communicative resources, even for people who are barely literate but who can draw on the writing skills of others to communicate in writing or to read texts. In other words, we should see literacy in relation to the wider social conditions for communication, and *as a factor changing* these conditions. In many places in the world, literacy is a very specialised and exclusive resource monopolised by specialised – or special – people such as scribes, clerks, notaries, teachers, priests or bureaucrats. This does not mean that such places, as a whole, are 'illiterate': it means that there is a highly selective distribution of literacy resources concentrated around a narrow group of specialised people and that rather than using 'literate–illiterate' distinctions, we should seek to specify the particular literacies that operate there. When such people perform their writing practices, these are special events, but still events that occur *within* a particular sociocultural formation. They are not *outside* that unit, but deeply within it, and very often quite centrally within it. It is the presence of such literate people that makes other members of that society 'illiterate'.

Julien and Tshibumba, to be sure, were such special and exceptional people who performed practices very different from those of most people in their sociocultural milieu. Their writings articulate a subjectivity – a sense of Self as agentive and relational – which needs to be understood as 'deviant', if only because such deviations offer us a window on the complexes of norms and expectations of 'normal' behaviour from which these practices deviate. There are two hugely inspiring examples for this exercise: Carlo Ginzburg's magnificent *The Cheese and the Worms* (1980) and *I Pierre Rivière* by Michel Foucault and his associates (Foucault, ed. 1975).

REFLECTIONS

In both books, 'extravagant' individuals are set against the patterns of 'normalcy' of their times. Ginzburg brings to life a 16th-century miller from Friuli in Italy, Menocchio, who got into trouble with the Holy Inquisition because of the unusual views he held on God, the Pope, and the creation of the world. Menocchio had read a few books and had extracted from these books a profoundly 'heretical' and critical view of religion, which he could not keep for himself but loved to spread among the customers of his mill. The books he had read were of course well known to the Inquisition, and the interrogation by the Inquisition at times becomes a discussion on the meaning of passages from these books. Ginzburg lucidly notes that the sharedness of sources did in no way cause similarity in interpretation: Menocchio and the Inquisitor belonged to very different worlds of reading, and '[e]ven if Menocchio's interpretation was triggered by contact with this text, its roots had distant origins' (Ginzburg 1980: 41). The literacy world of 16th-century Italy, we can see, was clearly divided into an elite and a non-elite segment, and different rules governed both segments. Foucault and his collaborators investigated documents that related to a case of multiple murder. In 1835 a young man called Pierre Rivière killed his mother, sister and brother. He was arrested and convicted and left (along with records of interrogations, witness statements and other official documentation on the court case) a long written 'memoir' on the wider conditions that prompted this slaughter. Foucault's analysis focuses on the way in which, around this case, forms of knowledge were gathered, organised and constructed that could lead to the definition of the perpetrator as a 'madman'. The various discourses documented in the archive on Rivière, in other words, show how someone's life can be re-situated against the normative, and 'normal', patterns of conduct, and so against a particular emerging regime of power.

Documents are in both cases the only 'data', and they are analysed in a way that shows a particular subject *in relation to larger normative complexes* that define him as a *particular* subject. There is nothing static or stable about subjectivity: its particular form is the outcome of specific practices organised in relation to norms and expectations that belong to the deeper fabric of societies and can be internalised as compelling models of conduct − in other words, as habitus. The fact that Julien and Tshibumba make such efforts at writing very specific genres, of which we know that they are beyond the reach of what they have in the way of resources, testifies to the way in which all of us want to be *particular* people in the eyes of others. It also testifies to the many ways in which such attempts can fail to achieve their aim − such as when people look Heideggerian to others.

The skeleton of literacy practices

Julien's and Tshibumba's documents give us an image of literacy reduced to its bare essentials. They thus call into question many of the features that are often, outside the milieu of advanced literacy researchers, assumed to be part of *every* form of literacy: the rather unproblematic accessibility of ortho-graphic norma-tive complexes including a democratically distributed standard written language variety, the existence of intertextual bodies of information which can be used as references or sources for later texts, the requisite material infrastructure of writ-ing, the presence of an identifiable audience – that is, the assumption of uniform literacy in society – and knowledge of the different forms of literacy we need in our lives. We have seen that in Julien's and Tshibumba's cases, hardly any of these assumptions could be upheld. Their writing proceeded in a context where no normative and standardised model of language and literacy was available to them, without access to the wealth of written information that we associate with a late-modern knowledge economy, without a community of readers who could assist them in the process of writing and editing, and with a very limited aware-ness of how to perform particular genres. As I said in relation to Tshibumba, the only resource he had for the realisation of the genre of historiography was *writing* itself: the bare essentials of putting graphic signs on paper as a result of 'thinking'.

I emphasise this point for three reasons. One, because I believe that inquir-ies into literacy should never take too much for granted, least of all the presence elsewhere of features of 'advanced' literacy regimes. Understanding what people actually do with literacy requires close attention to the local systemic conditions under which it occurs and is practised (I echo Street 1995 here). It is then that we start to see the limits of what they can do with it, and may understand why some of these practices fall short of institutionally defined (and often generalised) norms of literacy achievement. We sometimes need to delve very deeply into the soil of literacy, and we need to go and look at the elementary constituent practices and the material conditions of writing, before we can make reasona-bly accurate statements about what writers communicate. This, of course, is a cautionary note mainly directed to people outside the field of literacy scholar-ship (where much of what I say here is generally accepted), as well as an appeal that should be answered by a fully developed ethnographic inquiry into literacy. We do need to 'peel off' the many layers of institutional normalcy in which our understanding of literacy practices is now often wrapped.

Two: this, then, opens a wide spectrum of topics, related to the ways in which literacy is placed in the repertoires of its users. In a brilliant survey paper, James Collins, referring to Lévi-Strauss, remarked that writing 'seems to favor rather the exploitation than the enlightenment of mankind' (Collins 1995: 81). He also suggested that 'modern educational systems produce stratified literacies: elites are socialised to an interpretive relation to texts, and nonelites are socialised to a submissive relation to texts' (84). The problem then is one of determin-ing what sort of orientation to literacy we meet here and what functions can be attributed to it, and again, very little should be taken for granted here. Given the connection between literacy and subjectivities, it is not hard to appreci-ate that people attribute value to literacy, even if such literacy only exists in fragmentary and truncated forms. The specific value attributed to it, however, cannot be predicted but needs to be found in a thorough inspection of practices and products. We will find that, very often, what looks like ortho-graphy to us is actually hetero-graphy for them (the use of conventional graphic symbols for functions other than those of ortho-graphic writing) and vice versa. Graffiti, obviously, should be a case in point, where people 'write on the wall' and address us, while they use a code which is hermetic to us and can only be 'read' by fellow graffiti writers. There are plenty of instances where we see that orthographic resources are dislocated and creatively redeployed hetero-graphically. This should help us get rid of established ideas of the functions of 'writing', and teach us that such functions can often be far more numerous and complex than 'normally' assumed.

Three: we may find that, in such practices, there are very intricate tensions between knowledge and capability. People may know what 'good' writing is but they may not be capable of performing it; they can be able to read something but not write something similar, they can have been exposed to particular forms of literacy but not have absorbed their rules of construction, and so forth. The question, in sum, is that of determining what exactly we mean by literacy 'competence'. If we go back to our examples here, we saw how both Julien and Tshibumba oriented towards a distant genre and tried to perform it. They had knowledge of that genre, however incomplete and superficial this knowledge may have been, and this knowledge directed their writing exercises. Genre became a knowledge format for organising the writing: if things are written in this way, they will convey particular kinds of knowledge. While writing, there will always be such forms of knowledge about writing practices, and practices will display orientations to these bodies of knowledge – which is why the Congolese lady who was arrested by the Belgian police affirmed that she 'could write': she believed that her knowledge of elementary writing skills warranted this qualification. These orientations, however, do not immediately convert into actual capability. Julien and Tshibumba delivered very 'incomplete' versions of the genre they oriented towards; the Congolese lady, likewise, produced something that failed the test of literate genre writing in a legal context. If we want to understand 'competence', we need to cover the different aspects of these processes, and very often, we look at practices without inquiring into the forms of knowledge *about* practices that direct them. The specific metapragmatic – ideological – framing of such practices remains unexamined, and the information such frames may yield on the particular position of people in a larger literacy complex is not tapped. This is problematic because we need to understand what counts as literacy for people, how it matters for them, how they project identities, function and authority onto particular forms of literacy, and so forth. It is an area of inquiry we cannot afford to overlook.

Grassroots literacy, I submit, offers us a view of what literacy can *minimally* mean for people. It reflects the most peripheral kind of insertion in economies of language and literacy resources, and it teaches us that even when literacy occurs as a very restrained and constrained set of practices, it *functions* locally.

Such insights, I am sure, will teach us that we had better conceive of literacy as organised in relatively autonomous complexes that need to be described as such, rather than as part of large (for instance 'globalised') and abstract technologies of literacy. The rules that apply locally may differ significantly from those valid elsewhere, and an analysis of processes of transfer needs to be based on an analysis of the different regimes of literacy through which the texts move. These regimes can be (and are) influenced by one another; but that does not mean that they are commensurable, let alone identical to one another. This, too, is an argument in favour of ethnographic approaches to literacy, in which justice is done to the local organisation of literacy and in which the analyst abstains from quick generalisations and reductions of complexity.

Grassroots literacy in globalisation

Texts such as those treated in this book do move around, and models of literacy also move around. The regimes I described above as relatively autonomous are at the same time connected to others through processes of cultural transfer, some of which have a respectable age and some of which are very recent. Such connections are now understood in a theoretical framework of globalisation studies, and the good thing about such studies is that they force us to accept the world as a unit of analysis and a context for action. They force us, simply put, to situate literacy practices in Central Africa in the same time and space as literacy practices in Central London or Beijing. Consequently, they force us to recognise that developments in the centre of the world also have effects on the margins of the world.

I must be insistent and precise on this point: the different places in the world are connected, but that does not mean that they become uniform, and the point is to grasp the actual nature of such connections. Most people in the world do not immediately experience what we commonly see as the features of globalisation. They do not speak English, do not watch satellite TV, do not surf on the internet and have never heard of Harry Potter. That does not mean that they do not know that English, satellite TV, the internet or best-selling books exist, it merely means that the organisation of their lives develops outside the sectors of society in which such attributes circulate and have practical use. That also does not mean that they cannot be confronted with the realities of globalisation: when they move across different places and, for instance, apply for asylum in Western Europe, globalisation suddenly becomes a very practical matter, and knowledge of its emblematic and defining instruments is not sufficient.

I came across this phenomenon when I analysed a handwritten text from a Burundese man whose asylum application in Belgium had been rejected on the grounds that his Burundese identity could not be conclusively established (Blommaert 2004, Blommaert 2005a: Chapter 5). The appeal judge had given him what seemed like a straightforward assignment to prove his claims about Burundese citizenship: he had asked the man to write everything he knew about

REFLECTIONS

> **QUESTIONS:**
> 1. What language do you like most and why?
>
> the language that I like at school to learn English because that everybody
> they learn English because is a very nice language to everyone that they want
> to speak English.

Figure 9.1 Questionnaire response, Wesbank

his country. The result was a seven-page document in grassroots writing. It was a document that displayed many of the features we have encountered and discussed earlier: chapters, (incomplete) lists, drawings, unstable orthography and vernacular language varieties. If someone should give me such an assignment, to write 'everything I know' about Belgium, I would rush to an internet café and search Wikipedia and other sources for comprehensive and recent information on Belgium. The man from Burundi had not done that; instead, he had asked at least two other friends to help him remember facts about their country: the text showed traces of three different handwritings. The gaps in his memories, even if combined with those of others, remained big enough to produce what was considered by the judge to be an unsatisfactory result. There is little doubt that these people were familiar with internet cafés, and that they had a more or less developed idea of what their function could be. But it was also quite clear that they did not know how to operate this complex information technology, and how it could serve as a useful back-up for their own personal memories. Knowledge of globalisation processes does not equal the capacity to use them; knowledge of resources does not equal their absorption into repertoires.

I also came across this phenomenon during research in township schools around Cape Town, South Africa. Students of a secondary school in one of these townships articulated very strong beliefs in the emancipatory power of English. If they could learn English well, they would be able to get into mainstream middle-class life trajectories (Blommaert et al. 2005). English there carried the heavy ideological load it has acquired in contemporary globalisation: it is the language of upward globalised mobility. The ideological load of English, however, was not matched by actual resources. Consider the following example, a written questionnaire answer to the question 'which language do you like most, and why?' The student, a 16-year old girl, clearly 'writes well' (see figure 9.1 above). This is what she wrote:

> the language that I like at school to learn English because that Everybody
> they learn English because is a very nice language to Everyone that they want
> to speak English.

The grassroots traces are clear: the sentence, however aesthetically crafted, contains hardly any punctuation and we see unwarranted capitals in 'Everybody'.

In addition, the English carries traces of vernacular local norms: 'because is a very nice language'. Clearly, the actual language and literacy resources this girl has acquired do not match the criteria of upward globalised mobility. It will not get her out of the township, it is more likely to keep her in the township. It is *locally* good English that loses value and function as soon as it leaves that particular social space. And while in the township, this could qualify as good English and good writing, it becomes township English and grassroots literacy as soon as it leaves that space.

The margins of the world very often prove to be a most fertile terrain for investigating globalisation processes. That is: places where globalisation appears to be minimally present are very often the places where one can see it at work. In a shopping street in Banjul, Gambia, for instance, one can find shop signs that read 'HARLEM NIGGAZ'.[3] The environment is one of grassroots literacy, and Gambia is seriously peripheral in the world of economic and political globalisation. Yet, we see how fully globalised forms of literacy penetrate such peripheral places: the shop sign expresses orientation towards a globalised Hip-Hop culture in which the hetero-graphic spelling of 'niggaz' is a politically correct self-qualification of black people (while 'niggers', ortho-graphically realised, would be a white racist slur) and in which 'Harlem' signals a connection with centres of globalised Hip-Hop prestige. All of this dense indexicality is produced by a particular written form, a form that responds to 'peripheral normativity' (Blommaert et al 2005): it needs to be written in this precise 'sub-cultural' and 'non-standard' way, and not, for instance, as 'Harlem niggers'. These globalised rules are known, but that does not mean that more general ortho-graphic rules would be known or convertible into 'normal' writing.

Similarly, when I first visited Tanzania in 1985 I was struck by the way in which people used plastic shopping bags. They would be sold as separate items at stalls in the street and people would use and re-use them until they fell apart. The bags carried bootleg images and (often English) inscriptions, of Rambo, Ferrari, Marlboro and other globalised status items. In my home society, plastic shopping bags were among the least valued possessions – a visit to the super-market would saddle one with six or seven such bags, most of which made it directly to the dustbin. In addition, even if such shopping bags carried inscriptions – the name and logo of the supermarket, for instance – no one would ever consider them literacy objects. Plastic shopping bags are not made for reading. In Tanzania, however, people would actually choose a particular bag on sale – Rambo or Marlboro? – be fussy about their choice, and then display the inscription on the bag on every possible occasion. The bag was made for reading, because its inscription signalled globalised prestige and the choice of a particular inscription identified the person who had chosen it (Rambo would typically be chosen by young men, and not by young women). Later in life, when the 'big brands' hype hit my consumer society, I saw that people would walk around with plastic bags carrying Gucci, Armani or Puma logos, and would proudly display them. These bags were not purchased separately, they were items that came with buying Gucci, Armani or Puma goods, and globalisation was here expressed not just through the bags but through what they signalled: that people could afford to shop at Gucci, Armani and Puma. In 1980s Tanzania, the goods could not be purchased but the bootleg bags were on sale: in the absence of full insertion into the globalised consumer culture, its absolute peripherals – cheap bags with prestigious English and brand logos – were the things that signalled globalisation. This was not about consumer products, it was all about signs on a bag. I suddenly saw a literacy object that I had never considered as such before, and I saw a minimal, absolutely marginal trickle of globalisation in the plastic bags carried around by people in Tanzania. Again, places and regimes were connected, but in highly unpredictable ways.

Globalisation there, as in Gambia, appears as *a little bit* of language and literacy, not as a huge and overwhelming complex. Thus, there is a connection between regimes and places across the world, but in this case that connection is minimal, niched, and not generalisable. The conclusions we draw about shop signs and plastic bags should not seduce us to make, for instance, generalisations about literacy in education. The task is to find the precise niches in which such little bits of globalised form enter societies, how they come to mean something for people, and how such meanings can be played out in practices. It is obvious that the dichotomies mentioned above – oral versus literate, traditional versus modern, and so on – are unhelpful in such an effort. We need a new vocabulary for such an exercise.

History from below

It seems to me that such an exercise may benefit historians too. The problem of 'evidence' in texts, or rather the complex set of problems, is well known and has been addressed by generations of historians under the label of historical criticism. Often, the focus was, and is, on 'truth', on the way in which distinctions can be made between 'facts' and 'not-facts' in documents, the ways in which forgeries can be identified, the way in which documents can disclose 'truthful accounts' of historical events.

From the perspective outlined in this book, there are three points we need to make. First, a distinction should be made between 'old' and 'historical'. Often, documents are called 'historical documents', whereas in fact, prior to historical–methodological inspection, they are merely 'old'. They *become* historical because of scholarly, disciplined and methodical interpretation. This distinction between what a document *is* and what it *becomes* was a central concern in this book, and I hope to have demonstrated the amount of complex work involved in that. Texts do not immediately become 'historical', and thus do not immediately, out of their sheer existence, become 'memorable' bearers of historical meaning. This leads to a second point. Many historians have advocated the use of linguistic techniques as part of the necessary toolkit of historical criticism. Long ago, Marc Bloch already paid tribute to the precision and usefulness of linguistic analysis (Bloch 1953: 126ff). But I'm afraid that Bloch as well as others gave too much credit to the historical sensitivity of linguistics. As I hope to have demonstrated in the preceding chapters, we need *a particular kind* of linguistics to suit a historical project. Third, the issue of truth versus fiction/interpretation/forgery is obviously one that does not stand the test of postmodern critiques of positivism and truth. Rather than truth, *voice* should be central to the historical inquiry into documents. Consequently, and connected to the previous point, we need an analysis that starts investigating documents long before they were produced – pretextually – and questions the conditions of production, interactional functions, entextualisation patterns and so forth. We also need to address issues of genre, seen as organised ways of dealing with received (or locally constructed) models of text and communication.

The texts by Julien and Tshibumba were *reluctant* documents, documents which do not quickly surrender their historical meaningfulness to readers who live in other sociocultural environments. They were, both, not immediately 'memorable' texts: they were perhaps remarkable and special, but at the same time easily dismissed as bearers of historical information. The point was that the historical 'facts' they reveal are very often a matter of the way in which the authors displayed degrees of acquisition and control of particular linguistic and stylistic, genre-constructing resources. In other words, perhaps the most telling bits of historical information emerged from the texts as soon as we analysed not their 'contents' but their form and shape. It was then that we started to realise that such documents bespeak a particular historical position from which the authors wrote: a constraining position that made it possible for them to write certain things in certain ways, and impossible to write other things in other ways. Historical 'facts' can only be articulated by particular, positioned voices, and many of these voices cannot be heard. The positioning of voices is in itself a highly informative historical 'fact'.

It is an awareness of such intricate, nuanced and delicate relations between signs and the economies in which they acquire value and meaning, and between which signs travel, that allows us to construct 'voice' for Julien and Tshibumba as people in history commenting on history. A blank, linguistic or propositional reading of the text doesn't produce anything that comes close to vindicating the document as a source for historical research. We need an ethnographic approach in which signs are seen as relatively fixed, hierarchised (or at least stratified) resources with attributable functions derived from their local economies, not from the single signs. This is a linguistics that is not linguistic, but one that addresses language as something into which people have made investments. And only through the application of such a linguistics can texts become historical documents. If not, they are merely old. For it is voice, its genesis, structure and the constraints under which it operates that inform us about history, and we can make texts 'historical' as soon as we are able to identify the voice they articulate. This is tough work, but it breaks the silence. It can be productively applied to subjects from Africa, Latin America or other disenfranchised parts of

REFLECTIONS

the world where regimes of language and literacy work in ways different from ours, and where knowledge, truth and historical experience consequently take on different shapes.

Conclusion

Tshibumba concludes his historical narrative with the words (page 69):

> L'Histoire n'a pas de fin
> ainsi écrit, dit déjà un grand
> travail.

Translation:

> History has no end
> thus written already speaks a great
> work.

A paraphrase of this statement could be: whatever has been achieved has been achieved, even if the job can never be properly finished. Here speaks a true intellectual, very much aware of the inevitably limited character of his own efforts and contribution. His *Histoire*, like Julien's three versions of his life story, is 'already a lot of work', but even so it is necessarily unfinished.

This book, too, is best seen as a necessarily unfinished effort, as something that under the best of circumstances opens some other people's eyes for the theoretical, descriptive and methodological issues that revolve around literacy and the ethnographic interpretation of texts made in sociocultural environments different from one's own, and invites these people to extend this line of work. The sheer complexity of these issues means that the effort is doomed to be fragmentary, unfinished and insufficient. Nevertheless, and I quote Dell Hymes looking back on his work on Native American ethnopoetics,

> [w]e must work to make visible and audible again that something more
> – the literary form in which the native words had their being – so that
> they can move again at a pace that is surer, more open to the voice,
> more nearly their own.
>
> (Hymes 1981: 384)

There is a tremendous amount of work to be done there, in helping to restore voice to those whose voices have been distorted or silenced. The huge and threatening problem such people are facing is one of inequality: their voices are *systematically* in danger of being misunderstood, dismissed or silenced, not because of choice but because of far more complex and difficult issues that have to do with the ways in which we work and live within relatively stable sets of expectations and norms with respect to meaning, truth and voice. Such issues are exacerbated by the processes of intensified flow and exposure we now call globalisation; getting to the bottom of them is an academic as well as a humanistic challenge.

Academically, we must be ready to revise some of our established views of language, semiosis and meaning; they no longer explain the complexities of this world. Academics tend to find such a challenge exciting and hard to resist, and some have embarked on such an exercise already. But it must lead somewhere, and this is where the humanistic challenge enters the picture. Part of what academics need to do in their societies is to provide hope to others: hope that problems can and eventually will be solved. Academic work has, in the eyes of others, very often such utopian dimensions, firmly grounded in the legacy of Enlightenment and Modernity: in the end, they think, scientific research will solve it. It is good to keep this in mind, because it allows us (even in the face of increasing pressures to become a sector of the knowledge industry) to apply our work to real-world problems. Such problems are plenty; they are important, and they are relevant. The academic who turns to them will find such problems fertile terrain, in part, for acquiring a sense of usefulness for his/her work. S/he will, however, also find that solving them requires the best possible work, because there is no room for errors, failures or half-baked work – people's fate may depend on it. Academic work improves through such confronting and challenging applications. And academics tend to find that, too, irresistible.

NOTES AND REFERENCES

NOTES

1 INTRODUCTION: GRASSROOTS LITERACY AND LITERACY REGIMES

1   Hymes emphatically dismisses connections between this 'practical structuralism' and 'structuralism' as 'what has been made of linguistic analysis in anthropology, semiotics, and the like' (Hymes 2003: 123). It is easy to be misled by terminology here, and Hymes is not always the most helpful writer in this respect (witness famously cryptic lines such as 'In aim, the method is structural, but in execution, it must also be philological' – Hymes 1966: 131). Hymes has maintained throughout his career a complex relationship with structuralism (see e.g. Hymes 1983).

2   The 'practical structuralism' shines through in statements such as this one: 'One must work out a "grammar" of the local world of discourse and work out the internal relations of a text in relation to that grammar before proceeding to analytic comparison and interpretation in terms of relationships found elsewhere'. (Hymes 2003: 126)

3   I can refer the reader to some very good sources. The period of the Congo Free State is covered incisively by Vangroenweghe (1985). There is a very good discussion on the Belgian colonial system, with focused attention on language issues, in Fabian (1986). The pre-independence and early post-colonial period is documented in an unparalleled way by Crawford Young (1965), and there is no better source on the Mobutu regime than Braeckman (1991).

2 THREE LIVES FOR MRS ARENS

1   I developed for that purpose a system of transcription in which graphic features of the handwritten text were maximally replicated in the typed version. I was of course inspired by conversation-analytic transcription systems, and thought that as much attention should go to the formal organisation of writing as to that of spoken speech. I will apply that system here in presenting examples from the texts. The organisation of text in lines, the alteration of lower and upper case, punctuation, strikeouts, self-corrections and super- or subscripted corrections will all be rendered as well as possible in the typed version. What this transcription system does not replicate, evidently, is the quality of paper and the particular 'feeling' of the handwriting. Also, wobbling or bending lines in handwriting cannot be replicated. Extracts from the texts are identified here by a figure referring to the version followed by the page number. Thus, 3/6 is page six of the third version.

2   During an interview I had with Mr and Mrs Arens in 1996, I inquired into their knowledge of Swahili. Even taking into account the time-gap of more than two decades since they left Lubumbashi, the result was meagre: a mere handful of isolated

NOTES

words and inflected verbs, bearing strong traces of pidginisation. In a letter written in August 1996, Mrs Arens listed 62 words, morphemes and expressions. The couple did not have any degree of fluency in Swahili, and neither could claim any knowledge of other locally widespread languages such as Luba. The couple confirmed that the language of interaction between them and their staff in Lubumbashi was French.

3 Ngandazika is probably Gandajika, a town close to Mbuji-Mayi in Kasai. As we have seen, Julien writes with an accent, and the spelling of this name probably reflects his pronunciation.

4 In contrast to the difficulties Julien has with spelling place names, the distances reported in his texts are in general quite accurate. The title he uses in this fragment suggests that he uses road signs as a generic blueprint and that he keeps a memory of the distances mentioned on such signs.

3 GENRES AND REPERTOIRES

1 The obvious fact that different genres in writing should be reflected in different genres of reading is, unfortunately, a poorly researched topic. The collection of essays in Boyarin (1993) offers some stimulating suggestions.

2 The Jamaa movement is in itself a highly interesting colonial and post-colonial phenomenon. It was initiated by a Belgian Catholic missionary, Placide Tempels (author of *La Philosophie Bantoue*, 1945), and developed into a large and culturally important charismatic movement. The relevance of Fabian's paper is, unfortunately, not matched by its minimal impact on mainstream genre theory. Linguists and sociolinguists rarely use Fabian's work, even if it is replete with superbly rich and provocative reflections on language.

3 This point is also emphatically made by Mayer and Woolf (1995) in their introduction to a volume on biography in early modern Europe. Mayer and Woolf emphasise 'the degree to which the late Renaissance experimented with genres *avant la lettre*; their formalization was a long, painfully combative process . . .' (1995: 7). They also list ten genre 'models' that could be found, to various degrees of replication, in early modern European biography. The use of such borrowed genres, and the experiments with innovation through them, 'suggests that humanist life-writing was not sufficiently formalized to be considered under the rubric of a single genre', and therefore 'any attempt to understand the nature of life-writing during and after the Renaissance must steer clear of generic prisons, while nonetheless remaining cognizant of certain constrictions of form, in part descended from ancient models.' (ibid.)

4 By signing the two versions in this way, Julien obviously refers back to the older, existing relationship between himself and Mrs Arens. But that is not all, he also creates an anachronism in signing with his 'Christian' or 'European' name. During the period of so-called 'Zairianisation', Mobutu decreed that all Congolese should adopt 'Bantu' names and stop using their former 'European' ones. Thus Joseph Désiré Mobutu became Mobutu Sese Seko. Practices developed in which people created double names, one 'Bantu' and another one 'Christian' or 'European'. Julien surely must have adopted such a 'Bantu' name, and the fact that he avoids it here illustrates how he frames his interaction with Mrs Arens in terms of their original labour relationship.

5 As in many other African states, the colonial system of education in the Congo did not vanish on the day of independence, of course. The education system continued to be 'Belgian' in design and structure, and for decades after independence Belgian missionaries and expatriate teachers populated the local education institutions.

6 We have seen in these fragments several instances in which Julien uses the inflectional suffix -aka. This suffix is alien to (Standard) Swahili but quite frequent in other regional languages such as Lingala. See Schicho (1990) for an overview.

204

NOTES

7   The use of the locative particles 'ku' and 'mu' is evidence of influence from Luba languages; it is alien to Standard Swahili.
8   Julien uses a similar phrase in version two (2/10). His use of 'democracy' here reminded me of a passage in André Yav's *Vocabulaire*. Yav writes 'na vile tulikamata Indépendant yetu hiyi ya kuwoza-woza' – 'and thus we got that rotten Independence of ours'. Yav writes this in the concluding sections of his text (page 33 of the facsimile, Fabian 1990a: 31), and the phrase sums up the continuous and escalating crisis in the early post-colonial Congolese state. It is interesting to see how terms that in an established Liberal discourse only have positive connotations – independence, democracy – can summarise a very negative process and state of affairs for people such as Yav and Julien. Julien, clearly, seems to agree with something Eric Hobsbawm lucidly wrote: 'Democracy can be bad for you' (Hobsbawm 2001).
9   In Blommaert (1999) I discuss the history and standardisation of Swahili, and I have to refer the reader to that source for further details. Fabian (1986) is a splendid analysis of the genesis and development of Swahili in the Congo.
10 Mrs Arens reacted with irritation to Julien's increasing religious zeal. She herself professed to be a militant agnostic.

4 WRITING, REMEMBERING AND BEING

1   Research among African asylum seekers made it clear that many of them do not possess that sort of archive. Consequently, remembering details of past experiences (ranging from the date of birth or marriage to trivia such as the family names of relatives and friends) is rendered very difficult, and this in turn jeopardises the chances of asylum applicants for obtaining a favourable outcome of a procedure strongly focused on narrative autobiographical detail. See Blommaert (2001b, 2004). Vincent de Rooij, in correspondence on this topic, mentions that he has noticed that people in urban Lubumbashi do keep an archive of pictures and notes and attach great importance to it. While this may be true for some (groups of) people, the structure of Julien's texts makes it clear that he, like many others, does not possess such an archive.

5 TSHIBUMBA: ARTIST, PAINTER, HISTORIAN

1   Fabian's lecture, entitled 'Africa's Belgium', later became Chapter 10 of Fabian (2001). My work on Tshibumba's documents was fed into the MA dissertation projects of some of my students, and this led to a magnificent and extensive study by Maya Schiffer (M. Schiffer 2005). In this study (only available in Dutch), Schiffer reconstructs the oeuvre of Tshibumba – wider than the collection shown in Fabian (1996) – and analyses the paintings as well as the texts. Maya's sister Ellen also produced a dissertation (in Dutch) in which she provides a comprehensive historical context for Tshibumba and his oeuvre, including his contacts with expatriate academics in Lubumbashi (E. Schiffer 2005). Both studies have been sources of inspiration for me. Together they form perhaps the largest and most comprehensive corpus of scholarship on Tshibumba.
2   See also the literature reviewed in Chapter 1 above.
3   These three people, by the way, became the most important collectors of Tshibumba's works.
4   There is a very intriguing passage in the conversation with which Fabian opens his *Remembering the Present*, illustrating the double-sidedness of this relationship. Fabian inquires into the type and volume of work Tshibumba produces. After having mentioned that landscapes are not quite his thing, Tshibumba says: 'I'm good, for instance, at the kinds of pictures you have in the house, the historical ones. [. . .] I'm strong in history' (Fabian 1996: 6). This may be the moment when both people

205

NOTES

discover their shared interest in history. At the same time, since Tshibumba was out to sell paintings, it may also be the moment where Tshibumba identifies Fabian as a potentially interesting customer: Fabian's choice of paintings in his house signals his preference for genres in which Tshibumba is 'strong', and thus the possibility to sell such paintings. Perhaps even a good number of them; Tshibumba continues: 'Of the flogging there [. . .] I can do three a day. Pictures of Lumumba I can do two a day, if I work hard'.

5 Tshibumba's Swahili is amply documented. The 'Archives of Popular Swahili' website offers the original transcripts in Swahili of the conversations between Fabian and Tshibumba. (See *History of Zaire as told and painted by Tshibumba Kanda Matulu in conversation with Johannes Fabian*, http://www2.fmg.uva.nl/lpca/aps/tshibumbaintro.html.) References to fragments from this source will be made as 'APS' followed by the session number of the recording on the website. Thus 'APS 1b' is session 1b on the *Archives of Popular Swahili* website.

6 The *Union Minière du Haut Katanga* was the major industrial power in the Shaba/Katanga mining areas, and its plant dominated the city of Lubumbashi to the extent that it became emblematic of the place and central to historical narratives such as that of the *Vocabulaire d'Elisabethville*. It also figures in a good number of Tshibumba's paintings.

6 THE AESTHETICS OF GRASSROOTS LITERACY

1 Some exceptions deserve to be mentioned. Fabian (1982) describes code-switching in Shaba Swahili as a primarily 'poetic' phenomenon. Silverstein's analyses (e.g. 1985) of the indexical structuring of conversations equally emphasise the poetic dimensions of such interactions. And the 'ethnopoetics' developed by Dell Hymes (1981) and Dennis Tedlock (1983) explicitly assumes the poetic structuring of narratives as its point of departure. For a discussion of the latter, with special emphasis on Hymes' work, see Blommaert (2006).

2 If we turn to that other remarkable document from Katanga, the *Vocabulaire*, we see similar things. There is a drawing of a political symbol (a rooster in a circle and star-shape) on page 6, and every page is lined by means of patiently typed '%' symbols: an immense calligraphic effort.

3 Jim Cummins reminds us of the fact that 'native speakers of any language come to school at the age of five or so virtually fully competent users of their language. [. . .] Yet, schools spend another 12 years (and considerable public funds) attempting to extend this basic linguistic repertoire into more specialized domains and functions of language' (Cummins 2000: 59). The task is thus to understand what these twelve years actually achieve. See also Hymes' (1980) very important remarks on this topic. Bourdieu and Passeron's (1970) views of disqualification – *méconnaissance* – are obviously inspirational here. I find Foucault (2003a) indispensable to grasping issues of normalcy and abnormalcy.

4 In environments where *plenty* of resources are available (think of the contemporary multi-modal and multi-media classroom in Western societies) students will still use anything at hand, and one will often see elaborate experiments in calligraphic text design. Curious fonts, colours, computer-generated images and graphic shapes may be employed and the text looks like a poster rather than like a school essay. Think also of the use of emoticons in mobile phone texting and internet chatting. Of course, while these processes develop in a context that has its own constraints, the range of choice is infinitely wider there than in the grassroots literacy environments discussed here.

5 Based on contacts with both, Maya Schiffer (2005: 328) reports that Jewsiwiecki and Vinck did not initially attach great importance to their contacts with Tshibumba.

206

NOTES

The interest came with Tshibumba's work acquiring the character of (what was believed to be) reflections of popular historical consciousness.

6 The conversation can be found in APS 3b. Ellen Schiffer reviews this fragment in her dissertation (E. Schiffer 2005: 118–19).

7 Far clearer and more elaborate cartoon features can be found in the work of a number of contemporary Congolese painters, most prominently in the work of Chéri Samba.

8 As for traces of spoken vernacular, we saw in the fragment from the letter to Vinck how Tshibumba wrote 'mandier' instead of 'mendier' ('to beg'). The nasalised [ã] of Standard French is widely realised in vernacular varieties as a denasalised vowel close to [a]. The two vowels in 'pendant' would have a similar quality in Standard French; yet they are written differently. An intuitive writer would judge the 'a' grapheme to more closely reflect the vowel quality than the grapheme 'e'. Elsewhere in the *Histoire* we find examples of similar patterns, where French vowels are qualitatively changed in local vernaculars, and where this vernacular form is written. Thus, for example, we see 'injirier' instead of 'injurier' ('to insult, hurt') on page 36 and 'reïssi' instead of 'reussi' ('succeeded', 'achieved') on page 16.

9 One is reminded here of the 'Plinian races'. Pliny, in his *Naturalis Historia*, described various exotic 'races', creatures such as Cyclopes and 'Chiropodoi' (people with one leg and a foot so big that, on very hot days, they would lie in its shade). There is, of course, a very long tradition in Europe of perceiving 'exotic' people as monsters, and in fact, the very label of 'exotic' often suggests monstrosity; see Mason (1987) for an insightful survey and discussion. Tshibumba's description here is proof of the fact that such European stereotypes were well known among the 'exotic' people and were part of their experience of the colonial system (see Scott 1990).

7 SOURCES AS RESOURCES

1 The particular form in which Tshibumba writes *Iᵉ* reveals accent again. The Latin 'I' is, of course, pronounced as *premier* in French, and when this word is used as an ordinary figure it would be written as 1ᵉʳ. In royal names, however, the Latin 'I' would suffice. Note that this peculiarity only occurs in *premier*, and not in *deux*.

2 Inspiration for this particular analysis was found in Carlo Ginzburg's essay 'Un lapsus du Pape Wojtila' (Ginzburg 2001, Chapter 9).

3 Another myth, specifically about Leopold II, was his connection with the very powerful Bishop Monseigneur de Hemptinne. In APS 1b, Tshibumba says about Leopold: 'up to this day there is the suspicion that he was also Hemptinne', a bastard son of the Bishop.

4 I myself was exposed to these versions of national colonial history as well in my primary school education; the way in which Tshibumba described the history of exploration and colonial development had a strange *déjà vu* effect on me. There has been very little research on colonial schoolbooks from the Congo, but a fine paper by Honoré Vinck (1995) must be mentioned.

5 'Armée Nationale Congolaise', later rebaptised as 'FAZ ', 'Forces Armées Zairoises'.

6 See http://www.dehemptinne.net/documents/felix/felix.htm (French-language site) for a biography of Monseigneur de Hemptinne. Fabian (1990a: 142) comments on the fact that de Hemptinne was popular among the 'right-wing' colonial establishment, and very controversial among the Congolese, notably because of his racist views. In the *Vocabulaire*, de Hemptinne is seen as a child of Leopold II (Fabian 1990a: 97 and 148). Fabian notes that this was 'a belief widely held in Elisabethville/Lubumbashi' (148).

207

NOTES

8 THE GRASSROOTS HISTORIAN'S CRAFT

1 Note, in passing, how a distinctly 'national' event such as the death of Lumumba is emphatically located in Katanga.

2 Such points were only conclusively established in the late 1990s in a book by the Belgian historian Ludo De Witte (1999). The book, which contained rich detail about the plot against Lumumba, the actual assassination, and the political forces covering it up, caused a stir in Belgium. A Parliamentary Commission of Inquiry was set up in 2000 and produced a sizeable report in 2002.

9 REFLECTIONS

1 E.P. Thompson's *Making of the English Working Class* (1963) was of course a profoundly illuminating example of how to interpret this tension between individuals and collective (structural) processes. Similar emphases can be found in Eric Hobsbawm's *Uncommon People* (1998). I have addressed the issue of choice versus determination at some length in Blommaert (2005a, Chapter 5).

2 This is one of the few problems I have with Niko Besnier's otherwise very stimulating analysis of literacy on a Polynesian atoll (Besnier 1995). Besnier argues that local literacy practices draw on 'traditional' concepts of personhood – the 'new' formats of literacy are filled, so to speak, with 'old' cultural contents. Many of his examples, however, suggest that writing *constructs* and *produces* personhood in ways not previously accessible.

3 I base my discussion of this example on brilliant pieces of work on literacy and English in Gambia by Kasper Juffermans (2005, 2006). Papen (2006) discusses very similar phenomena in Namibia.

REFERENCES

Agha, A. (2005) Voice, footing, enregisterment. *Journal of Linguistic Anthropology* 15/1: 38–59.
—— (2007) *Language and Social Relations*. Cambridge: Cambridge University Press.
Appadurai, A. (1996) *Modernity at Large*. Minneapolis: University of Minnesota Press.
Bakhtin, M. (1986) *Speech Genres and Other Late Essays*. Austin: University of Texas Press.
Bamberg, M. (ed.) (2007) *Narrative – State of the Art*. Amsterdam: John Benjamins.
Barton, D. (1994) *Literacy: An Introduction to the Ecology of Written Language*. Oxford: Blackwell.
Barton, D. and Hamilton, M. (1998) *Local Literacies: Reading and Writing in One Community*. London: Routledge.
Basso, K. (1974) The ethnography of writing. In Bauman, R. and Sherzer, J. (eds.) *Explorations in the Ethnography of Speaking*: 425–32. Cambridge: Cambridge University Press.
Bauman, R. (1986) *Story, Performance and Event*. Cambridge: Cambridge University Press.
Bauman, R. and Briggs, C. (1990) Poetics and performance as critical perspectives on language and social life. *Annual Review of Anthropology* 19: 59–88.
—— (2003) *Voices of Modernity*. Cambridge: Cambridge University Press.
Baynham, M. (1995) *Literacy Practices*. London: Longman.
Besnier, N. (1995) *Literacy, Emotion, and Authority: Reading and Writing on a Polynesian Atoll*. Cambridge: Cambridge University Press.
Bloch, M. (1953) *The Historian's Craft*. New York: Alfred Knopf.
Blommaert, J. (1996) A Shaba Swahili life history: Text and translation. *Afrikanistische Arbeitspapiere (AAP)* 47: 31–62.
—— (1999) *State Ideology and Language in Tanzania*. Cologne: Rüdiger Köppe.
—— (2001a) Context is/as Critique. *Critique of Anthropology* 21: 13–32.
—— (2001b) Analysing narrative inequality: African asylum seekers' stories in Belgium. *Discourse & Society* 12: 413–49.
—— (2004) Writing as a problem: African grassroots writing, economies of literacy, and globalization. *Language in Society* 33: 643–71.
—— (2005a) *Discourse: A Critical Introduction*. Cambridge: Cambridge University Press.
—— (2005b) Bourdieu the ethnographer: The ethnographic grounding of Habitus and Voice. *The Translator* 11: 219–36.
—— (2006) Ethnopoetics as functional reconstruction: Dell Hymes' narrative view of the world. *Functions of Language* 13: 229–49.
Blommaert, J. and Dong, J.K. (2007) Language and Movement in Space. *Working Papers in Language Diversity 1*, University of Jyväskylä. http://www.jyu.fi/hum/laitokset/kielet/wild.

REFERENCES

Blommaert, J. and Omoniyi, T. (2006) Email fraud: Language, technology, and the indexicals of globalisation. *Social Semiotics* 16/4: 574–605.

Blommaert, J., Creve, L. and Willaert, E. (2006) On being declared illiterate: Language-ideological disqualification in Dutch classes for immigrants in Belgium. *Language & Communication* 26/1: 34–54.

Blommaert, J., Huysmans, M., Muyllaert, N. and Dyers, C. (2005) Peripheral normativity: Literacy and the production of locality in a South African township school. *Linguistics and Education:* 16: 378–403.

Bourdieu, P. (1984) *Distinction: A Social Critique of the Judgment of Taste*. Cambridge MA: Harvard University Press.

—— (1990) *The Logic of Practice*. Cambridge: Polity.

—— (2000) Making the economic habitus: Algerian workers revisited. *Ethnography* 1: 17–41.

Bourdieu, P. and Passeron, J.-C. (1970) *La Réproduction*. Paris: Minuit.

Boyarin, J. (ed.) (1993) *The Ethnography of Reading*. Berkeley: University of California Press.

Braeckman, C. (1991) *Le Dinosaure: Le Zaire de Mobutu*. Paris: Fayard.

Briggs, C. (1997) Notes on a 'confession'. On the construction of gender, sexuality, and violence in an infanticide case. *Pragmatics* 7/4: 519–46.

Caplan, P. (1997) *African voices, African lives: Personal Narratives from a Swahili Village*. London: Routledge.

Castells, M. (1996) *The Rise of the Network Society*. Oxford: Blackwell.

—— (1997) *The Power of Identity*. Oxford: Blackwell.

Collins, J. (1995) Literacy and literacies. *Annual Review of Anthropology* 24: 75–93.

Collins, J. and Blot, R. (2003) *Literacy and Literacies: Texts, Power, and Identity*. Cambridge: Cambridge University Press.

Cummins, J. (2000) *Language, Power and Pedagogy: Bilingual Children in the Crossfire*. Clevedon: Multilingual Matters.

De Fina, A., Schiffrin, D. and Bamberg, M. (eds.) (2006) *Discourse and Identity*. Cambridge: Cambridge University Press.

Derrida, J. (1996) *Archive Fever: A Freudian Impression*. Chicago: University of Chicago Press.

De Rooij, V. (1996) *Cohesion through contrast: Discourse structure in Shaba Swahili/French conversations*. Amsterdam: IFOTT.

De Witte, L. (1999) *De Moord op Lumumba*. Leuven: Van Halewijck.

Fabian, J. (1974/1991) Genres in an emerging tradition. Chapter 3, in *Time and the Work of Anthropology*. Chur: Harwood.

—— (1982) Scratching the surface: Observations on the poetics of lexical borrowing in Shaba Swahili. *Anthropological Linguistics* 24: 14–50.

—— (1983) *Time and the Other: How Anthropology Constructs its Object*. New York: Columbia University Press.

—— (1986) *Language and Colonial Power*. Cambridge: Cambridge University Press.

—— (1990a) *History from Below*. Amsterdam: John Benjamins.

—— (1990b) *Power and Performance*. Madison: University of Wisconsin Press.

—— (1993) Keep listening: Ethnography and reading. In Boyarin, J. (ed.): 80–97.

—— (1996) *Remembering the Present: Painting and Popular History in Zaire*. Berkeley: University of California Press.

—— (2001) *Anthropology with an Attitude*. Stanford: Stanford University Press.

Fabian, J. and Szombati-Fabian, I. (1980) Folk art from an anthropological perspective.

REFERENCES

In Quimby, I. and Swank, S. (eds.) *Perspectives on American Folk Art*: 247–92. New York: Norton.

Foucault, M. (1975) *Surveiller et Punir: Naissance de la Prison*. Paris: Gallimard.

—— (2002) *The Archaeology of Knowledge*. London: Routledge.

—— (2003a) *Abnormal*. New York: Picador.

—— (2003b) *Society Must Be Defended*. New York: Picador.

—— (2005) *The Hermeneutics of the Subject*. London: Palgrave.

Foucault, M. (ed.) (1975) *I, Pierre Rivière, Having Slaughtered my Mother, my Sister, and my Brother . . .* New York: Random House.

Gee, J. (1990) *Social Linguistics and Literacies: Ideologies in Discourses*. London: Falmer.

Giddens, A. (1991) *Modernity and Self-Identity*. Cambridge: Polity.

Ginzburg, C. (1980) *The Cheese and the Worms: The Cosmos of a Sixteenth-Century Miller*. Baltimore: Johns Hopkins University Press.

—— (1989) *Clues, Myths, and the Historical Method*. Baltimore: Johns Hopkins University.

—— (2001) *A Distance: Neuf Essais sur le Point de Vue en Histoire*. Paris: Gallimard.

Goffman, E. (1975) *Frame Analysis*. New York: Harper & Row.

—— (1981) *Forms of Talk*. Philadelphia: University of Pennsylvania Press.

Goody, J. (ed.) (1968) *Literacy in Traditional Societies*. Cambridge: Cambridge University Press.

Gradoll, David, Janet Maybin and Barry Stierer (eds.) (1994) *Researching Language and Literacy in Social Context*. Clevedon: Multilingual Matters.

Hobsbawm, E. (1983) Introduction: Inventing traditions. In Hobsbawm, E. and Ranger, T. (eds.) *The Invention of Tradition*: 1–14. Cambridge: Cambridge University Press.

—— (1987) *The Age of Empire, 1875–1914*. London: Weidenfeld and Nicolson.

—— (1998) *Uncommon People*. London: Abacus.

—— (2001) Democracy can be bad for you. *The New Statesman*, March 5, 2001 (http://www.newstatesman.com).

—— (2007) *Globalization, Democracy and Terrorism*. London: Little, Brown.

Hymes, D. (1966) Two types of linguistic relativity (with examples from Amerindian ethnography). In Bright, W. (ed.) *Sociolinguistics*: 131–56. The Hague: Mouton.

—— (1972) Models of the interaction of language and social life. In Gumperz, J. and Hymes, D. (eds.) *Directions in Sociolinguistics: The Ethnography of Communication*: 35–71. New York: Holt, Rinehart and Winston.

—— (1975/1981) Breakthrough into performance. Part 2 of *In Vain I Tried To Tell You*. Philadelphia: University of Pennsylvania Press.

—— (1981) *In Vain I Tried to Tell You: Essays in Native American Ethnopoetics*. Philadelphia: University of Pennsylvania Press.

—— (1983) *Essays in the History of Linguistic Anthropology*. Amsterdam: John Benjamins.

—— (1996) *Ethnography, Linguistics, Narrative Inequality: Toward an Understanding of Voice*. London: Taylor & Francis.

—— (1998) When is oral narrative poetry? Generative form and its pragmatic conditions. *Pragmatics* 8: 475–500.

—— (2003) *Now I Know Only So Far: Essays in Ethnopoetics*. Lincoln: University of Nebraska Press.

Irvine, J. and Gal, S. (2000) Language ideology and linguistic differentiation. In Kroskrity, P. (ed.) *Regimes of Language*: 35–83. Santa Fe: SAR Press.

Jakobson, R. (1960) Closing statement: Linguistics and poetics. In Sebeok, T. (ed.) *Style in Language*: 350–77. Cambridge MA: MIT Press.

REFERENCES

Jewsiwiecki, B. (1993) *Naître et Mourir au Zaïre: Un Demi-Siècle d'Histoire au Quotidien*. Paris: Karthala.

—— (ed.) (1992) *Art Pictural Zairois*. Sillery: Septentrion.

—— (ed.) (1999) *A Congo Chronicle: Patrice Lumumba in Urban Art*. New York: Museum for African Art.

Juffermans, K. (2005) *English Writing Contest, English Writing Contested: An Explorative Analysis of Metalinguistic Compositions of Gambian Lower Basic School Children*. Ghent: Vakgroep Afrikaanse Talen en Culturen (research Report 4).

—— (2006) *English and Literacy Practices in The Gambia: Sociolinguistic Investigations in Education, Media and Public Life*. Unpublished MA dissertation, Ghent University.

Kress, G. (1997) *Before Writing: Rethinking the Paths to Literacy*. London: Routledge.

—— (2000) *Early Spelling: Between Convention and Creativity*. London: Routledge.

Kress, G. and van Leeuwen, T. (1996) *Reading Images: The Grammar of Visual Design*. London: Routledge.

Malkki, L. (1995) *Purity and Exile: Violence, Memory, and National Cosmology among Hutu Refugees in Tanzania*. Chicago: University of Chicago Press.

Maryns, K. and Blommaert, J. (2002) Pretextuality and pretextual gaps: On re/defining linguistic inequality. *Pragmatics* 12/1: 11–30.

Mason, P. (1987) Seduction from afar: Europe's inner Indians. *Anthropos* 82: 581–601.

Mayer, T. and Woolf, D.R. (1995) Introduction. In Mayer, T. and Woolf, D.R. (eds.) *The Rhetorics of Life-Writing in Early Modern Europe*: 1–37. Ann Arbor: University of Michigan Press.

Papen, U. (2006) *Literacy and Globalization: Reading and Writing in Times of Social and Cultural Change*. London: Routledge.

Prinsloo, M. and Breier, M. (eds.) (1996) *The Social Uses of Literacy: Theory and Practice in Contemporary South Africa*. Amsterdam: John Benjamins.

Radley, A. (1990) Artefacts, memory and a sense of the past. In Middleton, D. and Edwards, D. (eds.) *Collective remembering*, 46–59. London: Sage.

Rafael, V. (1993) *Contracting Colonialism: Translation and Christian Conversion in Tagalog Society under Early Spanish Rule*. Durham: Duke University Press.

Schicho, W. (1980) *Kiswahili von Lubumbashi*. Vienna: Institut für Afrikanistik und Aegyptologie.

—— (1982) *Syntax des Swahili von Lubumbashi*. Vienna: Institut für Afrikanistik und Aegyptologie.

—— (1990) Linguistic notes on the 'Vocabulary of Elisabethville'. In Fabian (1990a): 33–54.

Schieffelin, B., Woolard, K. and Kroskrity, P. (eds.) (1998) *Language Ideologies: Practice and Theory*. New York: Oxford University Press.

Schiffer, E. (2005) *Historiografische Situering van Tshibumba Kanda Matulu*. Unpublished MA dissertation, Ghent University.

Schiffer, M. (2005) *Remembering the Past: Een Geschiedenis van Zaire, gezien door de ogen van Tshibumba Kanda Matulu*. Ghent: Vakgroep Afrikaanse Talen en Culturen (Research Report 1).

Scott, J. (1990) *Domination and the Arts of Resistance: Hidden Transcripts*. New Haven: Yale University Press.

Shulman, Lee (1986) Those who understand: Knowledge growth in teaching. *Educational Researcher* 15/2: 4–14.

Silverstein, M. (1979) Language structure and linguistic ideology. In Clyne, P., Hanks, W.

REFERENCES

and Hofbauer, C. (eds.) *The Elements: A Parasession on Linguistic Units and Levels*: 193–247. Chicago: Chicago Linguistic Society.

—— (1985) On the pragmatic 'poetry' of prose: Parallelism, repetition, and cohesive structure in the time-course of dyadic conversation. In Schiffrin, D. (ed.) *Meaning, Form, and Use in Context: Linguistic Applications*: 181–99. Washington DC: Georgetown University Press.

—— (1996) Monoglot 'Standard' in America: Standardization and metaphors of linguistic hegemony. In Brenneis, D. and Macaulay, R. (eds.) *The Matrix of Language*: 284–306. Boulder: Westview Press.

—— (2004) Cultural concepts and the language-culture nexus. *Current Anthropology* 45/5: 621–52.

—— (2006) Old wine, new ethnographic lexicography. *Annual Review of Anthropology* 35: 481–96.

Silverstein, M. and Urban, G. (1996) *Natural Histories of Discourse*. Chicago: University of Chicago Press.

Street, B. (1995) *Social Literacies*. London: Longman.

Szombati-Fabian, I. and Fabian, J. (1976) Art, history and society: Popular painting in Shaba, Zaire. *Studies in the Anthropology of Visual Communication* 3: 1–21.

Tedlock, D. (1983) *The Spoken Word and the Work of Interpretation*. Philadelphia: University of Pennsylvania Press.

Tempels, P. (1945) *La Philosophie bantoue*. Elisabethville: Lovania (Translated as *Bantu Philosophy*, Paris: Présence Africaine 1959).

Thompson, E.P. (1963) *The Making of the English Working Class*. London: Gollancz.

Vangroenweghe, D. (1985) *Dus Sang sur les Lianes*. Paris: Hatier.

Vinck, H. (1995) The influence of colonial ideology on school books in the Belgian Congo. *Pedagogica Historia* 23: 355–406.

Wacquant, L. (2004) Following Pierre Bourdieu in the field. *Ethnography* 5: 387–414.

Wallerstein, I. (1983) *Historical Capitalism with Capitalist Civilization*. London: Verso.

Williams, E. (2006) *Bridges and Barriers: Language in African Education and Development*. Manchester: St Jerome.

Young, C. (1965) *Politics in the Congo*. Princeton: Princeton University Press.

INDEX

Adula, Cyrille 149
Africa: artists' attribution xv; Julien's opinions 58–9; literacy in 142–6
African Voices, African Lives (Caplan) 10–11
Albert I, King 144–5
alcohol and drugs 52; Julien and 93
Alliance des Bakongos (ABAKO) 109
Arens, Helena xv; advice of 79, 81, 82; assigns writing to Julien 48–9; becomes addressee 56, 176; disappointed with writing 72, 73; Julien's effort for 37, 39–40; plans autobiography 42; possession of Julien's text 89; relationship with Julien 29, 31, 33, 35–6, 90–2; support for Julien 41, 52, 82, 83
Arens family 35, 81; chronology of 76; Julien works for 51–2, 53–4, 76; return to Belgium 59–60
autobiography: as history 85–6; within larger structures 187–90; memory and 74, 75–80; Mohammed's diaries 10–11; *see also* Julien

Bakhtin, Mikhail: speech genres 44; voices in discourse 46
Bakongo Kingdom 146; *see also* Congo, Democratic Republic of the
Barton, D. 89
Basso, Keith 12
Baudoin, King 109, 143, 145, 155; narratives about 132–3; warns against racism 143, 163
Bauman, Zygmunt: transmission of culture 44
Before Writing (Kress) 116
Belgium: aids Mobutu 110; chronology of kings 142–6; colonial history 108–10,

119–20, 146–8; Congo and 21–2; law and literacy 3; localism within 186–7
Belgium's Africa conference 99
Bloch, Marc 164; *The Historian's Craft* 137–8; linguistic techniques 197–8; on sources 146
Blommaert, Jan: *Discourse: A Critical Introduction* xiii; localism of upbringing 186–7; possession of Julien's text 89, 90; possession of Tshibumba's text 99
Boas, Franz 16
Bodson, Omer 119, 121, 151
Bourdieu, Pierre: ethnographic epistemology 87–9; habitus 188; inflected knowledge 157; predispositions 41
Burundi 11

Caplan, Pat 188; *African Voices, African Lives* 10–11
Charles, Prince Regent 143; rumours about children's eyes 155, 156
The Cheese and the Worms (Ginzburg) 190–1
Chomsky, Noam: scientific model 15
Collins, James 192
colonialism: anti-colonial voices 148–9; Belgian kings and 142–6; Berlin Conference 148–9, 162–3; history of 108–9; official Belgian history 146–8
communication: inequalities and xiv–xv, 23–4; spheres of 43–4; *see also* grassroots literacy; writing
Congo, Democratic Republic of the (temporarily Zaire): colonial context 50; colonised by Leopold II 142–6; democracy in 77; flags of 124–5; historical perspective 20–3; maps of 25, 26; Mobutu's propaganda 152–4; social

215

INDEX

context of Julien 41; tribalism 170; writing as a voice for 166–9; *see also* *Histoire* (Tshibumba)

culture: African literacy and 189–90; for elite from non-elite 176–7; transmission through genre 44–5; value of writing 117

Dédec, Père 173

Degueldre family 35

Democratic Republic of the Congo; *see* Congo, Democratic Republic of the

Denard, Bob 110, 168

Derrida, Jacques: 'archontic power' 86; objective narration 74

diamond mines 52, 93; slavery of 94

Discourse: A Critical Introduction (Blommaert) xiii

Elebe Lisembe 151

epistemology: inflected knowledge 157; subjectivity and 86–90

ethics xv–xvi, 20, 86, 89

ethnography: descriptive theory 12; methodology 13–15; philology and 15–18; status of linguistic data 47–8; subjective data 87–9; writing and 4–6, 12–15

Fabian, Johannes 19, 132; on chronology 127; commissions paintings 122–3; conversations with Tshibumba 139; creolisation of language 71; epigraphs 119; ethnographic data 88–9; evolving genres 46; *History from Below* xiv, 8, 50, 99–100; the how of documents 19; interpretive procedures 89; the Jamaa movement 47–8; on national viewpoint 161; origin of Tshibumba's text 99, 101; reception of *Vocabulaire* 178–9; *Remembering the Present* xiv; on Tshibumba and comics 126; on the *Vocabulaire* 8–10

Foucault, Michel 180; *Hermeneutics of the Subject* 95; *I Pierre Rivière* 190–1; positivity 139; regimes of power 188, 189

Franco (musician) 150

François, Bwana 173

French language: code-switching 68; grassroots use of language 175–6; Julien's use of 19, 30, 33–5, 37–8, 41, 56–9, 67, 79; Tshibumba's use of 107, 162–4

Gal, S. 114

genre: Bakhtin's spheres 43–4; colonial applications 50; cultural transmission 44–5; distant 7; for elite from non-elite 176–7; globalisation and 6; grassroots techniques 176; of history 185; Julien's perception of 49–50, 72–3; layering 47; shifts in footing 45–6; wider communication and 44

Giddens, Anthony 189

Ginzburg, Carlo: *The Cheese and the Worms* 190–1; evidential paradigm 14–15

globalisation: communicative inequalities 23–4; exclusion due to 4; flow of texts 6; grassroots writing and 194–7; inequalities of xiv–xv; linguistic relativity and 42–3; rhetoric of 189

Goffman, Erving: shifts in footing 45–6

Goody, Jack: *Literacy in Traditional Society* 190

grassroots literacy xiv; art in documents 113–18; Burundese asylum seeker 194–5; chapter and chapter titles 174–5; characteristics of 7–8; chronology and 172–4; constraints 10; for elite from non-elite 176–7, 186; function of 193–4; in globalisation 6, 194–7; judging Africa 189–90; reception of 178–82; techniques of 171; Tshibumba's text 105–7; *see also* texts; writing

Hamilton, M. 89

Hammarskjoeld, Dag 110

handwriting *see* ortho-graphy

Hemptinne, Bishop de 156, 160, 162, 176

Hermeneutics of the Subject (Foucault) 95

hetero-graphy 7, 117–18, 193; *see also* ortho-graphy

Histoire (Tshibumba): chronology of 126–9, 172–4; Katanga locus 157–8, 160–1; methodology 165–71; micro-narratives of 132–5; origins of 99–103; reception of 178, 179–82; sources 146–57, 162; summary of contents 108–12; 'un-aesthetic' 135–6

The Historian's Craft (Bloch) 137–8

historicism 48

history and historiography: autobiography and 74, 75–80, 85–6; documents and 137–8; genre orientation 185; grassroots constraints 18–19; inscribed on paintings 118–23; reception of

216

INDEX

grassroots 178–82; social context of facts 145; sources 146; subjectivity 86–90; Tshibumba's methodology 165–71; voice and truth 197–9; writing as a voice for Africans 166–9
History from Below (Fabian) xiv, 8, 50, 99–100
History of Rwanda (Kagame) 151, 162
Hitler, Adolf 167
Hobsbawm, Eric 24
Hymes, Dell 199; ethnography of writing 4–6; ethnopoetics 16–18; genres 45; linguistic relativity 43; story formation 53

I Pierre Rivière (Foucault) 190–1
identity: in autobiography 85–6; illegal immigrants xv; Tshibumba's claim to 19–20
Ileo, Joseph 149
immigrants, illegal: loss of official existence xv
Irvine, J. 114

Jacqueline (Julien's first wife) 35, 53; chronology of 76, 79; happiness of marriage 61
Jakobson, R. 113
Jamaa movement 47–8
Jewsiwiecki, Bogumil xiv, 19; academic climate 178–9; *Belgium's Africa* conference 99; *Histoire* written for 152; *Naître et Mourir au Zaïre* 11; origins of Tshibumba's text 100–3, 105
John Paul II, Pope 110
Julien xiv; assigned to write 48–9; chapters and chapter titles 174–5; chronology of 76–80, 127, 172–4; colonial context 50; compared to Tshibumba 103–5, 131, 136; context and pretext of 40–1; debts of 76; effort taken to write 38–9, 62, 64, 70; for elite from non-elite 176–7; employed by Arens family 51–3; as an exceptional person 190, 191; farms of 52, 60, 61–2, 76; genre awareness 49–50, 72–3, 176, 185; grassroots techniques 171–8; historiography of 19; identity of 85–6; illness of 77; jealousy of others 41; language use 30–5; life's story 35–6; marriages of 61, 76, 79, 94; memory and 75–80; possession of autobiography 89; problems with

Kalonda 80–4; reception of text 178, 181; religion of 93–5; resources of 186; rewriting 76; self-presentation 90–5; subjectivity 95–6, 138, 185–6; three texts of 29–30, 37–40; three versions of 51–65; use of French 56–9, 68–70; use of language 175–6; versions compared 65–8, 83–5; voice of 198–9
Julienne (Julien's second wife) 35–6, 61; chronology of 76, 79

Kabila, Laurent-Désiré 23
Kagame, Abbé Alexis: *History of Rwanda* 151, 162
Kalonda, Theo 35, 52; chronology of 76; Julien's problem with 80–4
Kalonji, Albert 22, 109, 149–50
Kalume 52
Kasabubu 109
Kasai: Bakuba kingdom 158; conflict with Katanga 54–6, 64; secession of 149–50
Kasavubu, Joseph 22, 149
Katanga, King 108, 121
Katanga region: conflict with Kasai 54–6, 64; construction of railroad 139; historical perspective on 21; independence movement 22; the Jamaa movement 47–8; as locus of Tshibumba's history 157–8, 160–1; Tshibumba's context 104, 108, 109; UN troops in 110; Yav's history of 138–9
Kimba 149
Kimbangu, Simon 121, 149, 173
knowledge economies 7
Kress, Gunther 42, 113; *Before Writing* 116

language: code-switching 175–6; creolisation 71; grassroots techniques 175–6; linguistic relativity 43; monoglossic 68; vernacular 7
Leeuwen, T. van 42, 113
Leopold I, King: in *Histoire* 108, 109; Stanley and 133–5; Tshibumba's confusion with Leopold II 134, 140–6; Yav on 139
Leopold II, King 21; colonial enterprise 148–9; photographic images 151; rumours of child 156; Tshibumba's confusion with Leopold I 134, 140–6
Leopold III, King 144–5
Lévi-Strauss, Claude 88–9
Lingala: of Congolese diaspora 3–4

217

INDEX

linguistics: ethnography and 12–13
Literacy in Traditional Society (Goody) 190
literacy regimes xiii; computers and
5; globalised language xiv–xv;
historiographic 18; sociolinguistics 5;
uncovering voice 18–19; *see also* writing
Livingstone, David 108, 140–1, 147
Lumumba, Patrice 22, 103, 108, 149;
narratives about 134–5; paintings
of 143; telling death of 167–8;
Tshibumba's *Histoire* 109–10

Malkki, Liisa 181; *Purity and Exile* 11
Marx, Karl: social being and
consciousness 188
Mbula-Matari 109
media and popular culture: as historical
sources 149–52
minority groups: ethnopoetics 16
Mobutu Sese Seko (Joseph) 22–3;
failure of governance 64; flag of 125;
propaganda 152–4; Tshibumba's
Histoire 110–11; Tshibumba's painting
of 118–19; visits Katanga 161; wedding
of 145–6
Mohammed's diaries 10–11, 188
Mouvement Populaire de la Révolution (MPR)
22–3, 110
Msiri, King of Katanga 108, 158, 160;
Tshibumba's paintings of 119, 120–1
Munongo Godefroid 168

Naître et Mourir au Zaïre (Jewsiwiecki) 11
Native American narratives: Hymes and
ethnopoetics 16–18
New Literacy Studies 6
Ngalula 150
Nguz-a-Karl-i-Bond 110
Nigeria 24

oral narratives: Fabian on 8–10; Hymes'
ethnopoetics 16–18
ortho-graphy: graphic aspect of writing
113–18; Julien's handwriting 57, 63;
Tshibumba's handwriting 106, 135–6,
159; *see also* hetero-graphy

Panda, John 121
Pétillon, Governor-General Leon:
Baudoin and racism 143; narratives
about 132, 134; rumours about 157
philology: ethnography and 15–18
Purity and Exile (Malkki) 11

Récits: genre of recollections 72–3; memory
and 74, 75–80; subjectivity of 95–6
religion: Julien's Christianity 93–5
Remembering the Present (Fabian) xiv
Ricoeur, Paul 48
Rwanda 11, 181; crisis of 1994 23

Schicho, Walter 71; grassroots use of
language 175–6
Schiffer, Ellen 101
Schiffer, Maya 104, 122
Shaba region: ethnic violence 104; wars of
110, 111
Shaba Swahili language 8; grassroots use
of 175–6; Julien's use of 19, 30–5,
70–2; Mrs Arens' assumption 37–8;
Tshibumba and 105, 130; varieties
of 34
Silverstein, M. 43
sociolinguistics 5
South Africa: graphic aspect of writing
114, 117
Spaandonck, Marcel van 29
Stanley, Henry Morton 21, 108, 141,
143, 147, 148; Tshibumba's narrative
133–5
structuralism: Lévi-Strauss 88–9
subjectivity: attribution of creative works
xv; epistemology of 86–90; Julien and
95–6, 138, 185–6, 190; Tshibumba
185–6
Swahili language: *Archives of Popular Swahili*
131; borrowings and code-switching
68–70; Julien and 29, 51, 59, 67, 70–2;
Luba-group 68; variations 69; *see also*
Shaba Swahili language

Tedlock, Dennis 46
texts 48; comic strips 126; ethnography of
12–13; expectations of textuality 10;
global flow of 6, 24–5, 37, 186; graphic
aspects of 123–7; indexicality of 16;
Julien's three versions 37–40; mobility
of xiv; practice of ethnography 12–15;
as products 13–14; *see also* hetero-
graphy; ortho-graphy; writing
Tshibumba Kanda Matulu xiv; art in
document 113; chapters and chapter
titles 174–5; comic strips and 126;
commissioned by Fabian 122–3;
on Congo's existence 139–40; dates
paintings 127, 128, 129; disciplined
voice of 162–4; for elite from non-elite

218

INDEX

176–7; ethnographical study of 13; as an exceptional person 190, 191; genre awareness 176, 185; graphic aspect of *Histoire* 123–7; grassroots techniques 171–8; handwriting of 135–6; as historian 180–2; historical paintings of 102, 103–4, 118–23, 143, 150–2; historiography of 19–20; language use 103; life of 103–5; methodology 165–71; monoglossic French 130–1; 'objective' history 138; origins of text 99–103; parallels with Julien 103–5, 107; resources 146–57, 186; sample of text 124, 125; school history 146–8; subjectivity 185–6; use of language 175–6; voice of 129–30, 198–9; *see also Histoire* (Tshibumba)
Tshinyama 150
Tshombe, Moïse 22, 109–10, 149, 150

Uganda 23
Union Minière du Haut Katanga 21, 109, 139, 172
Urban, G. 43

Verstappen family 35; chronology of 76; Julien works for 52, 53–4; Mrs Arens recommends 60

Vinck, Edouard 102, 123; letter from Tshibumba 104, 105
Vocabulaire de Ville de Elisabethville (Yav) 8–10, 50, 71, 111, 138–9; chronology of 172–4; kings and 144, 145; reception of 178–9

Wallerstein, Immanuel 24
Whorf, Benjamin Lee 16; linguistic relativity 43
witchcraft 52, 77
writing: affordances of 42; as drawing 113–18; ethnography of 4–6; for export 186; graffiti 193; judgements on Africa 189–90; practice and function of 191–4; value-attribution 117; as voice for Africa 166–9 *see also* hetero-graphy; ortho-graphy

Yav, André: chapters and chapter titles 174–5; for elite from non-elite 176–7; genre awareness 176; grassroots techniques 171–8; use of language 175–6; *Vocabulaire de Ville de Elisabethville* 8–10, 50, 71, 138–9, 144, 145

Zaire: *see* Congo, Democratic Republic of the

eBooks – at www.eBookstore.tandf.co.uk

A library at your fingertips!

eBooks are electronic versions of printed books. You can store them on your PC/laptop or browse them online.

They have advantages for anyone needing rapid access to a wide variety of published, copyright information.

eBooks can help your research by enabling you to bookmark chapters, annotate text and use instant searches to find specific words or phrases. Several eBook files would fit on even a small laptop or PDA.

NEW: Save money by eSubscribing: cheap, online access to any eBook for as long as you need it.

Annual subscription packages

We now offer special low-cost bulk subscriptions to packages of eBooks in certain subject areas. These are available to libraries or to individuals.

For more information please contact webmaster.ebooks@tandf.co.uk

We're continually developing the eBook concept, so keep up to date by visiting the website.

www.eBookstore.tandf.co.uk

CPSIA information can be obtained at www.ICGtesting.com
Printed in the USA
LVOW07s0214090815

449207LV00006B/39/P